PRAISE FOR *CONFLICT RESILIENCE*

"*Conflict Resilience* offers a powerful, practical recipe for true dialogue between people with opposing views. Robert Bordone and Joel Salinas have written exactly the book needed in our time."

—Daniel Goleman, #1 *New York Times* bestselling author of *Emotional Intelligence*

"Every leader—from the halls of Congress to C-Suites, to university administrators and local officials—should read this book. With its practical advice on how to constructively disagree, hold your ground, and still get things done in an increasingly polarized world, *Conflict Resilience* is simply the best book I know on how to respectfully talk about policy differences and find constructive ways to work together."

—Adam Kinzinger, former US Congressman (R) and *New York Times* bestselling author of *Renegade: Defending Democracy & Liberty in Our Divided Country*

"*Conflict Resilience* is a masterful, in-depth account of everyday conflict in which the authors share their original tools for finding greater connection amidst substantial disagreement. Knowing how to sit with uncertainty, find ease, and reach for the other side will be some of the most sought-after skills in the coming century, and Bordone and Salinas have delivered a grand gift in the form of their new book."

—Jenara Nerenberg, journalist and bestselling author of *Divergent Mind: Thriving in a World That Wasn't Designed for You*

"If you are fearful, or even just hesitant, to engage in the difficult conflicts in your personal or professional life, *Conflict Resilience* is for you. Full of penetrating analysis, practical hacks, and illuminating stories, and buttressed by relevant and accessible insights from neuroscience, the authors provide a roadmap through emotions that block our capacity 'to genuinely sit with and grow from conflict.' *Conflict Resilience* invites us into the humble yet hopeful work of learning to hold even deep disagreement."

—Dr. Amy Uelmen, Director for Mission & Ministry, Georgetown University Law Center

"[A] rare gift: a practical and entertaining book with compelling lessons for entrepreneurs, CEOs, and business leaders, as well as educators, students, and parents. Replete with vivid examples, supported by the latest brain science, and full of easy-to-implement hacks, it provides a brilliant roadmap for working through our disagreements in ways that help promote connection and creative problem-solving."

— Rob Waldron, chairman, Curriculum Associates

"Bordone and Salinas begin *Conflict Resilience* with an important but overlooked truth: Conflict is not the problem—we are. Accepting that truth means reckoning with the deeper, internal work that is too often brushed aside in favor of quick fixes. Thankfully, the authors offer powerful and practical methods for building our capacity to not only handle but embrace the messy (and essential) work of conflict. This book is essential reading for anyone who faces friction at work or in life—that is, all of us!"

—Jeff Wetzler, author of *Ask: Tap into the Hidden Wisdom of People Around You*

"Bob Bordone and Joel Salinas are uniquely qualified to give valuable insight into the conflict that exists in everyday life. *Conflict Resilience* is a great read that will add depth to your thinking and practical strategies for your acting to navigate conflicts big and small."

—Chris Voss, *Wall Street Journal* bestselling author of *Never Split the Difference: Negotiating as if Your Life Depended On It*

"I've read many helpful how-to guides, but none as practically useful and scientifically validated as *Conflict Resilience*. Bordone and Salinas...offer a compelling case for why learning to sit with each other in the discomfort of our disagreement...is the best (and perhaps only) way to deepen and build genuine connection with colleagues, fellow citizens, and even family. If you're sick of the avoidance, tired of the fighting, and looking for a way to be authentic about the conflicts within yourself and the disagreements you have with others, do yourself a favor and read this powerful and timely book."

—Tania Tetlow, president, Fordham University

"*Conflict Resilience* combines powerful neuroscience with practical expertise to redefine how we engage with disagreement. Bordone and Salinas don't just show us how to face conflict—they provide tools to transform our mental and emotional patterns for the better. They truly offer a paradigm-shifting approach to conflict. More than managing tough moments, *Conflict Resilience* teaches us to use conflict as a catalyst for growth, mental health, and stronger bonds. With an approach that blends science and compassion, this book is truly a game-changer for personal and professional relationships. Essential reading for anyone committed to mental well-being and healthy connections."

—Dr. Laura Erickson-Scroth, MD, clinical associate professor of psychiatry, New York University

"A masterful guide to overcoming the intense divisions engulfing our world. In this groundbreaking book, Bob Bordone and Joel Salinas uncover a surprising truth: that it is our discomfort with conflict that prevents meaningful dialogue. Offering a science-backed, practical roadmap, they empower us to embrace this discomfort and navigate tough conversations with confidence and courage. Filled with compelling stories and actionable insights, *Conflict Resilience* provides exactly what we need to bridge the divides in our personal and professional lives. I hope 'conflict resilience' will become the rallying call of our time, moving us boldly toward an era of greater connection."

—Daniel L. Shapiro, PhD, founder and director of the Harvard International Negotiation Program and author of *Negotiating the Nonnegotiable*

"*Conflict Resilience* is the book we need now to help us weather these polarizing times and thrive in the future. A ground-breaking guide to facing our most daunting conflicts with grit, authenticity, and creativity, it reassures us that, even when resolution seems unlikely or even impossible, we need not give up or get into a shouting match. Instead, we can negotiate our disagreements directly, with empathy and authenticity, and find a path to connection, personal growth, and enduring relationships. *Conflict Resilience* educates, entertains, and ultimately imparts a hopeful view of how conflict can change our lives—and our world—for the better."

—William Ury, coauthor of *Getting to Yes* and author of *Possible: How We Survive—and Thrive—in an Age of Conflict*

"*Conflict Resilience* is *the* book that I have long wished were available. It is vital, helpful, and profound. Every student, teacher, professional, and leader urgently needs the tools it offers, for the good of our society and our well-being."

—Jeannie Suk-Gersen, John H. Watson, Jr., Professor of Law, Harvard Law School, and contributing writer, *The New Yorker*

# CONFLICT RESILIENCE

ALSO BY ROBERT C. BORDONE

*Designing Systems and Processes for Managing Disputes*, 1st edition (2013), 2nd edition (2019)

*The Handbook of Dispute Resolution* (2005)

ALSO BY JOEL SALINAS, M.D.

*Mirror Touch: A Memoir of Synesthesia and the Secret Life of the Brain*

*Neurology Evidence: The Practice-Changing Studies*

# CONFLICT RESILIENCE

### NEGOTIATING DISAGREEMENT
### WITHOUT GIVING UP
### OR GIVING IN

## ROBERT C. BORDONE
## AND JOEL SALINAS, M.D.

**HARPER**
**BUSINESS**
*An Imprint of* HarperCollins*Publishers*

"Blessing of Courage" © Jan Richardson from *The Cure for Sorrow: A Book of Blessings for Times of Grief.* Used by permission. janrichardson.com

CONFLICT RESILIENCE. Copyright © 2025 by Robert C. Bordone and Joel Salinas, M.D. All rights reserved. Printed in the United States of America. No part of this book may be used or reproduced in any manner whatsoever without written permission except in the case of brief quotations embodied in critical articles and reviews. For information, address HarperCollins Publishers, 195 Broadway, New York, NY 10007.

HarperCollins books may be purchased for educational, business, or sales promotional use. For information, please email the Special Markets Department at SPsales@harpercollins.com.

FIRST EDITION

Designed by Bonni Leon-Berman

Library of Congress Cataloging-in-Publication Data has been applied for.

ISBN 978-0-06-327833-2

25 26 27 28 29  LBC  5 4 3 2 1

*To those who have stood by me and believed in my resilience:* Annie, Chuck, Daniel, Dan, Florrie, Jen, Jimmy, Krista, Kyle, Sarah, Susan, Toby, Zoe, Mom, and Dad.

*And*

*To all who strive to build bridges across lines of difference:* With admiration and appreciation for the lessons you share on how to come together in a conflicted world.

—RCB

*To my father,* Armando, whose grit, compassion, and unwavering integrity taught me how to find ballast in every storm. Your tireless work ethic and your resilience through hardship showed me what it takes to thrive in a world full of conflict.

*And to all who embody the spirit of the scientist*—those who follow truth with courage and boundless curiosity, even when the pursuit pains them, yet remain open to changing course when new evidence beckons. Your steadfast willingness to wayfind births progress.

—JAS

If there is no struggle, there is no progress.

Those who profess to favor freedom,
and yet depreciate agitation . . .

want crops without plowing up the ground.

They want rain without thunder and lightning.

They want the ocean without the
awful roar of its many waters.

—FREDERICK DOUGLASS

# CONTENTS

# CONFLICT RESILIENCE

# INTRODUCTION

We're an unlikely pair: a law professor and a neurologist. Whereas Bob has been teaching and writing about conflict resolution and negotiation for nearly thirty years, for the past twenty years Joel has been teaching and writing about people's brains and their behaviors. Now—together—we've written a book about something very different. It's called conflict resilience.

Though we come from different fields, we share deep academic and clinical experience in academia and a relentless desire to make a meaningful, practical, and lasting difference in the real world through our work. Coincidentally, we arrived at the same conclusion about a growing collective unwillingness to engage with political and other differences like—but not limited to—race, gender, class, and identity.

Bob noticed this reticence to confront conflict and differences first in his students, then in his professional and personal orbit. The range of views expressed both in the classroom and in his social interactions narrowed, significantly. Whatever expressions of difference he did observe often escalated in unproductive ways. Sometimes this was fueled by avoidance—whether through self-censure or moving past potentially contentious topics as if they didn't exist. Bob would witness this in his "The Lawyer as Facilitator" course, where he'd spend twelve weeks teaching law students the skills needed to facilitate hard conversations, such as creating a low-risk space where parties with opposing views can feel comfortable enough to express themselves openly. Yet on the last day of class, when the students' skills would be tested by facilitating a real conversation between real people who volunteered to participate in a group exercise discussing polarizing topics that were timely and important (abortion, police reform, immigration, climate change, gun rights/control, etc.), the result was often the same: the students serving as facilitators would skirt the most uncomfortable issues and would instead focus their time on softer topics where deep disagreement would be less likely to present itself. This pattern showed Bob that, even when these skills are taught, the instinct to avoid conflict is real and pervasive. And as harmful polarization intensifies, so do the stakes for our society; we risk catastrophic consequences if we don't learn to work through the discomfort of disagreement.

Bob also noticed the opposite pattern of behavior constricting the range of viewpoints expressed in law school classroom conversations. That is, aggression in the face of conflict—a steamrolling of opposing views until the other party was sufficiently vanquished. He observed this during a student takeover of Harvard Law School's student center following a series of events that began with unknown persons placing black tape over the portraits of Black professors at the school and ended with a small group of students taking over the largest public space in the student center. The takeover, which lasted the entire semester, sent the most vocal partisans into opposing corners; they then inadvertently silenced a broad swath of students caught in the middle, too terrified or too exhausted to join in even a civil conversation. Similar dynamics play out on university campuses across the country on issues ranging from Israel/Gaza to free speech and more.

Despite many well-intentioned—yet sometimes perfunctory—efforts by university administrators to promote "dialogue," the reality on the ground has veered toward aggression and forced silencing. Student takeovers of the most hallowed spaces in U.S. higher education— from Harvard to Columbia to UCLA and Dartmouth—along with doxing on university campuses, congressional witch hunts, and the use of disciplinary hearings, police, and sometimes even military force by college administrators, all signify an alarming unraveling in our cultural fabric. Similar dynamics play out on a much smaller but no less consequential scale in a wide range of contexts in workplaces and families across the country. For example, multiple supervisors over many years avoid a hard conversation with a challenging employee ultimately resulting in workplace dysfunction and low morale across a department; otherwise-loving siblings conspire silently to avoid a conversation with each other or their aging parents about end-of-life decision-making because they know it will be painful to navigate and that agreement will be elusive or perhaps impossible. And on and on.

It's not just a lack of communication or negotiation skills that plagues us, though that is certainly a problem. Something feels profoundly different and troubling in this moment. This unraveling is not simply because we can't reach consensus. Rather, it's because we can't seem to live—let alone thrive or celebrate—with the discomfort of our disagreements.

Bob knew from his longtime service on the Harvard Law School Admissions Committee that there was at least as much diversity of perspective at the law school years after his graduation as there was when he was a student in the late 1990s. Yet it seemed almost impossible to spark meaningful productive conversation or dialogue across lines of difference.

As Bob observed a disastrous "all-school town hall," he noticed a recurring pattern in each exchange. It was as if the students' skills were limited to either avoiding expressing their views entirely or forcing their views on others like battering rams. At the core of both approaches was a lack of capacity and, in particular, an almost complete unwillingness to be in a place of disagreement and discomfort with others. This was most noticeable whenever there was no quick and easy "resolution" to the disagreement, which happens to be the case in most of the controversial and pressing contexts we face as we begin the second quarter of the twenty-first century.

That's when the lightbulb went off. He needed to do more than just teach his students effective negotiation and conflict resolution skills; he also needed to persuade them of the personal and professional value of sitting in the discomfort of disagreement and offer a practical approach on how to be present with the discomfort itself. Without this fundamental conviction and related skill set, he realized, not only would they leave a fair amount of money on the table as negotiators, but they would also lack the skills to be effective leaders.

The urgency to develop this capacity to sit with the discomfort of disagreement and difference has intensified. Americans find themselves in a frightening climate of poisonous division and increasing political violence. While recently grading students in his Negotiation Seminar at Georgetown Law School, Bob was struck by this line—thematic of sentiments expressed by many of his students—taken directly from the student's final self-reflection essay: "I try to avoid tension in *any* way that I can in order to prevent myself from feeling uncomfortable."

This capacity to sit with others in conflict and do the hard work of both listening and engaging with them is what Bob has termed *conflict resilience*. It is related to, but different from, conflict resolution, negotiation, mediation, or facilitation. It is their antecedent, the essential ingredient needed if we truly want to "get to yes" or at least get unstuck from the bad decisions and bad habits that continue to sabotage and betray our best selves.

Bob eagerly shared this topic for the first time at a public talk for PopTech in 2018. To his great surprise, the audience reaction was overwhelmingly positive. What resonated with general audience members was not the promise of a quick-and-easy shortcut to a solution for conflict and negotiation, but his stark departure from the assumption that problem-solving or resolution was the primary goal of facilitated dialogue or engaging across a line of difference. Unlike resolution, conflict resilience was accessible and achievable, something within their own control. Conflict resilience finally gave them the precise language to describe what they didn't know they needed but, at a visceral level, had felt was at the core of their pain all long.

Enter Joel, who observed these same disturbing patterns of behavior among colleagues, students, and patients across lines of identity and generations at academic medical centers, where he teaches neurology and conducts clinical research, and throughout health systems, where he mediates difficult care decisions for patients and their families in settings where resources are limited and ethical ambiguities abound, often in life-or-death situations.

During our early conversations, Joel explained the neurological framework for what Bob recognized as a significant gap in his field. What Bob saw as personal and professional deficiency, Joel saw also as an evolutionary and physiological problem. Yet both of us agreed that improvement was possible with awareness, knowledge, and deliberate practice. This was when our collaboration started in earnest.

The more we riffed, the more we realized that a book marrying conflict resilience and negotiation with the latest cutting-edge research into brain science could make a consequential and timely contribution, one that could add value for everyone from executive leaders to government officials to friends and family members.

Like our own central nervous system, the "brain piece" of our work holds the framework and the various concepts and prescriptions of our approach together. It helps us understand how to make sense of a world that can feel utterly chaotic at times, how to overcome obstacles to sitting with moments of disagreement, and how to grow from them.

Neither exclusively about conflict resolution nor the neuroscience of human behavior, this book combines the practical applications of both fields to teach readers how to turn conflict and negotiation into an act of union, a chance to bring people together, and an invitation for radical transformation in how we interact with our friends and families, our coworkers, and our neighbors.

At the same time, you will learn how to change in your approach to moments of discomfort and conflict, which will empower you to engage both the substance and the emotion of an issue with skill, grace, and fortitude.

In brief, our approach sets this book apart from other books you may have read in this space in two important ways:

1. The special definition of what conflict resilience is: a leadership capacity that is *prerequisite* to conflict resolution and negotiation, and a capacity that is declining—but essential—in our society; and,

2. The precise coupling of this idea with the latest insights and practical tactics from brain science, providing a transformative application and a prescription that flows from it beyond the negotiation table.

We are excited to share with you what we've learned from our diverse professional backgrounds and expertise, our unique collaboration, and the transformative journey we've laid out for you in this book.

...

Conflict is getting the best of us.

If you're currently putting off a long-overdue conversation with your boss about your career or dreading your next family get-together with your uberconservative uncle or your superwoke cousin, you know exactly what we're talking about. Just the thought of them probably makes your teeth sweat with anxiety and your heart stutter with adrenaline.

From our homes and community centers to C-suites and the halls of Congress, disagreements are frequently treated like "zero-sum contests," winner-takes-all propositions that allow little margin for error and even less room for productive conversations or opportunities for collaboration. A presidential election framed *not* around competing policy choices or directions for the country, but rather in the most extreme terms around "saving" the country from utter destruction that the other side would bring about if elected leaves little room for productive conversation around lines of difference. This unhelpful framing puts a tremendous and untenable strain on our most important relationships and institutions.

We're losing our ability—and our willingness—to sit in moments of tension or emotional discomfort with anyone with whom we may have a conflict or disagreement—friends, family, and neighbors alike.

And we're all starting to suffer the consequences.

We're feeling more stressed, more alienated, and more hopeless than ever before.

Between 2018 and 2021, the percentage of US adults who reported symptoms of serious psychological distress almost quadrupled from 3.9 percent to 15 percent, while what used to be about 1 in 10 adults reporting significant feelings of loneliness crept closer to 1 in 5. This is a dramatic change in just three years.

Compounding this worsening problem, a recent Gallup poll revealed that three out of every four Americans are dissatisfied with the way things are going in the country, a complete reversal of the state of the union twenty years ago, when 3 out of every 4 Americans were satisfied with the way things were going.

While all of the above may not be a direct consequence of conflict, we are fully persuaded that a substantial portion is connected to and complicated by our inability to handle conflict well across multiple levels: individual, interpersonal, family, community, organizational, and national.

Joel notes this pattern both in his patients and in emerging studies from the fields of neuroscience and the social and behavioral sciences. While Bob works with clients to navigate stressful conflict resolution, negotiation, and mediation situations, Joel tries to help families like the Wrights who needed to make a panicked last-minute decision about their mother's end-of-life care, a traumatic moral crisis that could have been prevented had the family (and their oncologist) engaged in the difficult conversation about prognosis and advanced planning that had been put off for years because it was easier to avoid rather than acknowledge an unpleasant truth.

The reasons why we all avoid conflict and moments of distress seem obvious, but there are always deeper and often more influential factors commanding us below the surface. For starters, our brains are prone to perceive disagreements with the same neural systems they use to perceive physical injuries and attacks.

Correct: our brains register a disagreement as a literal act of physical violence against us.

Left on their own, these same neural pathways and networks, which govern our complex pain reactions, amplify their effects through experience-induced neuroplasticity and synaptogenesis. The same neural pathways and networks that make us respond to the world with the experience and expectation of pain become stronger, more severe, and more deeply ingrained. Put another way: neurons that fire together, wire together.

Faced with this mental and physical stress reflex, we come to see most conflict and instances of negotiation as "bad," or ultimately painful and costly, a constant threat we guard against or try to avoid at all costs. Immediately, our instincts kick in with one of the five Fs: *fight, flight, freeze, fawn,* or *fester.* To deal with this literal discomfort, we might shrink away to protect ourselves or take shelter in behaviors that make us feel better—retreating to our comfort cocoons, where we find respite in our like-minded and carefully curated communities, or by numbing ourselves to arguments and bad feelings with food, alcohol, and other indulgent habits for analgesia.

Alternately, because we recognize differences as a threat, we engage them with hostility. Discussion is often marked by defensiveness, rancor, acrimony, aggression, criticism, and contempt, an especially corrosive response because feelings of resentment fester or prompt us to counterattack with spoken or unspoken forms of disrespect, ridicule, name-calling—or, worse, acts of physical violence.

What makes this even more dire is the fact that conflict continues all around us, in many different forms. Or, as Bob likes to say, conflict is as much a part of our day as breakfast, lunch, and dinner.

Consider the following scenarios:

- After a long day, you finally put the kids to bed. You walked your dog, cleaned up after dinner, and sat down to stream your favorite show. But you get a text from your boss: "Do you have time for a quick chat?" Your stomach turns. Even as you consider ignoring the message, you put in your earbuds, respond with a thumbs-up emoji, and resign yourself to another forty-five-minute postwork rant.
- You've always admired your dad. Over the last few years, however, his political views have drastically diverged from yours. It's impossible to talk to him about the news and it's become harder to speak with him about almost anything going on in your lives. You're starting to realize you're better off, mentally and emotionally, not speaking to him at all, because being around him breeds only negativity, resentment, and stress. You're left wondering, "What happened? When did I stop liking my dad?"
- You knew you'd regret volunteering to serve as chair of the search committee to recruit the next head of your local park conservancy. After an exhaustive process, the committee is considering two worthy candidates: a young Black woman and a middle-aged White man. Despite your best efforts, competing camps have formed, more aligned on general preferences than specific qualifications. The heated conversation centers on minor distinctions and vague explanations around "fit." But you know what's really going on. On the one hand, you want to name the elephant in the room. On the other, you worry it will alienate half the committee. Even worse, you worry that speaking openly will unite both camps against you, putting a target on your back. You're stuck and don't know where to start. Or if it's even worth the potential blowback.

Frustrated. Exhausted. Overwhelmed. Terrified. While we all cry out for wise leadership and common ground, gridlock, resentment, and name-calling prevail.

Despite the pervasiveness of conflict, our ability to handle it has atrophied. Unable or unwilling to negotiate conflict with skill, we ignore it or avoid it for as long as we can; when we can no longer avoid it, we escalate everyday disagreements and temporary flare-ups as if they're battles to the death. Neither approach addresses underlying issues, promotes stronger relationships, or yields satisfying results.

That's the bad news.

The good news is anyone can learn to reclaim conflict as a transformative force and start engaging moments of disagreement more effectively, with greater confidence, more compassion, and better results.

Drawing on our respective fields of expertise, we propose a radical new approach to conflict, befriending it as a powerful ally rather than a must-be-avoided, worst-case scenario.

We call our approach conflict resilience.

Simply put, conflict resilience is the ability to *genuinely sit with* and *grow from* conflict.

Conflict resilience stands apart from conventional approaches to conflict resolution that largely frame conflict as something to be prevented, managed, or "resolved." Instead, we champion the courageous act of willingly venturing into internal and external discomfort. This is the only way we can get ourselves "unstuck" from the same self-defeating and polarizing approach to conflict that continues to inflict harm and impose costs on our families, friendships, workplaces, community, and country.

Combined, our areas of expertise put us in a unique position to explain and leverage the inner mechanics of conflict—literally what's going on in our bodies and our brains during moments of distress—and teach you how to cultivate conflict resilience and start negotiating conflict with empathy, authenticity, and accountability.

More than just a shift in internal orientation, conflict resilience champions a set of skills and behaviors that allow us to engage constructively and authentically with people we disagree with, while simultaneously remaining accountable to our own behavior and, yes, our own portion of responsibility in the fight. Like emotional intelligence, conflict resilience is at once a mindset and a set of actions we can practice and perfect over time. Every one of us—whether you think you're the world's greatest negotiator or the most hopeless conflict avoider you know—can level up this ability.

Though perfecting conflict resilience admittedly requires regular practice and continued effort, we promise that you will reap immediate benefits just as regular exercise engages and strengthens a particular muscle group. By figuring out how our brain reads and responds to moments of distress and discomfort, we can single out and harness our emotional and mental triggers before they have a chance to exert their full influence on our choices and our behavior. Believe it or not, it is entirely within our power to rewire, or reroute, the same neural pathways that determine our decision-making processes, dictate our patterns of behavior, and destabilize our ability to remain cool, calm, and collected in every situation. That's right—we can physically gain agency over our fight-flight-freeze-fawn-or-fester instinct.

What starts to take shape is a newfound psychological, emotional, and physiological resilience, which helps us endure discomfort and disagreement without buckling under internal or external pressures and empowers us to negotiate conflict and mediate differences from a stronger position of self-awareness and self-assuredness, and finally start engaging high-stakes situations and contentious moments that previously overwhelmed us.

This is what becoming conflict resilient means, and this is why becoming conflict resilient is so necessary today.

We've synthesized our framework to becoming more conflict resilient into three overarching steps so they are easier to remember and to increase the chances that you'll be able to invoke these skills in the heat of the moment:

Step 1. NAME (and dig deep)
Step 2. EXPLORE (and be brave)
Step 3. COMMIT (and own the conflict)

We've divided this book into three parts that correspond to each step of the conflict resilience "protocol." In each part, we break the macro-step down further into accessible, useful micro-steps with lessons, concepts, and skills that successively build on each other, culminating in choosing a way forward and imparting what you've learned within your organization, teams, communities, and the people you care about most. Each step is representative of the concepts and tools that come together to form the overarching framework of conflict resilience. Whatever disagreements or negotiations you encounter, you'll be able to cycle through these steps to navigate any conflict, leaning into them regardless of how the specific circumstances of the conflict may evolve.

Perhaps counterintuitively, conflict resilience invites us to start with ourselves. As an essential first step, conflict resilience asks us to recognize the role we play in a specific conflict and start to recognize how our learned responses to an external threat hinder our ability to mature, to move on, and to make progress in every aspect of our lives.

None of us are immune to the insidious ways conflict limits us, professionally and personally. From settling for a mediocre career and making poor managerial decisions, to staying in unfulfilling relationships or falling victim to default helplessness, we all have at one point in our life held ourselves back either because we were afraid of "starting a fight" or because we convinced ourselves "it" wasn't worth the trouble. And what do we have to show for it? Dissatisfaction and distrust. Cynicism and self-doubt. Anger and resentment. And other emotional precursors to pervasive feelings of inadequacy and shame and guilt, all of which exacerbate our already fraught relationship with conflict and concretize our unwillingness to engage it in any meaningful or productive way. This only perpetuates our patterns of bad behavior and compels us more deeply into our carefully curated silos, echo chambers, and superficial safe spaces that ensure we'll never again have to consider a single thought or preference or point of view in opposition to our own.

Why would we suggest learning how to sit *in* conflict rather than teaching you yet another way to get *out* of it? Because it's the only way any of us will ever start to move on from our personal and professional dissatisfaction, and it's the only real and effective chance for all of us to finally put an end to our current climate of suspicion and strife, acrimony and alienation.

When we sit in the presence of others with whom we may disagree strongly but with whom we can maintain civility and curiosity, we almost certainly discover domains of shared interest and connection. Even in rare circumstances when we fail to find these, we can often still develop a better—more useful—appreciation for why our family, friends, coworkers, and fellow citizens hold different views. At a minimum, we develop a greater sense of acceptance about the circumstances of the disagreement, and we are better equipped to handle the times when we're inevitably confronted with one of the many challenging and disturbing ways these disagreements can manifest themselves.

As a transformative force, conflict resilience can correct self-sabotaging or toxic patterns of behavior, help mend broken relationships, and lighten (or eliminate) the weight of family strife, all while relieving the constant stress and despair that come from active conflict or the impending doom it conjures in its absence.

Conflict resilience can also reverse the interpersonal breakdown you may be experiencing professionally due to stress, low job satisfaction, reduced creativity, high turnover, or lost revenue. The notion that professional organizations and communities are better when everyone in them agrees with each other and "gets along" simply defies decades of solid research that shows that every kind of diversity—including a diversity of viewpoint—enhances an organization, from the top decision-makers to the bottom line. Greater diversity and inclusivity in the workplace enhances the ability to recruit and retain talent, maximizes productivity, increases innovation, augments team performance, improves decision-making, and boosts financial performance across every metric.

At the same time, universities, companies, and other nonprofits succeed when they attract the best talent from every group—across politics, ideology, race, ethnicity, gender, religion, geography, and more—not just the "best" from the group of people who most resemble the way everyone else in the organization tends to think, look, and act.

But the value of diversity doesn't get accrued to anyone's benefit if people don't have the willingness, capacity, or skill to actually speak about those differences of viewpoint and approach them openly and constructively with each other. And even when they do have the willingness, capacity, and skill to do so, it doesn't happen if an organization doesn't have in place processes that create spaces or opportunities conducive to this highly advantageous conflict.

Individually and collectively, we need to start cultivating conflict resilience and practice it during moments of disagreement with the people we care about, people we don't, people we work with, people we live next to, and people we do business with—whether it's our uberconservative uncle or our superwoke cousin, our demanding boss who refuses to let us alone in the evenings, or an adversary sitting across the negotiating table or standing on the opposite side of the political aisle. The more quickly we figure out how to do this, the more quickly we can start to make meaningful and lasting change in how we handle conflict and turn even the most difficult, frustrating, and contentious conversations into opportunities for reconciliation and collaboration, career advancement, and personal transformation.

In the following pages, we'll teach you how to develop and flex your conflict-resilient muscles and start handling conflict without escalating it, avoiding it, or surrendering your most closely held values or most desirable outcomes. We will also explain in easy-to-follow language how our brains and bodies process conflict and teach you surprisingly simple (yet in no way simplistic) steps, strategies, and best practices on how to emerge from moments of conflict more empowered and with more equanimity—from uncomfortable family get-togethers and contentious PTA meetings to divisive political debates and the toughest negotiation tables. Drawn from emerging developments in neurology, psychology, and cognitive neuroscience and material developed by Bob and his colleagues over decades at the Program on Negotiation at Harvard Law School, these include self-diagnostic audits, best practices for developing better behavior, and—once you're ready—suggestions for picking the right time, the right place, and the right forum for engaging others.

To bring these lessons to life, we'll share examples of harrowing struggle and stirring success from our own professional and personal experiences, as well as stories of conflict resilience in action from courageous and resourceful figures across history, professions, political persuasions, and nationalities.

Part 1

# NAME
# (AND DIG DEEP)

## Chapter 1

# GETTING PAST EXCUSES
# TO DIAGNOSES

When Katie set foot in Bob's office, she was more exasperated and apologetic than most of the clients he coaches on conflict and negotiation issues.

She was in a fight with her mother. Again. This time about Thanksgiving. Katie wanted to celebrate in Boston, where she lives with her husband, Syd, and their three children. But to no one's surprise, her mother insisted they celebrate with her and Katie's side of the family in Columbus, Ohio.

This is the same power struggle Katie and her mother have had for close to a decade. Starting every Labor Day, Katie and her mom deliver the same lines and preheated arguments they rehearse every year, ending in the same inevitable and frustrating holiday "compromise."

Katie had always loved returning to her parents' home and spending the long holiday weekend with her siblings and extended family. This started to change after she met Syd fifteen years ago. Now married, Katie and Syd settled down a few blocks away from Syd's parents in Boston. Because their children regularly saw Syd's side of the family, the two agreed they would celebrate most holidays in Ohio. Thanksgiving was the exception. Since this holiday had special meaning for Syd and his family, they decided as a couple to alternate each Thanksgiving between the two families—one year in Boston, the next year in Ohio.

When Katie came to speak with Bob in early September, it was a Boston year. Or at least it was supposed to be. Her mom was already hounding her about her plans. ("Your father and I aren't going to be alive forever.") But what was different this year was that her mother's hounding was escalating into blame-shifting ("Your sister had such a rough year with her divorce. The least you could do is be here for her.") before finally shifting into hostile accusations. ("Syd brainwashed you! He's turned you against me and you know it!")

On some calls, Katie would fight back and defend herself. On others, she would fall silent and sullen, sick of the entire situation and how it made her feel.

Katie knew how this would turn out. Following another blowout fight with her mom and another stressful conversation with her husband, she would adopt an unhappy compromise and spend Thanksgiving Day in Boston with Syd's family, then fly out to Columbus first thing Friday morning. This would mean spending barely any time celebrating with Syd's family on Thanksgiving evening, followed by a frantic all-night packing session and an ungodly early morning flight—with three cranky children in tow. Then, when they finally arrived, exhausted and annoyed, her mother would harp about how terrible it was that she chose to miss such a lovely dinner and what a shame it was that the grandchildren couldn't all be together on such a special day.

Katie felt stuck and sad, angry and resigned. To make matters worse, her husband was upset that—once again—he had to give up time with his family on Thanksgiving. More troubling to Katie, he was growing increasingly frustrated with her reluctance to put her foot down and end this ridiculous fight.

"All I want is to get out of this mess," she confessed.

Bob is used to working with people who find themselves trapped in a no-win situation—stuck between a rock and a hard place. He runs workshops and executive coaching sessions, training experts and leaders in virtually every profession, from high-ranking members of the U.S. and other European and Middle Eastern governments to small business owners and entrepreneurs. He teaches professionals how to manage conflict and engage in mutual-gains negotiations—an approach to negotiation where the goal is to create more value for all parties rather than simply haggle over what is often mistakenly perceived as a fight over a fixed negotiation pie, the illusion that there is a limited set of resources and possible outcomes to a negotiation.

In recent years, however, ordinary people like Katie have started contacting Bob to help them negotiate their everyday conflicts and unresolved differences. Relatedly, many of the C-suite executives he coaches have started to use Bob to help them through matters unrelated to their work, often personal challenges with family and friends. At first he was surprised by this trend. But the more he sat with people and the more closely he listened to their predicaments, the more this uptick made sense. More and more Bob noticed that folks tended to shy away from conflicts, especially emotionally fraught ones. Avoidance instead of engagement has always been tempting, but in the last decade Bob has observed a marked uptick in this "run for the hills" kind of engagement strategy.

In parallel, Joel observed the same trend but through a neurological lens. One possible explanation for this behavioral pattern has to do with the concepts of salience and sensitization. Salience is a brain function that makes some things stand out more than others, which helps us determine whether something barely registers on our radar, or if it registers as a matter of life and death. With a lack of exposure to anything over time, the brain registers it as more salient—it stands out more—in a process of sensitization. Thus the brain focuses more intently on the novelty and, more often, all the possible dangers of this lesser-known thing, perceiving it as a greater threat. This is the opposite of desensitization (also known as adaptation), which lowers the urgency of an experience with repeated exposure—as the brain concludes "oh, that wasn't so bad," it eventually stops tagging future experiences as a potential danger. Through sensitization, the brain magnifies the potential harmful consequences of experiences that have become foreign, triggering the body's natural survival response to perceived threats. In other words, avoiding the negative feelings that naturally come with conflict by avoiding conflict altogether paradoxically leads to sensitizing the brain to conflict, increasing the level of perceived threat from conflict, and influencing how intensely we respond to these moments of potential distress. The more we avoid, the more we sensitize, the more motivated the brain is to avoid conflict—again and again until it's like we've become allergic to conflict.

This is what Katie was going through. Her back-and-forth from sullen avoidance to all-out battle reinforced her brain's perception that conflict was simply a no-win, dead-end proposition. Most of us, it turns out, have a similar evaluation of conflict in our lives. Katie was oblivious to how visibly distraught she had become in Bob's office. At the slightest suggestion of imagining conflict with her mother, her brain's survival reflex was in overdrive: she was jumpy, breathing shallow, clenching her jaw, tensing her shoulders high and tight.

"It's clear to me you care deeply about figuring this out," Bob said. "And it's also clear you've gone to great lengths to accommodate your mother."

"I've tried to," she said. "I really have."

Bob probed further. "What have you tried so far?"

"Well, I've asked my husband and friends for advice. I tried talking to my dad about it to get his help. I even talked to my in-laws to find out what they would do if they were in my shoes. But in the end, over and over again, I found myself struggling and failing in the same last-minute conversation, as if I were in *Groundhog Day*." Bob picked up on something important. She saw the options as either fight or flee. But she hadn't genuinely considered what it would be like to embrace and engage the conflict differently—as an opportunity with nuance, complexity, and possibility.

In that moment, Bob was tempted to give her an extended professorial lecture on why her strategies were both common and unlikely to succeed. Instead, Bob took an atypical approach by asking her if she knew anyone in her life who could handle a situation like this well.

"My older sister Becca would. She's just great at this stuff. It's one of the things I love about her."

"Great. Can you act out for me how Becca would handle this?"

Katie let out a long breath, straightened in her seat, and transformed into another person.

Her voice settled into a deeper register with a slower, measured pace. "Mom," she said with full confidence, "I've been thinking a lot about how every other year you and I get into a back-and-forth over how we're going to spend Thanksgiving. It's always a hard conversation for me, and I expect it's probably hard for you too. I was wondering if I could ask you about your experience of this dynamic, share how I experience it, and then perhaps we could find another way of talking this through some more soon..."

Katie nailed it. She was assertive about her experience, open and direct about what she hoped the conversation would be about, genuine in her willingness to listen and seriously consider her mom's concerns. She was also adroit in framing the dilemma as a shared problem.

"It seems you already know exactly what to say to your mother."

"In here, sure. But when I talk to her, I get all stuck and confused inside. I retreat into 'react' mode."

Bob realized he could have easily coached Katie in effective negotiation techniques and strategies, identified her walk-away alternatives, arming her with many of the time-tested tools of his trade. But, after running through this simple roleplay with Katie acting as if she were Becca, he realized this would be the wrong move for at least two reasons. First, because Katie knew what to say. She had just done it as Becca. So giving her some lines or a script would be unhelpful; secondly, while a dress rehearsal and some practice might be useful, it was unlikely to address the bigger issues underlying Katie's discomfort.

First, Katie's challenge here was not understanding what to say or how to frame the issue. It was identifying what made it hard for her to enact those behaviors in the conversation with her mother as herself, not just when channeling her sister in a coaching session with Bob. And, related to this was a second issue, one that we see increasing at every level of contemporary life—namely, the extreme discomfort of raising a hard topic for fear that it is pointless or beyond resolution. So often in our work we hear a common lamentation, "But even if I engage this, I'll end up in the same spot, so why bother with the hard work, the emotion, the exhaustion, and the discomfort?"

Yet what we know from all the evidence available is that engaging in the discomfort of conflict is almost always worth it. It is not pointless. There is value that comes from direct engagement. It may be different for each person based on the specifics of the situation, but you need to trust us that it's there.

Like many of us, when confronted with conflict in her family, Katie became tongue-tied and stuck. No matter how differently she tries to negotiate conflict each time, escalation or escape always seems to come up as the only viable option for confronting a problem that is unlikely to yield a fully satisfying solution.

Figuring out how to sit in conflict constructively, even in situations where there might not be a perfect or "value-creating" solution, is not unique to Katie. We see it all around us—at the level of family life, community and organizational decision-making, and national policy formation and consensus: there seem to be a growing number of situations where the issue to be "negotiated" is or feels zero-sum, where the space for problem-solving seems limited, and where the instinct to either avoid completely or fight to the bitter end seems like the only option.

In the early days of his start-up company, Joel found himself deep in the turbulent chaos of creating an early-stage business out of nothing—armed with only an innovative idea and a passion to see it come to life. As Joel and his cofounder Julius were figuring through their go-to-market strategy and still testing out their value proposition, a superstar growth hacker—whom we'll call Laura—reached out to explore the possibility of joining their team. The timing, market, and business they were building were just right for her. Joel jumped at the opportunity to bring on someone with her level of skill and experience, because he believed she could catapult them into the next stage of their business much sooner and faster than they'd be able to on their own. Julius, though, wasn't so sure. He felt they should wait until they had secured more funding before investing in an expensive hire, even if her talent was unquestionably top-notch.

Joel was sympathetic to Julius's "roll our sleeves up" mentality, but he also knew that such an approach had its limit, namely time, energy, personal resources, and opportunity. You can only roll your sleeves up for so long; the longer you do it, the more you sacrifice, the greater the risk of being made obsolete by a competitor that made the investment you didn't. And Laura wasn't going to wait on them forever to decide. Time was running out and over the course of a month Joel and Julius's disagreement bubbled up daily, often in the form of little debates between them on the merits and demerits of whether to hire Laura or keep "white-knuckling" with what they had to work with. But in a way, this series of highly intellectual, logic-driven debates was an easy way to avoid the tense feelings that were simmering underneath the disagreement.

It was only when they shifted the conversation by asking each other in earnest, "What are you really worried about here?" that they began to find clarity around how to move forward. That was when Julius confessed that he couldn't stop thinking about one of their former competitors that had to shutter their business because they ran out of funds; they had hired too many senior team members too early and he was terrified of making the same mistake. Joel, meanwhile, revealed his apprehension over the potential fallout from excessively self-assured white-knuckling—thus making the ultra-lean approach to their operations ultimately pointless.

Keeping their dialogue focused on the substance of the conflict all-too-conveniently avoided the emotional piece that was motivating at least part of their disagreement. What followed in that conversation was a conversation about a whole host of emotions each of them was feeling about their joint venture, everything from fear, exhaustion, and weariness to hope, anticipation, and pride. Not engaging on an emotional level up until that moment surely had an aesthetic appeal—giving the impression that they're a team of perfect high-performing professionals without a trace of messy "unhelpful" feelings. But in this case, the feelings were as much part of the conflict as the supposed "facts" and figures. Avoiding talking about them did not help. Moreover, as you'll discover later, suppressing your feelings can make it harder for you to engage with people when you disagree and make you less effective at harnessing the upsides of conflict and managing its downsides.

Especially for those of us who fear the pain and messy chaos of conflict with the people we care about most, imagine what would be possible if we unlearned our belief that successful personal and professional relationships require us to always be in a state of harmony. Imagine if we replaced that unrealistic and unachievable "ideal" with a more authentic truth: engaging with and working through conflict directly and authentically can bring you closer and make you happier and more successful.

Going a step further, we propose that conflict not only brings us closer together, but is indeed the *only* way to cultivate enduring relationships or succeed in mining the benefits of a diverse team, workforce, or even country.

Yes, engaging conflict directly can sometimes lead to the end of a relationship. But the only way forward and deeper in a relationship that can hold together and be real is to navigate through the toughest conflicts. That process can fortify and lead to new levels of understanding and connection.

## IF YOU CAN'T STAND THE HEAT, HOW WILL YOU LEARN TO COOK?

It's totally understandable for conflict to trigger a feeling of dread and repulsion when it increasingly seems like you're damned if you do, damned if you don't. Regardless of the "hot-button" topic, genuine dialogue with people who have different opinions and perspectives often feels nearly impossible; most of us are just not equipped for it. When civil dialogue does occur, instead of being celebrated it's often decried as capitulation, betrayal, or pointless—especially when the dialogue fails to result in a tidy fairy-tale resolution. If we avoid confrontation, we might feel that we dodged a bullet, but it doesn't take long for that sense of reprieve to morph into a sense of impending doom. We feel something is amiss, a pernicious gnawing that slowly eats away at our self-confidence and self-worth. Over time, what's left is self-doubt and self-loathing, which manifests outwardly as resentment, distrust, and isolation. Like Katie, we end up feeling stuck and annoyed, dispirited and dismayed, and maybe even a bit hopeless.

Whether we examine these issues at a macro-societal level or at the micro-relational level, like in the case of Katie and her mother, some of the root causes and some of the prescriptions are the same.

Yes, it is important for us to know *what* to say and *how* to say it.

But that is only half the battle. We first need to undergo a fundamental reckoning of how we perceive conflict in our lives and our own willingness to engage the discomfort and uncover its many benefits. Put another way: learning what and how to cook is important, but you first need to learn how to stand the heat of the kitchen if you ever expect to make a meal.

Rather than focusing on devising a strategy to solve the "Thanksgiving problem" or finally "win" this ongoing argument, Katie instead needed to reckon with something more fundamental at the heart of why so many of us struggle with conflict today.

And so do we.

The hard truth is that conflict isn't the problem.

We are.

It's easy to think that Katie is being ridiculous and just needs someone to snap her out of it. But most everyone has a hard time reckoning with conflict in at least some contexts and will act in ways similar to Katie when they pop up. At some point you're going to need to have a difficult conversation, perhaps with a boss or colleague. Maybe you're feeling frustrated that you've been doing the yeoman's share of work on a project with a coworker, and you've exhausted all the conversations with them and so now you need to talk to the boss. Or maybe you're overworked and need a break. Or you deserve a promotion. Or you just accepted a job with a manager in another department in the same company. In any case, it's convenient to blame 100 percent of the distress we feel about needing to have this difficult conversation on our boss; and, if you're anything like us, there are allies in our lives who will be a little too willing to join us in the blaming and scapegoating. We too often believe the problem is limited to "them," the situation, or both. We are quick to cast the other as the villain and ourselves as either the hero or the victim. In the face of a challenging conflict or conversation, we are the ones who become reluctant to speak up for ourselves and we are the ones who fail to listen to those with whom we disagree when they speak their minds. Becoming conflict resilient means digging deep into ourselves and being honest; it means acknowledging our personal contribution to the situation and to our own distress.

Consider a recent executive coaching session that Bob had with the CEO of a large progressive advocacy organization in Boston. In the session, the CEO bemoaned the fact that there were warring constituencies within the organization who would bring up issues of microaggressions (Gen Z complaining about Gen X) and ageism (the other way around). Were these issues being brought up in direct conversation? Absolutely not. Instead they were raised directly with the CEO, and the complaining party demanded that the CEO discipline or otherwise solve the problem on behalf of the aggrieved party.

Where the CEO was stuck is that, in every single circumstance, when the CEO asked about the parties' willingness to have a direct one-on-one conversation, even if mediated by a facilitator, the answer was some version of "No. It's not my job to fix this. It's yours."

Of course, from the CEO's perspective, it was nearly impossible for him to address the situation if he had no permission to describe the offending behavior to the accused employee. What would have been an admittedly difficult yet appropriate one-on-one conversation was turned into a demand for an adjudicated disciplinary response without evidence or explanation for the accused, leaving the CEO stuck.

From Bob's perspective, it was yet another example of a situation where an unwillingness to handle uncomfortable conflict directly resulted in high costs, greater misunderstanding, and dysfunction.

Again, the difficult truth is this: There are times we all act like Katie or the staff at the nonprofit. We fall for the lie that conflict is bad or that the other person is the *real* problem.

But conflict resilience teaches how to reframe how you think about conflict and, just as importantly, how you perceive your role in it. Regardless of your previous responses to conflict, it is entirely within your power to transform even the most impossible-seeming situation into an opportunity for joint learning, advancing your interests, and improving relationships.

Acknowledging you are part of the problem sets you on this path toward conflict resilience. But it's only the first step. Katie was avoiding conflict with her mother, because she had become terrified of it and its potential consequences. Like Katie, you're going to keep repeating the same default reactions to conflict that leave you chasing your own proverbial tail unless you start to figure out, moment -to-moment, how you're thinking and feeling about the conflict.

To be clear, you must understand how and why you react to conflict the ways you do before you can expect to level up your skill to effectively negotiate conflicts. And this requires—in part—figuring out how your brain works.

## YOU ARE *NOT* A RATIONAL BEING AND IT'S NOT YOUR FAULT

Despite how well-intentioned they may be, we think that an important reason why some efforts to create healthier relationships (to coexist in society or at home) and healthier democracies (to coexist domestically or globally) fail is that they're not rooted in truly understanding human cognition. At the micro and macro levels, it helps to learn about how your brain works and how it navigates the world around you, so you can catch when it might be leading you astray and then course-correct, making better choices that are more aligned with your values and your interests.

Learning about your brain gives you greater agency.

The more aware you are of how your brain naturally works when experiencing conflict—and the tricks it can play on you—the better you are at learning how to work *with* your brain rather than against it. Just becoming aware that your brain plays a role in your experience with conflict already empowers you to be more mindful and intentional in how to make different, better choices in the future. It also takes away some of the shame and judgment we usually associate with reactions that are just a part of being human.

Most of us aren't taught very much about what's really inside the mysterious black box that holds our mind, let alone how it all works. To become more effective at handling conflict and negotiations, it helps to remember that you—your body—are the product of over 6 million years of evolution. Humans are still around today because our bodies evolved to be exceedingly good at surviving through our capacity to learn and adapt. Just as we evolved legs that allow us to move more easily toward dinner and away from danger, we also evolved a brain that allows us to perceive, predict, think, plan, and act so we can be better at surviving.

Our brains evolved to be our most effective survival hack, granting us the ability to perceive and recognize harm, predict potential harm, and take actions to stop or prevent that harm. Because of this, we now have 100 *billion* neurons wired together through 100 *trillion* connections that coordinate together in systems, like musicians in a 100-billion-piece orchestra—strings, woodwinds, brass, and percussion players all coordinating together to play the epic improvised symphony that is your life.

The most complex biological structure known to science is your brain. But you don't need to function at the level of a neuroscientist; it's fine to start with just the basics. For starters, your neurons send signals up to 1,000 times each second (that's 1 quadrillion information relays every second of your waking life). And let's not just give credit to your neurons. There are billions of supporting and immune cells of various types performing different jobs. At a high level, your brain can be divided into sections with distinct roles—from breathing and heart rate to coordinating movement and involuntary reflexes. The most developed part, the cortex (the outermost layer of your brain), does most of the computing, holding memories and your ability to plan, think, learn, organize, imagine, dream, and hope. Above all else, the cortex is responsible for making predictions of the future.

Whether accurate or not, predictions help us survive, allowing us to act to avoid potential danger or move toward promising resources. Everything your brain does, it usually does to protect you and the people you care about. It's just that these same evolutionary survival tactics are not as effective in some aspects of the present-day environment, an ecosystem that has evolved way faster than the human brain. In fact, these same neurological tactics can sometimes work against you, especially with regard to how they advise us when it comes to conflict.

Consider Iris. When she and Cass disagreed during their Monday morning team meeting over which social media platform to target in their new marketing campaign, Iris's neurologically wired instinct to avoid the threat of conflict led her to cancel their follow-up discussions for the rest of the week. This delayed the campaign's launch and introduced both chaos and a harmful tension within the team's dynamic. But fortunately, much like it's possible to forget a bad habit or learn a new language, your brain is "plastic"—ever-changing in response to experiences—and slowly over time you can reprogram, rewire, and reshape your brain. Even in the short term, you can learn to regulate your brain's survival reflexes, especially how you process and respond to them.

## THIS IS YOUR BRAIN ON CONFLICT

You have a perceiving-predicting system that helps you recognize conflict when it's happening or mentally simulates possible future conflict scenarios (based on past scenarios you've been in that have led to conflict) and pairs that with information to play out what might happen. If you've had relevant past experiences that were negative or if you don't have complete or accurate information, your brain's survival system registers a negative emotional signal using valence ("How good or bad is this?") areas and habit-forming areas. This negative signal is experienced as painful, because it uses the same exact brain areas involved in physical pain and, if it registers as significantly painful, it will set off your brain's safety alarm—"Danger! Danger!"

This triggers a cascade of adrenaline and other chemical signals that flood our body to prepare for urgent action (e.g., your heart races, your breath shortens, your muscles tighten). If the negative signal is overwhelming, our brain's higher-order system (for thinking, planning, deciding) is bypassed and our survival system triggers an impulse reaction, usually an old habit we learned to protect ourselves from harm or painful negative feelings. If the negative signal isn't overwhelming or we regain control in time, our higher-order system gets us to deliberate through pros and cons of possible options, make a plan, and ultimately act.

So, if certain conflict situations trigger especially painful negative signals for you (like high-stakes disagreements with your boss, spouse, or parent), chances are your brain will make it all too easy for you to react by choosing your go-to option among the five Fs: *fight* (combative overcompensation or counterattacking), *flight* (avoidance), *freeze* (stonewalling or experiencing feelings of disconnection with your body or surroundings, known as depersonalization, dissociation, and derealization), *fawn* (placating or inappropriate yielding), or *fester* (numbing or suppressing, often with behaviors and substances that in excess are highly destructive or deadly).

However you react, the painful negative feeling usually decreases, which, through a system that involves dopamine, makes your brain remember what happened with greater intensity so the next time the conflict situation comes up (perceived or potential) you'll be more likely to react the same way again and again. This negative cycle creates a loop that will shortchange you and the people around you—if not immediately, in the long run.

Consider Bowen, who is a self-identified lifelong "people pleaser." When a librarian asks him to pay a late-return fee that he doesn't actually owe, he considers contesting it. But his brain starts sounding the conflict-danger alarm so loudly that he immediately goes to his default reaction to "fawn." So instead of disagreeing with her, he thanks her for catching that and ponies up the money with a smile and a pained "No worries! Thank you so much. Have a wonderful weekend!" Now imagine what happens with this negative maladaptive behavior loop when Bowen's significant other, whom he's definitely fallen out of love with, turns to him and sweetly says, "Hey, what do you think about us moving in together?"

While falling into a nearly-automatic response that barely even registers as a "choice" may seem like a grim, inescapable reality, in later chapters we will cover the specific skills to help you break and retrain this habit loop in your brain, so the next time you encounter conflict you will be equipped with an upgrade—from a state of default helplessness to one of learned effectiveness. For example, a strategy we can use to trigger a breaker for these onerous brain circuits, especially the circuits that have become deeply hardwired habits, is to get better at "meta cognitive skills." That is, thinking about thinking.

## GETTING META

If you're like most people, when put in Katie's position in the Thanksgiving dilemma, your brain probably saw the situation immediately as a zero-sum scheduling problem. That is, your brain registered the gestalt of the problem as a matter of how to take a finite resource (i.e., your time) and split it evenly among the people who want some of it.

No matter how intensely your mind thinks and feels that finding the right division of time is the correct solution, it may not be that helpful at all. It's hard to redirect the brain's thinking once it's anchored to its assessment of the situation, which of course then influences what you believe to be the best approach. This is why it's so important, as early in the process as possible, to pause and reflect—to assess what is going on below the surface of the problem. It's also important to spot all the underlying issues in a context like this so that you can assess for yourself that, though it appears zero-sum in nature (i.e., How will you divide the Thanksgiving holiday?), it is far from zero-sum. For example, even from what little we've learned about Katie's situation already, it becomes clear that some of her mom's interests—having the grandchildren be together, spending quality time with Katie in Mom and Dad's latter years, and having Katie support her recently divorced sister—can be met in creative ways that don't require mandatory and annual attendance at Thanksgiving. With even more exploration of what's important to Mom and to Katie, a keen negotiation analyst can make the zero-sum gremlin disappear. But it's hard to get to this more analytical and academic analysis if your mind has quickly coded the conflict as zero-sum: how to allocate a fixed resource, time, during a holiday. That's why having the tools from the field of negotiation and conflict management paired with skills in handling your brain's many tricks really matters.

Like Katie, if you feel like none of your attempts at a conflict have worked, it's very possible that you're unaware that your thinking is stuck on using a specific set of approaches based on a limited or even cramped conception of what the conflict really is. Katie had been using the same ineffective approach to the dilemma with her mother: avoiding direct engagement and instead asking others for advice. A central part of Katie's distress—central to what's making this dilemma extra painful for her—is that she needs to slow down, take a step back, and reassess the correct diagnosis underlying her painful dilemma. She needs to invite herself—genuinely, nonjudgmentally—to think about her thinking. Thinking about thinking can help make conflict feel less "hot" and less distressing for her, making it a little easier for her to sit and be more present and constructive with the conflict in the moment and for the future. This requires learning new metacognitive skills that will complement any negotiation skills that she has or will learn. And the investment of time and effort is worthwhile. One study even found that among sixty people who underwent metacognitive skills training, 57 percent of them continued to experience the distress-lowering benefits of the training after almost a decade.

## ACCEPTANCE IS A VIRTUE, AND A WAY FORWARD

To make progress, you—like Katie—must first accept the often-difficult truth that, in any conflict, you are an important part of the equation. In fact, you are the only part of the equation that you have any real control over. We find ourselves in a culture and society that sees conflict as poisonous and to be avoided or "winner-takes-all." We often live and work in environments—families, social circles, schools, churches, organizations—that paint conflict in a negative and destructive light. Then add to that your brain's natural tendencies to make the conflict much more challenging to navigate; you're more likely to act against your will in ways that are not constructive, if not counterproductive.

So, it makes complete sense that neither you nor any other human is perfect at conflict. Without a proper toolkit of familiar skills and a healthy dose of metacognitive regulation to keep your default reactions in check, your brain is prone to treat conflict situations as an existential threat, a legitimate death threat. Remember, your brain only wants to protect you—that's what it evolved to do well and it is hardwired to learn how to do better. It's no wonder Katie has done everything *but* constructively engage the conflict with her mother.

Rest assured, though: with a little bit of courage and a little bit of practice, your reactions to conflict—within your brain, heart, mind, and body—are 100 percent manageable. You just need to know where to start, and in the following chapter we'll teach you how to rethink your relationship with conflict and, ideally, befriend it.

## Chapter 2

# RETHINKING YOUR RELATIONSHIP WITH CONFLICT

### The Value of Becoming Conflict Positive

## HARVARD LAW SCHOOL—CAMBRIDGE, MASSACHUSETTS

The last streaks of dusk slip behind the horizon of the Harvard campus. Hunkered down inside three polished Harvard Law School conference rooms, a group of bright twentysomethings work in pairs, hovering over sleek laptops, writing down last-minute notes. They're law students, but they aren't preparing for a mock trial. Instead they're preparing to facilitate small groups of real-life citizens engaging in conversations on some of the most controversial issues of the day: abortion, LGBTQ+ rights, health care, police reform, recent presidential elections, racial justice, and immigration.

Today is the capstone of a groundbreaking new class Bob created at Harvard Law School, "The Lawyer as Facilitator," which envisions a new role for lawyers—not as advocates for a client, but rather as "holders of space" for people in conflict. Unlike litigation, winning is not the goal, and, unlike mediation, resolution is not the prize. The primary purpose of the course is simple: to teach students how to create a low-risk space where those with opposing views feel comfortable enough to express their own perspectives, have those opinions acknowledged by the others present in the group, then be ready to listen to the views and reasoning of peers who hold opposing stances.

Over twelve weeks, a dozen promising Harvard law students have worked with Bob, learning how to facilitate hard conversations.

Facilitating challenging conversations is an essential skill that lawyers and leaders are constantly called upon to do but typically have no formal training to help them execute successfully. In this unique class committed to the notion that facilitation can transform conflict, build relationships, and help parties achieve better outcomes, the students practiced skills like deep listening, empathy, and process design. They also learned how to ask "image building" questions to get participants to open up and give time and attention to strong emotions—all the while making sure to encourage participants to dig deeper in their reflections and comments and ensure that every voice is heard.

This last day of the class is the students' opportunity to put their books down and test their skills in dialogue sessions with real citizens recruited for this specific purpose.

As the sessions begin, Bob wanders from room to room, anxious and hopeful on behalf of both his students and the participants. His sleeves are rolled up and his arms are crossed. What hot-button topics, he wonders, would the sessions bring to the fore? How would his students handle personal attacks? What would they do if a participant breaks down in tears, or if one of the dialogues devolves into a shouting match?

Much to his surprise, however, none of this happens.

The student facilitators lead the participants through long-winded get-to-know-you icebreakers. Then, despite their assigned task, the facilitators steer the conversations away from open disagreement toward more unifying themes at the slightest hint of tension. In most of the dialogue sessions, participants who seem adamant about expressing their view are regularly shut down so the larger group can come together around shared—and less "explosive" or "divisive"—opinions.

This was definitely *not* what Bob had in mind. Each time he sees this happen, he crosses his arms tighter and tries not to hang his head lower.

At the start of a dialogue session on race and community-police relations, the facilitators asked dialogue participants, including several police officers, what they each believed was at the heart of the matter on this challenging issue. They responded one at a time:

**White Police Officer 1**: Training budgets

**White Female Participant**: Love

**White Police Officer 2**: Unfair media coverage

**Black Female Participant**: White supremacy

The facilitator heard the list, paused, and declared, "Let's focus on this idea of love."

The faces around the entire table immediately relaxed.

Conflict averted.

Ninety minutes later, the facilitators call the sessions over. The participants leave the oak and ivy of the Harvard campus behind them and return to their concrete and asphalt communities around Boston. While the student facilitators exhale and congratulate each other for avoiding hurt feelings or discomfort, Bob is convinced that his new class has failed miserably.

The post-dialogue debriefings of class participants confirm his suspicion. The students agreed the conversations were "well organized," "decent," and "mostly respectful." But in interviews with dialogue participants afterward, a different narrative emerges. While they agree the sessions were "pleasant" and "polite," none of them feel as if they had the opportunity to dive into any real substantive differences in the way they had hoped. And most leave a bit deflated about the purpose or value of dialogue across lines of difference.

Reviewing the students' post-dialogue reactions and the participants' feedback afterward, Bob wonders to himself, "What went wrong here?"

## LAKE PLEASANT—OTISFIELD, MAINE

Several months later, several hundred miles north, we find a cohort of young people who gather at a lakeside summer camp for nearly three weeks. These emerging leaders come from some of the most brutal and contentious conflict zones in the world: Israel, Palestine, India, and Pakistan. Called Seeds of Peace, the program is a self-described experiment that asks, "What would happen if we brought young people from opposite sides of conflict and gave them an opportunity to come together that would otherwise be impossible?"

When Bob first started working with Seeds of Peace more than a decade ago, the idea was that he would bring a team of negotiation students from Harvard Law School to work with graduates of the Seeds of Peace program to teach them skills of negotiation, mediation, and facilitation. Over time, though, even as he continued running workshops in Jerusalem, Tel Aviv, Cyprus, and Dubai, he learned so much more about handling conflict from these young leaders in action than he could have shared from the research and theory of a classroom.

During a much earlier summer session, captured in the award-winning documentary *Seeds*, 166 young teenagers anxiously started the first day of the camp with a commitment to focus on the long term. All they knew with certainty was that they would participate in daily dialogue sessions around the existential conflict engulfing their home.

After breakfast, twenty students sat together in a cramped cabin for their first "active listening" exercise. Tension escalated quickly.

An Israeli boy started by saying, "We need a country of our own. There's always a desire to come back to where you came from."

A Palestinian girl immediately replied, "But not 'a country of our own' as in '*take* at the expense of other people'!"

Clicking his teeth at the Israeli boy, a Palestinian boy shouted, "Why don't you go back to your land?"

The Israeli boy gripped the edge of his chair, readying for a fight.

"What the heck did you just say?! Go back. You don't deserve to be here."

A counselor facilitating the conversation interrupted the exercise. Instead of trying to ease tensions, the counselor asked all twenty students to stand up and walk to opposite sides of the room—those who support the Israeli position on one side, those who align with the Palestinian perspective on the other. As you might expect, all the Israelis stood together on one side of the room and the Palestinians stood on the other. From separate sides of the room, they stared into the eyes of the fellow Seeds, and the counselor let the tension continue to mount. The students' hearts pounded. Their breathing shallowed. Some were no longer able to hold back tears and wept.

"Finally," the counselor explained, "the bubble has popped."

Acknowledging the uncomfortable space between them, the Seeds sat down again in this literal space and, on their own accord, reflected on their commitment to make it through the conflict before them.

The daily dialogues were tough. At times, participants and facilitators wondered about the value of continuing. After all, their efforts are unlikely to fundamentally change the counterparts' views on the conflict. And it's almost certain that these dialogues would not be the catalyst that brought peace to their homeland. So, it's only natural to ask, "What's the point?"

But twenty-one days after they arrived, on the final day of camp, everyone agreed on one thing: something had clearly changed. "Once we actually listen and hear what the person is trying to say," a Palestinian Seed shared, "then there is actual progress. People start to say, 'Oh, I didn't know that.' 'My family didn't tell me this.' 'I wasn't taught this in school.'"

The story captured by the documentary mirrored the experience Bob witnessed in his own work with Seeds of Peace many years later, even as tensions in the region escalated and violence worsened. More than passively bearing through the experience, the Seeds engaged in the deliberate—and decidedly more difficult—practice of genuinely participating in their dialogue sessions, which empowered them to return home and start applying the skills they learned at camp and become better people and more effective leaders. The way they saw conflict changed gradually day after day, one dialogue after another, until one day, the natural distress of their conflict was less a terrifying searing pain to escape or to snuff. Through their differences, they found connection, community, and shared humanity. A solution to the turmoil in the Middle East? Certainly not. A genuine reorientation in the direction of shared humanity and solidarity? Without question! And, importantly, even as political peace in Israel/Palestine seems far away, many of the young people who participated in Seeds dialogues over the years have committed themselves to working in solidarity with each other to promote change, mutual dignity, and justice across ongoing lines of profound and painful difference.

Let's consider the stories side by side. On the one hand, highly educated, successful, intelligent Harvard Law School students struggled to engage conflict directly and with skill. Even after more than forty hours of in-class training in facilitating groups in conflict, their primary focus seemed to be avoiding it at all costs. Low in conflict resilience and worried about creating discomfort, they exerted more energy tending to a sugarcoated version of "dialogue" than they did diving into the most controversial and uncomfortable feelings and viewpoints of the participants.

On the other hand, the Seeds were adolescents, many of whom were groomed by their homelands to see the other as a mortal enemy. Yet they remained open and willing to sit with their adversaries and listen to their stories, as painful and triggering as that experience may have been. Whether by dint of their youth or the conditions in their home, in many respects, they have the enviable and undeniable capacity to experience conflict without running away from it or escalating it.

Unlike Bob's law students, who conspicuously shied away from open conflict, the Seeds came to understand that you can't get past conflict by going around it; you have to go through it.

Acknowledging this unpleasant truth, the Seeds exhibited an attitude of conflict resilience, which put them in a mental and emotional position of strength to stop seeing conflict as an enervating threat and to start embracing it as a transformative opportunity for personal growth and better outcomes for themselves, their families, and their communities.

Although the Seeds initially struggled with listening, almost all of them—regardless of what they believed—came to handle conflict with a fierce sense of integrity. They did this work in the context of a total and immersive experience for several weeks at an important developmental moment in their lives, and with a huge amount of support from counselors, context, and an intentionally designed environment that lowered the risk of engaging in hard dialogue, thus creating a space that encouraged it to happen.

This is what we mean by reshaping how we relate with conflict toward becoming conflict positive.

## BEFRIENDING CONFLICT

The aversion to truly open expression of differences—whether about deeply held political beliefs or about why you don't want to have your cousin in your wedding party—is understandable. We have fewer mainstream examples of healthy, robust, open, and respectful dialogue across core, value-laden differences. In their place, we instead have what can be considered mindless regurgitating of superficial talking points, mudslinging, and ad hominem attacks. Wanting to avoid the latter at all costs and not knowing what the former might look like, we unwittingly conspire to keep all potential conflict out of the room.

Additionally, finding a way into deep and genuine dialogue around differences takes time. It can be challenging for two people—let alone a group—to feel comfortable enough to engage at a deep and personal level, regardless of whether it's during a ninety-minute dialogue or a multi-week dialogue camp in the middle of the woods.

And so, in many cases, we abort before we attempt.

But befriending conflict empowers us to stick with it, just as Dr. Anthony Fauci was able to do early in his career, during the height of the AIDS/HIV crisis.

As director of the National Institute of Allergy and Infectious Diseases at the National Institutes of Health (NIH), Fauci was in charge of the government's efforts to identify a treatment for the disease that was ravaging the LGBTQ+ population. When most elected leaders refused to utter the word *gay* in public, Fauci was among the fiercest advocates inside Ronald Reagan's conservative administration working around the clock to combat a virus that was killing an entire segment of the population that many dismissed as unworthy of public support, resources, or even basic protection.

With this backdrop, Fauci woke up on the morning of June 26, 1988, and read an open letter in the *San Francisco Examiner* by Larry Kramer, the firebrand founder of ACT UP (AIDS Coalition to Unleash Power). "Anthony Fauci, you are a murderer," Kramer began his letter before declaring, "You should be put to a firing squad."

Fauci could have crumpled up the newspaper and tossed it in the trash. He could have penned his own response. Or he could have threatened legal action against Kramer and ACT UP, silencing their criticism.

Instead, he picked up the phone.

Despite the very fresh knowledge that Kramer wanted him dead, Fauci summoned the courage to reach out. Rather than chastising Kramer for his public condemnation or rushing to defend his efforts to help Kramer and the entire LGBTQ+ community, he asked Kramer what motivated him to write—and publish—his letter. To his credit, Kramer explained that the letter was his attempt to get the federal government's attention and respond with the urgency the epidemic demanded. "I was the face of the federal government," Fauci later told the *New York Times*. "I was the one out there trying to warn the public, and he [Kramer] was, too. That was his way of saying, 'Hello? Wake up!' That was his style. He was iconoclastic, he was theatrical—he wanted to make his point."

Impressed by Fauci's willingness to reach out to him, Kramer put Fauci in touch with a couple of ACT UP activists in the Washington, D.C., area who agreed to meet with Fauci. Eventually, this sit-down with the D.C. activists turned into regular dinner parties! Together Fauci and the activists shared glasses of red wine, plates of charcuterie, long-held grievances, and festering bureaucratic frustrations. To be clear, the activists and Fauci continued to break bread together even though, by the time everyone was through with their dessert, they had ventured into deep and often emotional disagreement. Indeed, just a few months later Fauci's dinner companions organized a massive demonstration on the NIH campus, erecting an effigy of Fauci's head impaled on a spike. Later that evening, ACT UP activists burned the effigy on Fauci's front lawn, in front of the same house in which he regularly welcomed them.

In a 2020 interview, in the middle of the COVID-19 pandemic, Fauci explained what inspired him to stay engaged. "It was time for me to put the theatrics aside and listen to what they're saying."

Despite often not seeing eye to eye on many issues, his ongoing conversations with the ACT UP activists, which were never easy, gave him perspective and empathy and caused him to change how he thought about clinical trials, which led to better studies and better treatments for all diseases. Under his direction, the NIH diversified clinical trials for early drugs like AZT and, eventually, persuaded the federal government to overhaul its HIV/AIDS legislation and research funds.

For us, Fauci and the ACT UP activists who engaged him had befriended conflict. As head of the National Institute of Allergy and Infectious Diseases, Fauci purposely shifted his mindset on conflict, reappraising it from something "bad" to be avoided at all costs to something fundamentally good, an opportunity to open up new options for how he could respond, become a more effective leader, and achieve better research and clinical results. In the process, he strengthened his conflict resilience skills through an almost literal baptism by fire. Little did he know then how much he would need to draw upon these conflict resilience skills nearly three decades later to help him through the catastrophic COVID-19 pandemic and the complicated politics and polarization that accompanied it.

This orientation to approach conflict as a positive value-creating experience may seem more appropriate for handling political differences, making healthcare policy, or navigating issues of war or peace. But it matters just as much in determining how much we can fully participate in everyday life and thrive at getting what we want and need most in our personal and professional endeavors.

Consider the case of Trevor.

Following the murder of George Floyd, Trevor got involved in the Black Lives Matter movement. Over time, he began advocating for the removal of Confederate statues across the country. To his surprise, his grandmother saw his efforts as an attempt to rewrite history, a form of artistic and political censorship.

At one level, Trevor believed that his grandmother's views on this were part of the problem, the blindness that contributed to White supremacy. A side of Trevor wanted to avoid an unpleasant conversation trying to change her mind. Another side motivated him to engage in a conversation—not just to persuade her, but also to begin to understand why someone he revered so much could have what he considered a profound blind spot. He felt stuck.

So, to help manage his distress around engaging in the conflict with his grandmother, we would coach Trevor through a four-step process for self-reflection:

1. PAUSE. And breathe.
2. Write down reasons why it is important to engage this hard conflict or conversation and why you want to avoid it.
3. List what you want out of the encounter (your core interests).
4. List what your counterpart might want out of the encounter (their core interests).

## 1. PAUSE. AND BREATHE.

This may sound simple. But simply taking ten seconds to pause and breathe will open up space for self-reflection. We go into more detail on this step in Chapter 3.

## 2. REASONS TO ENGAGE AND REASONS TO AVOID

Before sitting down with his grandmother, Trevor needed to increase his awareness of the conflict, acknowledging his conversational partner as a real-life person (rather than an idea or an imaginary political foe on this issue) and account for the stakes of the discussion. Trevor needed to take stock of his own contribution to the misalignment of views with his grandmother.

To do this, he wrote down the reasons *why it was important to engage* and *reasons why he'd prefer to avoid* the hard conversation with his grandmother. Among the reasons why it was important to engage the conflict included:

- It's important to understand my grandmother.
- I want to be more assertive about things that matter to me.
- I want her to know how strongly I feel about this.
- If I don't speak up, nothing changes.

A few of the reasons why he didn't want to enter conflict with his grandmother were:

- I want to be respectful.
- She won't change her mind.
- She is just one person and not an "influencer"; it won't impact others.
- I always feel like I'm the one who has to raise different viewpoints in my family and it is exhausting.

### 3. WHAT YOU WANT (YOUR CORE INTERESTS)

Trevor identified the specific interests at play in his decision to engage. The core of what Trevor was looking to acknowledge is what he honestly hoped to gain from a conversation with his grandmother. This may require a fair amount of willingness on his part to be vulnerable enough to get to the deepest *core interests* he might not usually give voice to. We'll dive into this concept in more detail in Chapter 6.

### 4. WHAT THEY WANT (THEIR CORE INTERESTS)

Trevor then imagined what his grandmother's interests might be for engaging the same conflict space, affording her the same courtesy of reflection and respect he allowed himself.

This process gave him a deeper appreciation of the internal and external landscape of this conflict. He knew what the possible outcomes might be and how much he was willing to stake personally in each outcome. He also figured out how he might open and navigate the conversation, because he understood finally why it was such a hard one to broach, for him and for his grandmother.

Ultimately, he decided to have the conversation.

As he suspected, the interaction was tense and emotionally fraught. Ultimately, neither Trevor nor his grandmother changed their views. But it was worthwhile. Trevor learned from his grandmother that her mother grew up in Germany in the 1930s, when there was increasing repression of political expression and art from the government in the name of racial purity. Because these stories were seared into his grandmother's memories, her rejection of efforts to remove any kind of political expression or public art remained unwavering.

For Trevor's part, he was able to share his perspective that there were more effective ways to teach and remember history than public statues. Specifically, he shared his own pain and confusion at seeing statues that seemed to celebrate the lives and actions of individuals who directly supported White supremacy. He also saw the resistance to dismantle them less as a desire to teach history and more as a deliberate and not-so-subtle reminder to Black people to "know their place."

Though he didn't change his grandmother's opinion, Trevor was able to communicate his perspective authentically to his grandmother, while still acknowledging her point of view and her feelings. He was also able to empathize with her values and continue to honor his own, distinguishing between the political climate in America today and the climate in 1930s Germany. To his surprise, Trevor learned that part of his grandmother's view on this issue was rooted not just in the issues themselves, but also in her own sense that staying firm on free expression was a way to honor and remain loyal to her own mother. In a way, the entangling of a substantive issue with a theme of loyalty to a deceased family member shed a different light on the situation for Trevor. While he still wished his grandmother could see things differently, he could appreciate why a woman he admired for her general openness to rethink her opinions might be a bit more stuck when issues of fealty to a deceased mother were in play in the background.

Trevor had befriended conflict, which ultimately yielded something of real value, though it didn't produce any concrete "win." By befriending conflict, Trevor deepened his relationship with his grandmother and discovered a more grounded resolve about his own commitments and next steps. All by learning how to respond to conflict as an opportunity to voice his point of view and his most closely guarded values with authenticity, assertiveness, and accountability.

## THE PAYOFF

Generally, we need better coping strategies than the five Fs, especially in situations that may not seem ripe for resolution or problem-solving or "fixing." For those situations, the kind of conflict resilience Trevor demonstrated emerges as the better choice because it invites us to begin inward, with ourselves. And, in moments when we can't change others' views, when we can't obliterate or ignore them, the one thing we can change and work on is ourselves. It is a far better investment of the limited time and effort available in our single lifetime to focus on what you can control and what is possible right now. To change something or resist change you don't want, especially when the world feels upside down and every conflict seems overwhelming, you must dig deep and change yourself first.

In almost any situation where you will experience conflict or the need to negotiate, conflict resilience builds your capacity to engage constructively, opening up a creative space for identifying common ground where it may exist or finding the bright spots in situations that may be overwhelming or seem completely impossible to overcome. The parallel stories of Dr. Anthony Fauci and Trevor learning how to befriend conflict show what's still possible in what seem to be impossible or intractable situations.

Better than avoiding or combative overcompensation, befriending conflict helped Fauci accelerate the federal government's response to the AIDS epidemic, even though he never fully gained the trust of Larry Kramer and the ACT UP activists. At the same time, while Trevor couldn't persuade his grandmother to accept his viewpoint that he was on the right side of history, he did learn more about his grandmother's thinking in a way that helped him appreciate why shifting her views might be harder than just persuading her on the merits. In the process, he learned how to state his opinion in full to someone he respected and cared about without being petrified by the fear of doing irreparable harm to their relationship. The experience gave him not only some real-life exposure and practice, but also tangible tools he could use later in every other aspect of his life, including his activism.

By rethinking his relationship with conflict and becoming more conflict positive, Trevor made the process of conflict more manageable, something tangible that he could get a handle on. Thanks to the four-step audit, he was able to weigh why entering into a space of conflict was worth the risk, while simultaneously gaining a deeper appreciation for the core issues of his lingering "fight" with his grandmother. He was empowered to name the hardest part of the conversation, then properly tailor his process of engagement, framing the conversation in a way that was actionable and appropriate to what was really at stake.

Though we can't say for certain that Fauci engaged in a similar audit, his process of befriending conflict runs in tandem with Trevor's. And, in the end, Trevor and Fauci were both *much* better equipped to take that chance. Because Fauci and Trevor both chose to befriend conflict, they found it easier to stay and do the hard work, and, over time, they would become more comfortable sitting *with* and *through* this conflict, which made it possible to uncover previously unimaginable paths forward.

With the foundation of reorienting how you perceive conflict to make it easier for you to value it as a positive opportunity, you are now ready to learn the skills to literally change your brain as we coach you on how to train your tolerance to conflict. In the next chapter, we'll provide a practical toolkit to help you better recognize and hold conflict so you can better handle it, hot-wiring your brain and gaining increased mastery of your cognitive and behavioral responses to conflict.

# Chapter 3

# UNDERSTANDING YOUR CONFLICT TOLERANCE

## Your Experience of Conflict ≠ Their Experience of Conflict

You are one of six members of the Immigration Appeals Board authorized to determine whether undocumented persons should be allowed to stay in the country. Three of the seven individuals before the board will be granted amnesty, and the other four will be deported. All seven have compelling stories in favor of amnesty. The task for the committee? Arrive at a unanimous agreement within the allotted time. Failure to do so would mean that all seven candidates will be sent back to their homelands, where danger, punishment, and maybe even death await them. How should you decide who stays and who goes?

Bob has used this same simulation for years in his advanced multiparty negotiation and group decision-making classes. Ideally, students who do this exercise will agree upon a set of criteria by which to assess each candidate's worthiness. Typically, it's a fraught and difficult negotiation, fueled by a clash of values, priorities, and sympathies—some deeply held—that the students need to hash out. Who is more deserving? An LGBTQ+ person who, if deported, will face persecution and perhaps torture back in their home country? Or an undocumented worker who, if sent back to his home country, won't be able to find the work he needs to feed his family of eight? Or is it better to send a cancer-stricken mother of four young children back to a place where proper care is unavailable when state-of-the-art treatment in the U.S. has a 90 percent chance of curing her?

Despite the agonizing and consequential decisions facing the committee, today one group of six students returns to the classroom in a mere twenty minutes, well ahead of schedule, full of smiles, and with a unanimous agreement.

"What happened?" Bob asks, looking perplexed and concerned.

"Oh, we're done!" one of the students crisply responds.

"But how did you do it?" Bob asks.

"Oh, well, we went around and said whom we each preferred and all of us had the same people for two of our three selections. Because we each had someone different for our third, we just decided to pick the person who had the most votes."

From the perspective of getting a quick and unanimous decision, it's hard to criticize what the students did. But from the perspective of identifying a set of criteria that could be used to explain their process to the four people who weren't chosen—much less the broader community—their approach was deficient. It put the fate of seven vulnerable people in the hands of a committee that treated the question like a popularity contest, not as a serious policy matter with a reasoned decision-making process that might yield defensible reasoning that could be shared with these seven candidates and their families, as well as applied to future candidates, when similarly hard choices presented themselves.

As Bob challenged what he saw to be serious problems with a "popularity" straw-poll approach, one of the students raised their hand and asked, "But Professor Bordone! If we had started to really discuss the issues the way you are suggesting, it would have gotten very messy and very stressful. We all have very different views about so many of these issues and it would have been very hard. Do you have any ideas of how we could have this conversation and have it not be hard?"

Upon hearing this, Bob replied, with frustration in his voice, "No, to be honest, I do not. I have no ideas about how to talk through a hard decision like this—one that involves conflicting values, beliefs, principles, and human life—without creating discomfort. If you ask me, 'Do you have ideas on how to make the process better, more fair, more efficient?' I do. But how to get into the really hard questions without it feeling hard and full of tension and conflict, sorry. I got nothing."

Bob went home troubled by the student's question, even if unsurprised. More and more, Bob observed the tendency toward studied avoidance. If students in a leading American law school where conversations about hot topics should be seen as par for the course were wringing their hands about having a consequential policy debate, what hope could there be that these conversations might occur outside the controlled environment of an intentional classroom experience set up for just such a discussion? The palpable anxiety and kryptonite-like vibe around conflict—functions of both an antipathy to personal discomfort and a profound lack of skill for handling differences adeptly—had creeped even into a law school environment. People don't even want to openly acknowledge the possibility that there may be a disagreement, because they don't really know how to approach it constructively.

Joel has seen emerging studies that support this observation with increasing levels of social anxiety among young adults in recent years. Although specific causes remain unclear, this trend may be leading to more interpersonal dilemmas, difficulty with keeping relationships, and problems at school and work.

It would be nice to produce wise and sustainable outcomes in our private and public life without conflict and without any disruption to our sense of friendliness and calm in relationships, but it's simply not a realistic aspiration.

Even law students who had already devoted two semesters to intensive courses learning conflict resolution and negotiation skills were loath to make decisions that would make them feel uncomfortable.

As Bob thought more about it, he also remembered that the same student who was hesitant to engage in this exercise had no difficulty advocating with great gusto in an earlier simulation on behalf of a client. What registers as conflict for one person might be a piece of cake for someone else. Someone might be a fierce bulldog in the workplace but a scaredy cat at home; someone else might be able to maintain their equanimity when dealing with a difficult client but yell at a neighbor who leaves their empty trash bin on the curb long after the garbage truck has made its rounds on a Monday morning.

Conflict resilience depends on a set of skills, which we will teach you—deep listening, effective assertion, careful framing—but it also requires something else, what we refer to as *conflict tolerance*. Conflict tolerance involves two distinct "subcapacities" as components that work together and are prerequisite to being truly effective in conflict. The first is *conflict recognition*. Conflict recognition relates to our internal barometer for coding an interaction as "conflict" in the first place. The second is *conflict holding*. Conflict holding relates to our ability to sit with and work through an interaction that we have coded as "conflict" without shutting down, acting out, or jumping to easy and superficial decisions, such as the one Bob's students made in their effort to avoid hard things.

For Bob's student to understand why she was so avoidant in one situation and so confrontational in another, she needed a deeper understanding of herself and her experience when engaged with others across lines of difference.

In this chapter, we give you tools for understanding your own conflict tolerance—the relationship between your ability to recognize conflict and your ability to hold conflict. We examine how differences in recognition and holding can make engaging differences with family, friends, and colleagues either more fraught or more productive.

As we unpack these concepts and raise your own awareness about yourself, we hope you'll feel more ready to grapple with hard stuff. Wherever your conflict tolerance level is currently set (low, high, or in between), this chapter will give you prescriptions to retrain your brain so that your conflict tolerance threshold grows. We'll give you access to inner resources that will allow you to sit with the discomfort of conflict so that you can make informed and wise decisions about whether and when to engage directly with the tough stuff.

## YUP, THIS FEELS LIKE A CONFLICT: RECOGNITION

Conflict recognition relates to our perception of being in a dispute or conflict with another. Whatever formal definitions may exist for conflict or dispute, each of us has our own unique barometer of what we would consider being in a state of conflict. The difference in the way each of us might perceive a particular interaction relates to our conflict recognition. What one person thinks of as conflict is barely even noticed by the other.

A lively staff meeting where colleagues are hashing out different approaches on how to position the new product rollout feels to Tao like an energized and spirited conversation; to his colleague Elle, however, it feels tense, contentious, and conflict-filled. If the meeting were videorecorded and broadcast on YouTube, there would be plenty of viewers who would line up with Tao, and others with Elle. Some would likely have interpretations in between the two.

Is there a right answer to this? Almost certainly not. It's simply a reality that, by dint of personality differences, culture, and our family of origin, among other factors, what registers as "conflict" differs for each of us. Becoming more aware of our own recognition "default" and how it differs vis-á-vis other people is critical to one's efforts to become more conflict tolerant. To help you assess your own conflict recognition baseline, take the quiz below.

### Conflict Recognition Quiz

Please rate the following on a 1-to-5 scale, where 1 is "severe, potentially relationship-ending conflict" and 5 is "very mild, barely discernible misunderstanding."

1.  You are hoping to have an early dinner with your significant other and get a good night's rest for a busy weekend; they want to get the weekend started with late dinner and drinks with friends at one of the city's newest hot spots.

2.  Spending time with extended family over the holidays, your cousins from Michigan suggest that they believe there may have been voting irregularity in the recent election, making the president's election fraudulent. You disagree. A lengthy conversation ensues between you and them, only ending when it's time for the family to begin the meal and say grace.

3.  A Democratic and Republican senator on a Sunday morning talk show spar with each other on immigration policy at the southern border of the United States.

4.  You and your spouse have different views, despite many conversations, on whether to respect your thirteen-year-old child's request to be referred to as "they" instead of "him."

5.  Your team is deciding between two competing advertising campaigns, pitched by rival advertising firms. Opinions are divided and there exist major differences between the two proposals.

Total up your score.

If you scored between 5 and 12, your conflict recognition threshold is *low*, meaning that you tend to see many disagreements—even relatively minor ones—as more serious and uncomfortable conflicts. If you scored between 12 and 20, you have a midlevel conflict recognition. And if you scored greater than 20, you have a *high* recognition threshold, meaning that you are more likely to see differences between parties as expected and not necessarily bothersome or relationship-threatening.

Before reading on, notice your responses to each of the individual prompts above. What patterns might you observe? What, if any, insights might that yield for you with respect to how your own recognition is calibrated? Perhaps your recognition is more sensitized in workplace versus personal contexts? Alternatively, maybe for you the aphorism "avoid conversations about politics or religion" fits aptly because you see all disagreements in those domains as conflict. What might register as deep and foreboding conflict when discussed in a meeting of your church's vestry might be part of the regular back-and-forth policy debates that your campaign team working on behalf of an aspiring state senator has almost daily. What is most complicating about recognition is that it often varies across relationships and contexts.

Later in our book, we discuss how the mix of organizational culture and assumptions impacts our ability to be conflict resilient. But for now, we want to focus simply on the individual differences in the way we recognize the very existence of conflict in our midst.

We (Bob and Joel) are fortunate to have a strong personal friendship with each other in addition to our colleagueship as coauthors. In writing this book, we handled differences constructively (mostly!), working hard to model our own advice.

At the same time, Bob has come to understand that certain kinds of behavior that he engages with regularly with some of his lawyer friends would be experienced as highly contentious and perhaps even rude and hostile if he used them with Joel. Similarly, Joel knows he can express a certain level of disagreement with Bob, who will not lose an ounce of sleep afterward, whereas if Joel used that same behavior with one specific neurology colleague, it would suggest the entire relationship was in jeopardy.

So, *conflict recognition* relates to how each of us experiences interactions as being "in conflict" or not. One's recognition is not an inborn or immutable trait like eye or hair color, but it is more "baked-in" than our sense of style or clothing choice. It's a complex product of personality, culture, upbringing, and socialization, all within the contours of a particular situational context and relationships or system of relationships. It is the first part of understanding our own conflict tolerance.

## LEARNING TO STAND THE HEAT: HOLDING

The second "subcapacity" of conflict tolerance is conflict holding. Holding relates to our ability to sit with or be in the presence of a conflict as we are experiencing it rather than either fighting it or running from it. Once we acknowledge the presence of conflict, are we able to sit with that experience of conflict, to examine it, hold it, and work through it with the others who are involved?

Importantly, it is possible to have a high recognition threshold and a low capacity for holding it. That means it takes a lot before you realize you're in a state of conflict ("Why did they suddenly become so defensive?") and, once you do, you immediately want to escape the situation ("No, thank you!").

This describes Bob well. Partly because of his professional training in law, partly by dint of his upbringing, he tends to see most disagreements as ordinary parts of life, not as relationship-threatening conflict. But when something does register for him as "conflict," such as having to back out of a previous commitment he made when he knows it will seriously disappoint the other person, his comfort with conflict can be extremely low. He would describe himself as having a "high recognition" threshold and a "low holding" threshold. He realizes that this is partially what drew him to a career in conflict resolution in the first place.

Meanwhile, Joel tends to label more interactions as conflicts (low recognition threshold) and has a lower capacity to sit with those uncomfortable feelings (low holding threshold). If you identify as a "people pleaser," you probably relate with this combination. As a result of it, Joel tends to notice small changes in people's behaviors in great detail, which might explain his interest in neuroscience. He also experienced significant bullying at a very young age, which wired his brain to be extra sensitive and on the lookout for conflict. His natural tendencies and those early experiences made him highly adaptive and attuned to potential threats—better to avoid them than to endure them. This must have been especially useful when sitting near bigger, scarier kids on the school bus ride home, but that same stance has become less helpful and quite tricky to navigate as he moved on to engaging with a much wider array of people and situations later in life, potentially missing out on valuable opportunities, friendships, experiences, and points of view. His determination to address this was part of his attraction to this work on conflict resilience.

To help you assess your own conflict holding capacity, take the quiz below.

### Conflict Holding Quiz

Please rate the following on a 1-to-5 scale, where 1 is "I find it extremely difficult to stay in the conflict without impulsively reacting to it or avoiding it," and 5 is "I am very comfortable holding the tension of the conflict without impulsively reacting to it or withdrawing."

1.  You've spent months organizing a group event, and you've often noticed tensions growing between various individuals. During what was supposed to be the last planning meeting before the event, a colleague criticizes the venue choice, saying it's too far for most people to attend and that they dislike how you have been organizing it. They suggest that someone else should be put in charge.

2.  During a dinner with long-time friends, someone brings up your recent decision to change your diet, and another friend jokes about how "it's just a phase." You feel misunderstood.

3.  Your partner tells you that they feel you've been distracted and less attentive lately, particularly when they need to talk. You feel hurt because you believe you've been trying your best.

4.  At a holiday gathering with your family and friends, your aunt and uncle start arguing loudly about immigration policy, and your aunt looks to you for support in her argument. You feel pressure to take a side.

5.  Your team is debating two marketing strategies, and the exchange is intense. One person accuses another of "not thinking things through properly, as usual." You feel emotions in the room rise.

Total up your score.

If you scored between 5 and 12, you may find it difficult to sit with conflict without feeling the need to react impulsively or avoid it. This suggests that conflict holding is an area for growth in learning how to stay present even in discomfort. If you scored between 12 and 20, you have a mid-level capacity for holding conflict. You may be able to stay present during conflicts in some situations, but may still find it challenging in more emotionally charged matters. If you scored greater than 20, you are likely very comfortable with conflict holding, meaning you can stay in the presence of a conflict without needing to fix, escape, or react.

Before moving on, reflect on your reactions to each prompt. What patterns do you notice? Are you more comfortable holding conflict in certain settings, such as work or family, but not in others? Consider how improving your ability to hold conflict could impact your relationships and decision-making.

Similar to the differences in conflict recognition and holding that we've noticed between ourselves, we meet people with all sorts of configurations. Perhaps for you, your brain labels (and your body experiences) small disagreements as conflict, but your holding capacity is high enough that you don't feel the urge to fight, flee, freeze, fawn, or fester. Whatever your conflict tolerance is today—whether low or high—the good news is that it is not fixed. There are steps you can take to train your conflict tolerance.

Of course, these differences in how we recognize and respond to conflict reflect our unique experiences and perspectives. For example, even if your brain labels minor disagreements as conflict, your capacity to manage those feelings might prevent escalation. The important takeaway is that conflict tolerance isn't set in stone—it can be shaped and strengthened. To begin, it helps to understand how your mind and body recognize conflict in the first place.

## UNDERSTANDING YOUR RECOGNITION DEFAULT

To be clear: there is no "right" combination you should be striving to achieve. The goal is not to lower or raise your own conflict-monitoring tendency to meet some unchanging statistical "average," as if such a thing exists. Some of us who are neurodivergent, prone to anxiety, or have tendencies more similar to people with an avoidant personality disorder may have brains that are more hypervigilant and have a harder time navigating interpersonal nuances, while—on the flip side—these same brains may have a natural aptitude for creativity and innovation (coming up with new ideas with the same ease as we come up with all sorts of creative worst-case scenarios when left to our own devices). Trying to train people to have identical recognition capability would be like forcing an extreme extrovert to become an extreme introvert—or vice versa.

Instead, like stretching every morning to become slightly more flexible, the work here is to expand your range of flexibility within the spectrum of recognition, becoming slightly more aware of the distance between what you gauge to be conflict and what may or may not be labeled as conflict in the eyes (read: brains) of the people around you.

First, there is enormous value in simply increasing your own awareness of defaults and situational patterns. You can start simply by paying attention to how you physically feel in different conflict situations and putting a deliberate name to your experience. For example, if you notice a tightness in your chest when disagreeing with your partner about where to go for dinner, you might label this feeling as "anxiety," perhaps signaling a need to explore what it is about this specific situation that creates a sense of potential threat in you. This process activates more frontal-lobe brain systems responsible for deliberating and higher-order judgment, which simultaneously has the effect of almost turning down the volume of noisy parts of the brain involved in triggering strong positive or negative emotions. So, rather than falling into a default reaction or behavioral pattern, this act of naming increases your control over intense experiences, making it easier for you to then identify how, when, and where you can allow yourself to shift your behavior and push for your own growth.

There are different vectors or factors that can influence our own conflict recognition.

- What we label as conflict varies depending on whether the disagreement occurs in the workplace versus home or among a friend group.
- For others, disagreements about issues they code as "intellectual" or "rational" or "policy-oriented" track differently from those they code as "personal" or "emotional" or "identity-based."
- For some, the vector of conflict recognition might relate to a sense of physical threat, but for others, the vector might relate to emotional or psychological threat. And, of course, at times the level of that threat is beyond emotions and at the level of trauma, a topic we take on in more detail later.
- Sometimes the vector of what feels like conflict is heavily influenced by your physical state and "interoception," how your brain registers what your body feels (e.g., you have a headache, stomachache, the flu, or you're sleep-deprived). Think of a time you were physically ill and in pain or, just the opposite, physically relaxed and euphoric. Were you more or less prone to detect an exchange with a friend, child, or coworker as a high-threat conflict? Even mere words that make you vividly imagine bodily sensations (such as "stabbing back pain" or "warm secure hug") have the potential to powerfully influence how threatening your brain registers your surroundings and your interactions with other people.

For most of us, the ingredients that cause us to label an experience as "conflict" are a combination of the above along with other conditions like the culture of a workplace, timing, and mood on a given day.

Recently, as Joel left his gym's locker room he overheard a staff person, speaking in Spanish, make a crude homophobic comment with respect to him. But what the staff person didn't know was that Joel is bilingual. Joel immediately experienced a wave of distress, intense negative feelings both internally and in relation to this staff person. Flooded with overwhelm, Joel did nothing in the moment— he walked away. Only later did he reach out to the gym manager to report the incident and discuss what might be appropriate.

In a case like Joel's, so much is going on: the substantive "conflict" about what are appropriate ways to refer to LGBTQ+ people, the emotional reaction of hearing yourself referred to with a slur in a way that is intended to be derogatory, and then the experiential and historical context of living in a world where acceptable social behavior for some includes part of your identity being openly subject to ridicule, discrimination, and hate.

All of this came to the fore immediately for Joel. To him, the recognition of conflict was palpable. He registered this as a disagreement about what is socially acceptable behavior, what constitutes a severe violation of respect for another person, and what kinds of speech are almost as harmful as an overt act of violence—and all of these layers of conflict were occurring across lines of difference too—even though there was no open engagement with the employee.

Because Joel's historic tendency with respect to "holding" is low, immediate exit came naturally. But being able to later name the difference in recognition (how his brain coded the situation compared to the staff person's) and call out his low holding gave him a degree of self-control and autonomy. He could regain his bearings, contextualize what was going on, and allow himself to reengage in a productive way on his own later.

Indeed, heightened self-awareness of the factors that influence your conflict recognition is not just an academic exercise or an action taken in service of some elusive self-enlightenment. To the contrary, research suggests that self-awareness actually increases your ability to handle conflict effectively and negotiate better outcomes. Certainly, we're not opposed to self-awareness for the purposes of enlightenment. But we just want to assure you that this very hard work has very practical benefits for better outcomes in your day-to-day life.

Once aware of your own recognition tendencies—and the factors that tend to influence them—remember two things:

First, your recognition tendency is bespoke—entirely unique to you.

Second, that tendency is neither right nor wrong; neither too much nor too little.

What this means is that trying to *change* you or the other person on whether they are experiencing something as a conflict is an exercise in futility. When you are enraged, for example, that your younger brother doesn't understand that needling you about your liberal political views in a family of die-hard conservatives feels like a personal attack, it might not be because he is purposefully trying to upset you or pick a fight. It might be that it just isn't registering for him as conflict in the way it feels to you.

It doesn't necessarily mean he's a bully or a dolt or thickheaded. All of these are, of course, possible. But it's equally possible that he just doesn't experience conversation like this as tearing at the fabric of the relationship in the same way you do. For him, it might even be a way of connecting with you because perhaps for him, seeing you get riled up is a sign for him that you are engaging with him, and engagement is what he really wants.

The fact that he is different from you doesn't mean you need to accept the situation as it is. But it is genuinely possible that you each have very different recognition thresholds, and that this difference—perhaps more than even your divergent political views—is something that each of you needs to find a way to talk about.

Understanding that your own *recognition* differs from others' helps you avoid the tendency to attribute bad motivations to others or to cast aspersions on their character. It also helps us short-circuit the downward spiral we may find ourselves in.

For Bob, this self-awareness has been deeply empowering, helping him understand why he can engage endlessly in highly contentious situations in some domains and not others. As long as his brain is seeing the differences as "differences" or "conversations" or "opportunities for connection," he's all in. But as soon as his brain recognizes something as "conflict," the low holding capacity sets off all sorts of alarms. This self-knowledge helps him move past the initial internal spiral and judgment and move toward a more constructive form of self-knowledge.

The awareness around recognition and holding also gives you constructive language to engage with your colleagues, children, parents, friends, or lovers about these differences. Conversations about how we recognize and hold conflict go a long way toward understanding and enabling conflict resilience—even when the substance of the disagreement remains as deep as ever.

For example, while Kendra may be assuming that her brother Jonathan is an insensitive jerk for continuing to needle her about her political beliefs in a way that gets her upset and emotional, Jonathan may often see Kendra's reaction to his "joking" as a sign that she is "weak" or unable to stand the fire of a good challenge. Of course, neither of these may be true. But in the moment, this additional layer of evaluation, attribution of intention, and judgment of character ends up fueling the conflict and the bad will.

A conversation where you discuss the experience of the interaction for each of you—tough or strange as this may be—can provide a genuine moment of connection, especially if both sides agree that the point is not to persuade the other that they are either too sensitive or too obtuse, but just that they are different and have something to learn from each other.

Consider this first exchange:

| | THINKING (BUT NOT SAYING) | ACTUAL SPOKEN EXCHANGE |
|---|---|---|
| JONATHAN | I think I know what Kendra thinks about this but I am guessing this will get her engaged and riled up a bit so we can have some fun! | Don't you think all these kids who introduce themselves using preferred gender pronouns are just a little too precious? |
| KENDRA | I can't tell if he is just trying to make me mad or if he wants to get into a fight or if he has actual concerns about the use of pronouns, but this is exhausting. | Well, two things. First, no, I don't think so. I think it's something we can learn from. And second, we don't say "preferred" pronoun because it is just their pronoun. It's not preferred. |
| JONATHAN | I can't believe Kendra has fallen for this. | Really? You got to be kidding. There are all sorts of things we can add to our name. "Hi, I'm Jonathan, a Christian." Or "Hi, I'm Cyndi, East Bostonian." Why are we appending gender pronouns and not a bunch of other descriptors? It's just another example of woke gone wild. You can't really have fallen for this stuff, hook, line, and sinker, Kendra. Be real! |
| KENDRA | Why is he making me feel so stupid? Rather than have an honest debate, he basically says if I believe this, I've just adopted some mob mentality. I just want to end this conversation. | [Shaking head] Jonathan, you're impossible. Honestly, sometimes you're just a complete Luddite. You're lucky I'm your sister! |
| JONATHAN | Why doesn't she want to have this conversation on the merits? I hate when she tries to weasel out of thinking beyond her little liberal bubble. | No, I'm not letting you off the hook, Kendra. Don't fall for this PC crap. This is the kind of ridiculous woke stuff that screws kids up. Boys are boys, girls are girls, and we don't need to announce our pronouns whenever we meet each other. |
| KENDRA | Why can't he get the hint? I think he just likes to fight. | I just don't want to talk about it while we're visiting Mom and Dad. Just drop it. |
| JONATHAN | It's so frustrating to never be able to have a real conversation with Kendra because she just shuts it down. It's clear she just hasn't thought the issue through very well and doesn't want to be challenged. | OK. Whatever. |

When we pull back the curtain and see what Kendra and Jonathan are thinking but not saying, it's clear that part of what is making this conversation hard is *not* just their difference on the use of gender pronouns; it's also about the experience of the interaction for each of them and the meaning they are each making of the interaction, disconnected from the merits of the "pronoun" question.

Kendra experiences her brother's behavior as pugilistic and needlessly combative. Jonathan experiences Kendra as dismissive, weak, and disengaged. No one's interests are served and the siblings just feel alienated and further apart.

With greater self-awareness around conflict recognition, Kendra and Jonathan might have an entirely different conversation, one that might set them up to have more productive and mutually enjoyable conversations around their differences going forward and leading to more conversations that might build rather than slowly eviscerate their relationship.

Consider Kendra's different approach to the conversation:

**REVISED SCRIPT**
**(WITH KENDRA MODELING A MORE SKILLFUL APPROACH)**

| | |
|---|---|
| JONATHAN | Don't you think all these kids who introduce themselves using preferred gender pronouns are just a little too precious? |
| KENDRA | Jonathan—before we get into this question, I'd like to raise something with you.<br>　　There are times when you bring up a hot topic like this and ask a question that I experience as loaded or leading. I sometimes feel as if you are trying to pick a fight with me and I'm not sure what to do about that.<br>　　When that happens, instead of engaging the issue, I feel that I want to escape.<br>　　I'm not sure how you experience the dynamic, but I am often left feeling stuck and confused.<br>　　I thought I should share this with you and ask you how you experience these conversations? |
| JONATHAN | I'm not trying to fight, just trying to get you to engage. |

| KENDRA | Hmmm . . . And it sounds like for you, a way to get the engagement is to get me a bit riled up? |
|--------|------------------------------------------------------------------------------------------------|
| JONATHAN | Yes. I know you'll have a few good retorts. And I like seeing your passion.<br><br>It kind of stinks that you tend to shut the conversation down immediately, but I suppose that's because you know I won my point. |
| KENDRA | So, for you the shutting down is my way of conceding without conceding? |
| JONATHAN | Yes. Obviously. You often just don't think things through and as soon as I point it out, you're defeated, so you just try to shut down the conversation rather than give me the win. |
| KENDRA | I'm really glad I'm asking you this because I think when you open a conversation topic like this in a very loaded way, you do get a strong initial reaction.<br><br>And you are right to notice that I shut down and change the subject quickly. |
| JONATHAN | For sure! |
| KENDRA | This is helpful. For me, I am shutting down because I experience the way you raise issues like this not as you wanting to engage with me, but more as you trying to debate me or win a point or browbeat me. I experience them not as a disagreement on views, but rather as combative conflict. |
| JONATHAN | Well, that's not what I mean. I mean, sometimes I do like to debate. But mostly, I just think we need to be able to disagree and if we can't do that, then it's just no fun. |
| KENDRA | I think where we agree is that we want to find a way to have these conversations together where we can disagree and still have fun and where we can also learn to see other perspectives. And I think part of why I'm raising this with you is I feel that the current way we are doing it stops us from having a conversation and turns it more into an uncomfortable fight that has me shut down rather than engage.<br><br>For example, I tend not to experience a loaded question as an invitation to a real conversation but more as the initiation of conflict. And when it goes from conversation to conflict with me, you might get a few sparky responses but ultimately I just shut down.<br><br>Instead of having the deeper conversation you seem to really want, I think I just leave feeling like you were picking on me.<br><br>And it's sad because I know I could learn a lot from listening to your perspective on this. I just find myself shutting down by the way the conversation gets going.<br><br>So, this ends up not working for either of us. |

| JONATHAN | Hmmm. That's not my intention. For me it's just a way into a fun and sparky conversation. It would never even occur to me that you felt like it was a real conflict, though I do appreciate what you're telling me here.<br>    And it's helpful to know because when you shut down, I often take it as either lack of interest in having a conversation with me, which feels bad, or, sometimes, as a tacit agreement that I'm right. Either way, it sounds as if I am wrong about both of these conclusions, and we are both really missing the chance to have a better conversation around an issue where we still probably don't agree. |
| --- | --- |
| KENDRA | Yes, I think that's right. That's why I wanted to raise this. I thought that if we could have a conversation about how we experience these interactions it might actually help both of us have the conversation around the issue itself for the first time. |
| JONATHAN | Yup. I get it. How about we agree that if you're feeling like the intensity is high, you'll let me know and I can try to engage differently? |
| KENDRA | I'd love that. And maybe if you feel that I am withdrawing too soon, just remind me that for you it really is a conversation from which you learn and I'll do my best to stick with it. |

Just realizing and appreciating that each of you may have different *recognition* thresholds can help you hold back from these unhelpful spirals. And it can give you a powerful shared vocabulary for talking through these sensitivities.

What might this look like in practice for you? You might ask yourself:

1.  What makes the difference for you between an ordinary disagreement and a distressing interpersonal situation (e.g., one that creates stress, roils in your brain, or keeps you up at night)?
2.  What are the discernible patterns that distinguish the two scenarios (e.g., context, subject matter, level of emotion, identity, experience, history of the relationship, something else)?

Even if one of your goals might be to change the other's perspective through a difficult conversation, it's easy to identify worthy—perhaps even more important—goals that can be achieved when such a conversation is entered into with skill and a willingness to sit in the discomfort of disagreement. For Jonathan and Kendra, there is the possibility of mutual learning, increased respect, and a closer and more trusting relationship. In our national politics, the possibility of improved trust, the discovery of unexpected stories and shared interests, and the learning that promotes respect and civility all open up space for collaboration on a whole host of issues, even if unrelated to the points of disagreement. Moreover, without this capacity, polarization and spiraling apart will undo us all. Imagine how different your relationships and public life could be if we could break out of the cycles of avoidance, incrimination, and siloed thinking that have become defaults in modern, social-mediated life. If we don't do this work, what's at stake is not only the relationships we hold dear, but also our ability to coexist in a united democracy and uphold a thriving, functioning society.

## UNDERSTANDING OTHER PEOPLE

For many years, Bob worked with a colleague, Nate, whom he would describe as having a high recognition threshold. Through many meetings, he would observe Nate dig into others' comments in ways that his colleagues experienced as personal and aggressive. Following these meetings, Nate rarely saw these situations as consistent with high (or even any!) conflict. Except when Bob pointed out to Nate that others had experienced him as tough, unkind, or ridiculing. Even when Bob delivered this feedback skillfully, Nate reacted defensively. Bob came to think of Nate as having a high recognition on most matters—except ones that challenged his self-image and identity. This was valuable information for Bob to have about Nate's conflict recognition threshold, so that he could share feedback in the future in ways that Nate could actually absorb and benefit from.

To understand how someone else might be registering conflict, first, when possible, look at their behavior in other contexts. Do they tend to be mild-mannered and matter-of-fact in general? Or are they easily agitated? As you observe the other person across contexts, are there some contexts that spark noticeably different patterns of behavior?

But observation alone is not enough. That's because as humans we are subject to selective attention biases. Once we have a story we tell about the other person, we tend to notice data that confirms our existing biases and assumptions about them. And we tend to downplay or ignore data that would tell a different story. That's why, in addition to honing your skills of observation, it helps to ask others who know the person what their experience and observations have been about the recognition defaults of the person with whom you may be in conflict.

How you do this matters. If you reach out to those who are sympathetic to you and frame your questions in ways that suggest you have a set of biases, you're more likely to find others corroborating your view of the situation. This will feel good. And it's also not helpful.

Instead, let those you reach out to know that you're trying to improve your own ability to interact effectively with the subject of your inquiry. Then ask them for their observations and impressions, without biasing them about your viewpoint. After you've heard that, share with them your impression of the person and then ask, "I'd love to hear, from your experience. What do you think I'm missing and what examples do you have that might show me this person in a fuller light than my initial impression?"

Consider Shania and her experience with her supervising partner at a major Los Angeles–based law firm. Over and over again she experienced this person as having an extremely high recognition threshold with others but not in conversations with her, where she felt an unusually high sensitivity to any arguments she made that contravened the partner's perception of how to proceed. In these situations, the partner would suddenly become deferential and apologetic, shutting down the substantive conversation Shania was inviting on the issue.

This dynamic confused Shania. Even worse, because part of her job was to dig deep on statutory history and legal precedent while the partner provided a big-picture strategy, she found herself stumped as to how to raise areas of concern without eliciting an instant apology and a quick retreat from the partner.

In talking with others at the firm, she discovered that years earlier, the partner's best friend in the firm had been accused of racial bias by a young associate, forcing him to leave the firm. This experience caused the partner to be highly sensitized and overly deferential to feedback from associates of color. Understanding this pattern of behavior didn't solve the problem—and it was a serious one—but it did stop the spinning in Shania's head and opened an avenue for how she might handle the situation. This included specifically asking for constructive feedback and even active pushback from the partner on her thinking. It also involved Shania sharing personal stories of how she thrived best when she was pushed in an almost back-and-forth Socratic Q&A way from mentors.

## BUILDING THE MUSCLE FOR CONFLICT HOLDING

As we mentioned, the second part of *conflict tolerance* is conflict *holding*. Building muscle for conflict holding, like building muscle for your arms, quads, or calves, is a process, not a one-and-done event. We don't recommend plowing headlong into the most difficult, triggering, or contentious conversation looming in your life. That may be a medium or long-term goal, but it's not a good starting point. It would be like beginning your fitness regimen by trying to do two thousand jumping jacks on day one. It will just lead to frustration and maybe to giving up the fitness regime entirely. Remember this because it will make it easier to allow yourself compassion when you—like all of us—inevitably fail spectacularly in a scenario that is particularly thorny for you.

And that's OK. There are many reasons why people are unable to make enduring substantive changes in their behaviors, but a common one is that they tend to go all out too quickly and then, just as quickly, they burn out and give up altogether.

Start low. Go slow.

We begin by inviting you to simply become more *self-aware* of the physical experience of being in conflict. Where in your body does that sense of conflict show up? Is it in your stomach? Your head? Your neck?

In those moments when you start to experience a sense of conflict with others, apart from the physical reactions, what kind of "automatic" thoughts come up for you? Are there any specific words or images? Perhaps you feel your stomach turn. Or, as Joel experiences it, perhaps your jaw muscles tighten and the tip of your tongue presses against the roof of your mouth. For Bob, his hands and feet feel colder. Maybe you notice a sensation, like a physical urge to rush to leave the room, you turn red-faced, or you feel your breath start to shorten.

How about the mental experience of being in conflict? Do your thoughts veer toward the temptation to change the topic or fall back on empty phrases, like "let's agree to disagree," as a means to shut down the bad feelings that the interaction has churned up? Does your mind go somewhere entirely different, like harnessing an arsenal of rational arguments about why you're right and they're wrong so that you can somehow vanquish them with superior knowledge and analytical capability?

Maybe you're the kind of person who starts to doubt yourself. Ten minutes ago, you were sure you knew that polarization in Washington, D.C., was caused primarily by the lack of congressional term limits, but now you're not so sure. Maybe your cousin is right that it's all about corporate money and lobbying.

Maybe when you find yourself in conflict, you immediately get curious. That would be a great automatic reaction. But it's not the one most of us have in the moment when conflict looms in front of us.

Our first task in building our *holding* muscle is the task of self-awareness and mindfulness. It's taking the time to PAUSE, breathe, and notice—without judgment—what is going on with us in the moment when we first experience conflict and the moments that follow.

Based on whatever your past experiences have been with a specific conflict-like situation (e.g., being told you're too inexperienced for a role), what type of person (e.g., authority figure, romantic partner), and where you might have been hurt or learned that there was some kind of potential danger there (e.g., in a one-on-one work meeting or your parents' house), whenever your brain is reminded of one of these past experiences it will literally re-create that same experience or echo of unpleasantness from the past using the exact same systems that process physical pain! That's right. You're using the same systems that your brain uses for physical pain to experience the pain or potential pain of conflict. And, if that pain is great enough, it might set off one of your brain's alarm systems to then put your whole body into a crisis mode in response to this detected threat. In many respects, this neural response is helpful. Our brains evolved to react quickly to do something to either avoid detected threats or lessen whatever pain is going on.

And our brain does this in sneaky ways. It relies on deeply ingrained, almost primitive, reflexes meant to help us survive in harsh environments. This is kind of like how you might duck or curl up to protect yourself. You may just end up relying on one of the five Fs that we've talked about before as your default reaction—because they've been successful in serving a purpose for you before: *fight, flight, freeze, fawn,* or *fester.*

So again, when you've recognized negative or distressing feelings of conflict, first PAUSE and take at least one long deep breath. It's OK if you need more than one long deep breath or if you'd like to use any other special breathing technique. The breathwork is crucial! Apart from oxygen going into your circulatory system and being transported to your body's cells and carbon dioxide being transported away, whenever you breathe you activate millions of nerves in your body. Breathe in and you activate your sympathetic nervous system, which increases your heart rate; your body releases norepinephrine ("adrenaline") and you feel more awake. In contrast, focusing on breathing out activates your parasympathetic nervous system, which triggers your brain to decrease your heart rate, relaxes your body, and makes you feel more calm. Some studies suggest that focusing on slowly breathing out can also cause your brain to release a special neurotransmitter called GABA, which will add to the calming effect on your nervous system.

One study divided a hundred people into four groups where one group was instructed to do mindful meditation without focused breathing while the other three groups were instructed to engage in different focused breathing techniques. They did this for five minutes daily for a whole month. Surprisingly, at the end of the study, the breathwork groups felt overall more positive, less anxious, and less stressed compared to the mindfulness-meditation group, suggesting that breathwork may have a greater effect on your emotional regulation than mindful meditation alone.

The group that experienced the most benefit? The one that focused on long, slow exhales using a technique called *cyclic sighing*. This involves inhaling quickly and deeply through your nose, holding it a second, then inhaling again just the last bit extra that you're able to, and finally exhaling that breath slowly through your mouth. (Safety note: The first time you try this, be sure to do it seated, as you might feel a little lightheaded.) If you are feeling better and calmer once you try this, it's because taking even just one of these breaths is the quickest physiologically validated method to instantly lower your stress level and restore calm. Repeated for five minutes once a day, cyclic sighing can greatly reduce stress while increasing your conflict-holding capability.

Another technique you might consider is *box breathing*. In this method, you breathe in through your nose for four seconds, hold for four seconds, breathe out through your mouth for four seconds, hold for four seconds, and then repeat. Box breathing is excellent for maintaining a steady rhythm and can be particularly useful in high-stress situations when you need to quickly regain focus and control.

So, whether you like box breathing or you prefer the deeper, stress-relieving breaths of cyclic sighing, both techniques have their unique benefits. Box breathing might be ideal for moments when your anxiety is rising and a rhythmic, repetitive pattern is more likely to help you stay calm, while cyclic sighing is an evidence-backed method to reduce overall stress and regain your bearings. Incorporating either or both into your daily routine can notably enhance your mental clarity, emotional stability, and ability to manage the stress and discomfort of conflict more effectively.

After your all-important breath(s), allow yourself to notice what is going on with your body. Are you clenching your fists? Are you leaning or backing away? Is your face feeling flushed? Heart racing? Stomach hurting? Jaw muscles tightening? Is your tongue outstretched and pushing against the roof of your mouth? These are signs of your sympathetic (fight-or-flight) nervous system activating—and may seem involuntary, but just like you can unclench a fist, you can start to counteract the sympathetic flow by starting to relax some of these muscles and engage your parasympathetic (rest-and-digest) nervous system.

You might be thinking to yourself now, "Um, actually, your suggestion doesn't make sense in the context of a real-life conflict." But we disagree and invite you to give it a try, even just once or twice. The intentional pause and slowing down helps both the person doing it as well as the others in the conflict. It slows the pace down and allows everyone to come back to something more purposeful and productive. For example, while Maya and her brother Lamont were on a long-awaited trip to explore Yamaguchi, Japan, Lamont grew tired with the minute-to-minute travel itinerary Maya had painstakingly crafted for them in the months leading up to the trip. Lamont snapped at Maya, "Hey, why don't we just scrap the itinerary altogether and have a more spontaneous trip? What happened to your sense of adventure?"

Although Maya could have snapped back by telling Lamont to go have his own adventure without her for the rest of the trip, she instead took an intentional pause, took a breath, and noticed how tense her whole body was feeling. She suggested taking a five-minute break and during that time she used her go-to breathing technique. The pause not only allowed her to gather her thoughts and calm her frustration, but also gave Lamont some time for himself to start thinking about what kind of an experience he really wanted out of this trip so he could articulate more clearly what it was that was so important about traveling with Maya: he missed spending time with his sister back home, which was almost impossible to do after she had her kids. He just wanted more relaxed downtime together. He wanted quality time and, in truth, Maya probably wanted the same with him. After the five minutes, their conversation ended up being much more constructive.

So, once you've allowed yourself to pause, breathe, and notice, there are some more questions to ask:

- To what extent is my reaction a subconscious default to moments of discomfort for me versus a truly purposeful, healthy, and useful response? From where does this pattern come in my life? And in what ways has it served me? And in what ways is it holding me back from being as conflict resilient as I would like to be?
- Separating out my own response and what I think I might be capable of, what are some other responses that I've observed or heard about that I'd like to add to my repertoire?
- What are the reasons or barriers that tend to prevent me from doing this in the moment?

## BARRIERS TO HOLDING CONFLICT

Some years ago, Bob was part of a group working on DEIB (diversity, equity, inclusion, and belonging) issues in an organization. This group was composed primarily of politically liberal, older, White, cisgender men. As part of the work, stakeholders in the organization participated in a workshop that challenged individuals to confront some of their own hidden biases. Workshop participants were invited to use some hypothetical scenarios to spur conversation about hidden biases. As he observed the group engage in these activities, Bob started to notice a pattern of engagement that felt like a default reaction to experienced internal tension and conflict. Specifically, rather than lean into the emotional and identity-based discomfort that the scenario was designed to evoke, the participants tended to fight the hypothetical fact pattern that was designed to spur conversation. They did this despite the fact that the workshop instructor was clear that the made-up fact pattern was not meant to be an accurate description of a real-life story. By sparring with the scenario, the group resisted engaging with the emotional and identity-based reactions it was designed to invoke. For example, the workshop participants asked lots of detail-oriented factual questions that were simply irrelevant to the main point of the exercise. "Did the racially motivated behavior occur during work hours?" or "The scenario doesn't say whether this behavior was a pattern or practice as opposed to a one-off incident."

Most of the participants in this workshop were trained as lawyers and it seemed that as their discomfort grew, their response was to engage not as persons exploring hidden biases but as lawyers quibbling over obscure and largely unimportant aspects of the made-up fact pattern. It wasn't until one of the trainers stopped, named the observed dynamic, and challenged the group to examine its own knee-jerk response to the discomfort that the exercise itself and the real work began.

Here are four common ways that people might fail to hold conflict:

1.  Grabbing the mantle of identity
2.  Putting a bow on it
3.  Externalizing the conflict
4.  Minimizing/maximizing

## 1. Grabbing the Mantle of Identity

In our highly polarized political climate, one common conflict-handling approach is to "grab the mantle of identity." What do we mean by this? It's the tendency to say, "Well, as a southern Christian . . ." or "As a first-generation college graduate . . ." or "As a Latino Millennial . . ."

The problem with this technique is that in the process of arming yourself against slings and arrows, you've also made it extremely challenging for someone who isn't of your particular persuasion or identity to voice their views without seeming to erase the validity and experience of everyone who belongs to your identity. Grabbing the mantle of identity often serves as a tactic to shut down differing viewpoints from being expressed by others, regardless of whether the identity is shared or not.

One of Bob's former colleagues at Harvard Law School had a rule in her teaching that forbade students from making a class contribution under the mantle of a particular group category. The purpose was not to invalidate the experience and perspective that certain racial/ethnic, gender, religious, or other identities confer upon us, but to protect space for disagreement without the fear that disagreement erased individual identity.

We are not suggesting that one's experience because of their association or involvement with a particular identity doesn't or shouldn't influence how they experience a set of issues. Of course, it does and it should. What we are saying is that as a way of engaging or holding the conflict, grabbing the mantle of identity may do more to shut down disagreement and authenticity and, thus, do more harm than good. One way of explaining how your identity informs your perspective without using it as a shield against different viewpoints might be to say, "Part of what informed how I came to see it this way stems from my background as . . ." This approach allows you to share the identity without unwittingly making it seem that you speak on behalf of all those who share that identity. It also provides enough space for others to disagree without feeling that they are attacking the experience or validity of everyone who may hold a particular identity.

## 2. Putting a Bow on It

Another common conflict-handling approach is to find some way to cabin the disagreement and "wrap it up" with a bow to minimize or even resolve it. What does this look like? Some time ago, Bob attended a panel on the U.S. role in the Israel/Gaza war that began after the October 7 attacks in 2023. Emotions ran high and the differences between the panelists were many, varied, and passionately held. At various times in the discussion, a panelist would make a reference to "genocide" or "antisemitism" or "colonialism" or "terrorism" in the context of their remarks. And each time, it would cause an uproar from other panel members. Admittedly, each of those words could be the topic of multiple panels. The notion that they could be adequately explored in a single panel is ludicrous. Worse, every time a hot-button topic was raised, the moderator steered the conversation away from a deeper conversation and toward a more anodyne subject. "Let's return to what our shared future might look like," he would say. Or, "I think we all agree that the situation is complicated for all involved." Or "May I ask that we return to a conversation about what the U.S. role can look like in the future?" Or, "Rather than focus on these complicated and divisive issues, let's focus on all you have in common with each other." For Bob, it seemed the panelists had very little in common with each other and that the moderator's strong desire to find common ground was actually detracting from a much more valuable and important conversation on the disagreement.

To us, this is what we mean by "putting a bow" on a conflict. We try to sidestep the heart of the matter because it feels so overwhelming and instead we say something placating and nice that we can all agree on in the vaguest of terms.

"Peace is good."

"Let's save the planet."

For most of us, it is hard to disagree with these more generic aphorisms and it is hard to dig into the conflict if we start and end there.

### 3. Externalizing the Conflict

Another common conflict-handling mode is to externalize the problem. For example, the personal aspect gets abstracted to something that feels more academic and distant: "Well, let's broaden our conversation from whether I should be composting and let me ask you something: Even if everyone composted in the U.S., would that make much difference given the behavior of large players like India and China who seem indifferent to climate change as they build their economies?"

A related form of externalizing is to shift blame away from our differences and suggest that the real problem is some external body—the government, the CEO, or Grandma's unreasonable holiday expectations.

## 4. Minimizing/Maximizing

A final common and usually unhelpful way of conflict holding is what we call minimizing or maximizing the conflict. What does this look like?

Minimizing is taking a point of disagreement and making it seem less than what it really is. "Now that I've heard your thinking on it, I actually think we largely see things the same way except for this tiny point..."

Now, when that's true, wonderful. But when the tiny point of disagreement is at the heart of what's being discussed, minimizing is just another way of avoiding.

Maximizing is the flip side of the same coin. "You are right. This problem is so consequential and beyond our scope that we really can't move forward until it is solved or until Adi decides." Again, at times this may be true. But often it's just a way to avoid engaging the conflict further by pushing it to another day or to somewhere outside the scope of the parties.

Recently, Bob participated in a weekend-long intergenerational dialogue of American Catholics. At one point, an older Catholic lamented, "These issues are so big, it just feels hopeless to be able to change anything."

A brilliant Gen Zer responded, "I hear you *and* we're here to see how we can change ourselves through relationship, connection, and talking through these challenges. I'm here to learn about accompaniment and relationship across the chasm of difference and divide. Tell me why our conversation has made you feel so powerless and without hope."

Talk about gracefully holding conflict to keep engagement alive!

## HOLDING ON TO CONFLICT WHEN YOU WANT TO LET GO

Being able to name your default reaction to avoid holding conflict is an important step toward understanding how to move toward more constructive engagement. The next time you find yourself headed to your default reaction, commit to three "conditioning" exercises so you can continue to hold conflict effectively:

1. Observe
2. Consider
3. Try

Let's break this down.

### Step 1. Observe

If you are like us, part of the challenge of handling intense conflict more adroitly is that we tend to go into an automatic or default "act-react" mode that spirals out of our control—either toward panicky avoidance or dangerous escalation. It's easy in that moment to believe that a purposeful response is out of reach. But here's the thing: no matter how difficult intervening mindfully and with purpose may feel for you at that moment, it is *not* out of reach.

One way of reconceptualizing the task here is not to think about a capacity you want to build or acquire, but to think about how to reclaim something you almost certainly had as a baby or young child. This capacity, simply put, is a highly curious and keen sense of *noticing*.

It's part of what makes a toddler both adorable and, at times, enraging. They seem easily distracted by anything that comes into their purview. Over time, the young toddler is taught—either explicitly or implicitly—to only notice things that are deemed important (perhaps by parents, society, schools, culture, or religious institutions), or that get them what they want, or that others think of as meaningful or worthy of attention. And so the general noticing ability fades away and is replaced by a more curated "noticing" based on the factors above.

Your task is to rekindle your own inner toddler who is attuned to noticing a whole bunch of things that we've been conditioned to ignore but that can make the difference in expanding your ability to respond. For Bob, he calls this going into "puppy mode." When Bob first became the human to his golden retriever Rosie, he often marveled at how Rosie seemed to notice *everything*—a leaf, a breeze, a bunny, a sound, a person, a flower. It was maddening at times—how could he get through a walk if every step opened a new and wonderful world of observation for Rosie?! At the same time, it was also eye-opening— and, to be honest, refreshing—for Bob to see this creature so enthralled with *everything* going on.

Though it may seem exaggerated, "puppy-mode" noticing is what we need when it comes to improving our conflict tolerance. The act of noticing and naming the many levels of what is happening in a moment of increased conflict and tension tends to reduce the emotional valence that drives that automatic reaction of the five Fs—fight, flight, freeze, fawn, or fester. Noticing and labeling helps us turn down the volume on the more reactive parts of our brains; it helps reduce the intensity of the emotions you might be experiencing, which will then allow you to perceive and assess the situation with more clarity. With the noticing and naming, you will come to appreciate that even if the sense of tension and anxiety you are feeling in the conflict isn't feeling great, it's almost never the case that the uncomfortable conflict is putting you in the kind of danger that would call for an automatic, reflex-like reaction. In the naming and the noticing, we realize, "Oh yes. This feels crummy. But I have the skill and capacity—the resilience—to get through it."

The act of observation then gives us space to move to step 2.

**Step 2. Consider**

This is your invitation to move from an automatic reaction to taking stock of the wide range of possible responses that might be possible, purposeful, and productive in the moment. For Bob, this means putting on his "negotiation professor" hat and saying, "If I were advising a student in this same situation, what useful suggestions would I offer them in this moment?" As soon as he can move himself into this "consider" stage, Bob can usually identify a range of behavioral responses that are more than his own tendency toward the binary reactions of "fight" or "run for the hills." For Joel, "consider" means putting on his "brain scientist" hat and challenging his working hypotheses about the situation: "What was the full collection of perceived stimuli and conditions that resulted in the observed behavior? What single parameter might I modify here to test one of those hypotheses that might lead to a different result?" Informed by what has been observed in studies examining which neural mechanisms are at work under the hood of altruism and other kind behaviors, he may start to wonder about how he can recalibrate his brain's reward-and-reinforcement pathways. Specifically, how he can get more of a positive "jolt" from directing his already-limited attention to focus on imagining a greater number of possibilities for what might be better responses to the current situation.

At this point, perhaps you will come up with nothing. Or maybe you'll think "I could punch them," or "I could run away to a foreign land and never return." Choices like these, of course, may feel worse than whatever your default reaction is. Which is why you go with your default reaction.

In some instances, the best way to figure out how someone is experiencing an interaction might be the hardest for some people: to talk about it. Initiating a conversation about it starts to get you out of your head and into the actual situation in front of you.

One hack that can work might be to ask, "Hey, I wonder if you'd be open to me sharing an observation about how I experienced your comment?" or "It's funny, but I realize that I had a strong reaction to the interaction we just had. I wonder if I could share that with you and get your thoughts?"

Admittedly, if their conflict recognition is very high and their conflict holding is very low (see below), talking about the experience, especially shortly after it occurred, may be very hard. But consider some other common responses:

- Getting curious about their motivation
- Listening
- Broadening the conversation to discuss a dynamic that comes up for you in the relationship, or even in relationships generally
- Naming what's going on for you
- Suggesting a way to have the conversation or disagreement in a way that all involved can engage

If you are still coming up with blanks here—don't worry. We're going to be offering you lots of useful responses in these pages and will elaborate on some of the ones above as well. And if you come up with a few ideas that are different from what you usually do but you're not quite sure if they're good or if you can do them, well, that's exactly where you want to be right now. Because the next step is . . .

## Step 3. Try

Yes, we are intentional about the word *try*. We aren't saying "choose the best response." Simply choose one of the other options that is not your default and that seems within the range of reasonable, and then just try it as an experiment. One part of this experiment is to see how you feel with a new response. And another part is to see how they react to the response.

Why this advice? Well, our experience is that part of what gets us stuck is that we are in "react" mode before we "observe" the dynamic. But another part is that, for some of us, we "observe" well, we see some other—possibly helpful—ways of holding the conflict, but we don't know which is better, which will work, which might flop, or how they might respond—so in despair and exhaustion, we fall back to the default.

As bad as the default is, it has an advantage that new approaches don't: a predictable outcome. The problem is that the predictable outcome leaves us still feeling dissatisfied and crummy. The lure of the predictable and manageable "crummy" can sometimes seem better than trying something new. The trouble with the routine is nothing changes. It's like resisting a new exercise regime because your muscles will be sore or your form might not be perfect or some of the exercise routine still won't give you the immediate results you hope for. All of this is true. And yet, if you don't try a new routine, your physical health is unlikely to magically improve on its own. Doing *something* is the first step toward improvement.

The same is true at this stage in your journey toward improved conflict holding! In this muscle-building phase, what you should be really working on is trying to get yourself to *think/feel* something different and *to do something different*, even if neither the thoughts/feelings nor the doing is "perfect."

One "brain science hack" to unblock this step involves considering the BBO, as Dr. Jud Brewer, a psychiatrist, neuroscientist, and director of research and innovation at Brown University's Mindfulness Center, likes to call it—the bigger, better offer (the BBO). By applying principles from neuroscience and our understanding of the brain's reward system, we can make it easier to break bad habits and try something different. If you're able to identify a different behavior that *might* provide a BBO than the current default reaction, you'll be much more likely to make the shift and make a new habit out of it.

First, identify the specific default reaction you want to change and what you would like to replace it with. Be precise about the actions you want to take. Work on understanding the triggers and the rewards associated with the default reaction to help you become more aware of the underlying mechanisms driving it.

Consider Carmen—a mindless apologizer. For her, taking the time to identify the situations that triggered empty apologizing and the rewards she got from it was a first step toward behavioral change. For her, the act of apology helped reduce stress and fear, associated with the possibility that she might have upset someone. Bullied as an adolescent in an all-girls school, Carmen learned to say "I'm sorry" as a way to both stop the bullying and reduce the internal stress. She carried this behavior to virtually every aspect of her life.

For example, on a date with her significant other, Shane, she might say, "I'm so excited to see the new Timothée Chalamet movie."

If Shane responded, "Ugh. I'm so *not* a Chalamet fan! He's just not 'all that,'" Carmen would instinctually respond, "Oh, all right. I'm so sorry. What should we do instead?"

From a neurologic perspective, during more threatening conflict situations, the amygdala becomes overactive, leading to impulsive reactions. Although the amygdala is often referred to as the part of the brain that processes fear or negative emotions, it's important to know that the function of the amygdala is more general—it processes and predicts the importance of various things you note in the environment, guiding your attention and facilitating decision-making based on your brain's previous experiences and predictions.

Aware of the source of the triggers, Carmen then had to develop a metric to track her progress. This can include the frequency of the new behavior, the reduction in the old behavior, or the improvement in associated outcomes. For Carmen, she decided to note the decrease in the number of times she used the word *sorry* in a disagreement. In addition, Carmen enlisted Shane and other trusted friends to interrupt her when they noticed the use of a mindless *sorry*. As Shane said, "You're not allowed to use the *s*-word unless there is something to be truly sorry about."

Ensure your goal is realistic and attainable, given your current circumstances and resources. One resource that is accessible to most in this regard is mindfulness. Mindfulness (in combination with breathwork) is important in habit change. It involves nonjudgmental awareness of the present moment. Mindfulness practices have been shown to reduce amygdala activation and increase activity in the prefrontal cortex, which is responsible for executive functions such as decision-making and self-regulation. Start with small, manageable steps and incorporate mindfulness techniques, such as meditation or breath awareness, to help you stay focused and present during the process.

Also make sure your goal is meaningful and connected to your over-all values and aspirations. Research highlights that tapping into your intrinsic motivation can help sustain behavior change. Reflect on why the new behavior is important to you and how it aligns with your values, such as improving your mental health, staying bravely with the discomfort of disagreement, or increasing your self-confidence. The orbitofrontal cortex is a part of the brain just behind the eyes that plays an important role in storing information about how rewarding a behavior or situation is or is not. For Carmen, part of the way she was able to motivate the behavioral change was to increase how rewarding her orbital frontal cortex registered that behavior. For example, reflecting on how avoiding the automatic sorry responses not only helped her be truer to herself, but also made her feel more present and genuine to friends, family, and her partner, Shane. Soon, even when others didn't necessarily notice a change, Carmen could take stock of—and actually experience the reward of—reflexive *sorry*s averted and avoided.

Finally, set a clear time frame for achieving your goal. This can be a specific date or a period within which you want to see progress. Keep in mind that behavior change takes time and being patient and com-passionate with yourself is a critical part of this process. Set a realistic timeline that allows for setbacks and gradual progress.

As a kid, whenever Bob resisted trying a new food—whether it was a vegetable or even a new ice cream flavor—his mother would say, "Just try it." As his mom would say, "What's the harm in trying? If you don't like it, you can try something else or go back to what you like." The invitation to try, knowing that he could "go back," lowered the stakes for him. If he hated the black raspberry ice cream, he could always go back to the cookies 'n' cream. If the Brussels sprouts turned out to be as gross as he expected, the carrots would still be on his plate and they were delish! Imagine, however, if faced with a range of choices, Bob were told, "Choose the best of the ice cream choices you have never tried," or "Choose the tastiest vegetable you have never eaten before." Bob would probably just say, "Ugh. Give me the cookies 'n' cream," or "I'll just stick to the carrots I know." The point here is that waiting to identify the "best" or the "most effective" way to handle a conflict before changing a default response raises the stakes and becomes an unhelpful excuse for doing nothing.

## AND THEN—TRY SOMETHING ELSE!

Once you've tried your new approach, take the time to observe again, asking some simple but key questions:

1. How did it feel for me to try something new?
2. How did it land on the intended recipient(s)?
3. What could I try next time?

### Question 1: How did it feel for me to try something new?

If it felt awkward or unnatural, you might also ask, "Did it feel as bad as I thought it might, or just awkward and a bit unnatural?" Our experience is that usually the idea of trying something new feels worse than the actual experience of doing it, even if the experience isn't exactly wonderful. Importantly, ask yourself, "Did the new behavior feel appreciably more awkward or difficult than other new tasks I've given myself in life?" And, even if the answer is some version of, "Yes. It felt excruciating," we want you to still celebrate the fact that you tried something else. When it comes to the discomfort of conflict holding, the very act of breaking the default is truly worth celebrating.

### Question 2: How did it land on the intended recipient(s)?

However it felt for you to try the new behavior, how did it land on them? Ideally, it was highly successful. Perhaps it opened up a new conversation you never had before, yielded a new set of insights, or gave you information to better assess how to approach the context or relationship in the future.

It might be just as likely that the approach didn't land as smoothly as you hoped. Perhaps your counterpart seems surprised? Confused? Or maybe a bit stuck about how they might respond? In our experience, even when the new behavior doesn't work perfectly as planned, it serves the purpose of breaking up the predictable and unproductive pattern that the parties have found themselves in. And that, in itself, is powerful. It helps move an interaction from a boring and predictably scripted play to an improv interaction that at least involves the relevant parties in something more interesting than reciting rehearsed and well-worn lines.

Carmen can remember vividly the first time she asserted a strongly held preference that was different from her group of friends. She said, "I know I usually say, 'I'm sorry,' or, 'I totally agree with you.' But, to be honest, as I think about it, I realize that I really don't agree on this and I'm trying to understand more. You all seem to think that authoritarianism is on the rise globally. I see that in some parts of the world. But not others. So, even if it might be increasing, it's far from obvious to me. Can you help me see what I'm missing here?" Externally verbalizing her internal thinking felt like a mind-blowing shift to her. And, to her great pleasure, it was received with joy and curiosity by the others at the dinner table. For the first time in a long time, Carmen felt like she was in the conversation *at the table* instead of the one in her head about whether her thoughts and feelings were worth saying aloud. She also realized that, even if it didn't land perfectly well, these were her friends. And she'd survive right on through dessert and an evening of playing Settlers of Catan as well.

If you've been in some kind of conflict rut for a long time and finally try something new, it's important to remember that your counterpart may feel confused and stuck as well. That's why allowing time for pauses, new reactions, and adjustment is important.

Frequently in Bob's coaching practice, he'll work with a client who is trying out some new kind of response with a boss or direct report or fellow executive committee member.

Following the experiment, Bob will ask, "Well, how'd it go?"

And the client responds, "It didn't work. A total disaster."

"Well, what happened?" Bob asks.

And the client says, "Well, there was an awkward silence for a long time and I couldn't tell what was going on. And then they (or I) muttered something nonresponsive or tentative or awkward..."

While we can appreciate why they concluded that the new move didn't work, we also think this conclusion is too extreme. The person on the receiving end of the new interaction is likely as confused and surprised by your new behavior as you are uncomfortable doing it. That means that there will likely need to be an adjustment time for them as well as you. It can help for you to explicitly acknowledge that you are trying something new and that you don't expect your counterpart to have an immediate perfect or satisfying response. The transparency of a communication like this can ease discomfort for everyone in the conversation. It can also be a place of connection even if the substance of your communication might be to create more "disagreement" because you are asserting a need, preference, interest, or opinion for the first time.

To go back to the fitness-training example, if you are working muscles in ways you haven't in years you're likely to experience some pain and stiffness before you start to feel stronger from the new routine.

Last year Bob's father had knee-replacement surgery. His friends and his surgeon told him it could take a year before his knee felt right.

For months his dad would complain of soreness, discomfort, even a clicking of the knee. Meanwhile, his physical therapist and his surgeon said that he was in the "top ten percent" of patients for recovery and rehabilitation for his age.

Was Bob's dad exaggerating or making things up? Neither are his nature. Perhaps the doctors were just sweet-talking Dad to make him feel better? Maybe, but also unlikely. The reality is that the rehabilitation and hard work of muscle strengthening was necessarily going to be awkward, sometimes painful, uncomfortable, and time-consuming.

And, in so many respects, that's the invitation of conflict resilience—it is awkward, sometimes painful, uncomfortable, and time-consuming. But if you push through it with determination, it will bring you to better health and better outcomes in your relationships and organizations. If we do the same collectively as a community and a country, we'll see ourselves break through this national moment of polarization—not to more agreement and consensus, but to more unity and shared purpose. That prospect makes the effort worthwhile. Whether we are trying to heal and restore Dad's knee or our individual and collective resistance to holding conflict, there is simply no path forward without the hard work and discomfort of working the muscles we've let lie latent for too long.

### Question 3: What could I try next time?

Next, and especially if what you tried didn't work perfectly, ask yourself, "What other responses, moves, or behaviors could I try next time?" In our experience working with clients, the biggest challenge is getting them to do something—anything—new in the interaction. Once they've done that, it usually opens cognitive and emotional space to identify a whole host of other responses they could make that perhaps they were less aware of before they broke the initial pattern.

Finally—as we urged above—be sure to take a moment to celebrate, even if the outcome wasn't all (or anything) you hoped for. Why? Because simply changing your typical response is the first step to starting to build new repertoire around conflict holding, and this is something that is essential if you are going to build the kind of conflict resilience in the long term that will make you agile, aware, authentic, and competent in the face of the wide range of conflicts that you'll find yourself in.

In Chapters 5, 6, and 7 we will break open some of the specific behavioral skills that will enable you to be more conflict resilient, but before we do, we dig even deeper inward, inviting you to better understand your own internal conflicts—your negotiations within—that can at times hinder your ability to be conflict resilient across the negotiation table.

# Chapter 4

# EMBRACING YOUR
# NEGOTIATION WITHIN

## The Self as the Starting Point for Conflict Resilience

Talia spent the better part of the last decade working night and day to build her small start-up into a multimillion-dollar company with hundreds of employees and offices around the country. She now had an offer to sell the company that would mean she wouldn't have to work another day in her life if she so chose. At the very least, she could start a family and begin to enjoy the fruits of her labor. This moment was all she had worked for; everyone in her life was cheering her on, thrilled for the imminent sale that would free her to live her best life. And yet . . . there was another side of her that felt uneasy and unsure about the sale, as irrational as it might sound to others in her life. If she really thought about it, she felt torn and worried about pursuing a post-start-up life; she felt sad and adrift at the idea of no longer growing her company and her amazing team. Instead of feeling excited about the road ahead, Talia felt unmoored and anxious about her future.

And then there's Thomas, who graduated at the top of his class, rocked the LSATs, earned admission to an elite law school, and was on his way to becoming the first in his family to earn a college degree. Thomas was proud of his achievements, but none of them compared to the thrill—and accolades—he got when he performed onstage in his university's musical production each semester. One part of Thomas reminded him that he'd be a fool not to accept the offer of admission from Georgetown Law; another part knew that his real joy came from performing, not from burying his nose in a constitutional law case-book and sitting at a desk. Thomas felt stuck.

Perhaps one of the above stories has some personal resonance for you. And perhaps not. Either way, if you are like virtually anyone we have ever met, there are times when you feel conflicted and torn on the inside—times when you feel stuck in an endless loop of "On the one hand... but on the other..."

Internal conflicts—those between two (or more) sides of oneself—are among the most challenging and complicated to take on. And they can also be among the most convenient to push to the back burner and avoid.

"But wait a minute!" you might be saying. "I picked this book up because I wanted some strategies for dealing with conflicts with other people. What does that have to do with my own internal dilemmas or sense of conflictedness?"

It's a great and fair question and one we can answer with great confidence: "A whole lot."

It's not hyperbole to say that the biggest hidden barrier to being conflict resilient stems from the inability or unwillingness to face and sit with our own internal conflicts—the negotiations between our divided and sometimes contradictory "selves." Even more surprising is that although there are dozens of self-help books on negotiation and conflict resolution, almost none of them spend any meaningful time on this critical *intrapersonal* barrier to handling conflict.

In this chapter, we look inward, examining the internal struggles and conflicts that hold us back from being conflict resilient. To be conflict resilient means facing our own internal contradictions, challenges, tensions, and conflicts with bravery, compassion, and aplomb.

## DYING WITHOUT FALLING IN LOVE

He had graduated from Harvard and Oxford University. Worked on a presidential campaign. Was awarded a Rhodes scholarship. Elected the mayor of South Bend, Indiana, and served in the U.S. Navy with a tour of Afghanistan. He was thirty-three years old and already on the radar of prominent Democrats such as Barack Obama and David Axelrod as a possible future leader in the Democratic Party. But as Pete Buttigieg tells it, despite that record of great professional achievement, he had never fallen in love. Indeed, it wasn't until he turned thirty-three and returned from his tour of duty in Afghanistan, with a fresh and lived awareness of the fragility and fleeting nature of life, that Buttigieg made the decision to "come out" as gay. He did this in the most public way possible, in an op-ed of the *South Bend Tribune*, the newspaper of record in his hometown—of which he was the current mayor. He did so only a few days before the U.S. Supreme Court declared that marriage equality was a constitutional right.

Perhaps your internal conflicts are not as high-profile as Buttigieg's but, whether they're mountains or molehills, one thing is for sure: it shouldn't take facing possible death in a foreign war zone to force you to confront them head-on. But, like Buttigieg, if you confront your internal conflicts head-on, with courage and integrity, it's more likely than not you'll achieve outcomes that far surpass your expectations. In his memoir *The Shortest Way Home*, Buttigieg talks about the fear he had that coming out might cause him to lose his reelection as mayor of South Bend, a city not known to be on the cutting edge of progressive politics. To the contrary, he was reelected in a landslide and by a much wider margin than his first race. He went on to be the first openly gay presidential candidate to win the Iowa caucus, the first openly gay person appointed to be a member of the president's cabinet, and the first openly gay person to be shortlisted to serve as the vice presidential candidate for the Democratic Party—all before he reached his mid-forties. It's hard to imagine Buttigieg being seen as the persuasive and authentic communicator he is had he not worked through his own complicated internal dilemma related to sexuality, success, ambition, and authenticity.

### TO RAISE OR NOT TO RAISE?

When was the last time you felt a disagreement with someone—whether a boss, a parent, a friend, a customer—but didn't raise it with them directly? Write down a few of the reasons why you didn't raise it. Some simple ones that might come to mind are:

- It's not that important.
- They just won't understand.
- They'd see me as a troublemaker, selfish, stubborn, annoying, etc.
- I really don't feel *that* strongly about it.
- They care about the issue more than I do.

Your list might be very different, but likely can go on and on.

Now that you've made a list of the reasons why you decided *not* to raise the issue with them, identify that part of you that still disagrees with them—that voice that still says, "Yeah, but . . ." For some, that voice will be easy to identify and loud; for others, it might take a bit of work.

For example, it might say:

- Yeah, but even if it is more important to them, it still irks me to remain quiet.
- Yeah, but maybe this isn't being selfish. Maybe it just expresses what matters to me.
- Yeah, but even if they experience me as being annoying, I can't expect more from them if I don't let them know what I'm thinking or what I need.
- Yeah, but I shouldn't always be letting myself down.

The point is that whenever we register dissonance with someone else and don't raise it with them, there are two sides of ourselves: the side that notices and cares a lot, or maybe just a little; and the side of ourselves that for whatever reason decides it's best to let it drop.

And, lest we be misunderstood, in many times and situations there are lots of very good reasons why we should just let things drop. But in many situations, "letting things drop" can become problematic, both in our relationship with the other person *and* in our relationship with ourselves and with those parts of ourselves that continually get silenced and that genuinely need *and* deserve to be expressed. We can never be fully conflict resilient if we simply avoid the across-the-table "conflict" by remaining silent and pretending that the conflict we're feeling within ourselves isn't really there and affecting us in some way. When we consistently silence a part of ourselves that rears its head over and over again, we end up suffocating something within ourselves that is valid and real—something that needs to be said, heard, or acknowledged even if it stands in tension with other "sides" of ourselves. To be conflict resilient, then, we have to listen to and hear the voices inside us that are telling us different, often conflicting or contradictory stories. This is what we mean by the negotiation within.

In their 2009 book, *Immunity to Change*, psychologists Robert Kegan and Lisa Laskow talk about five successive "orders of consciousness" in adult mental and emotional growth: the impulsive mind, the instrumental mind, the socialized mind, the self-authoring mind, and the self-transforming mind. At the stage of the fifth order, the self-transforming mind, the authors discuss the idea of being able to hold multiple selves, some of which are contradictory in nature. Individuals at this stage understand that any one system of meaning is partial and they are thus more open to the contradiction and transformation of these selves. In our work and practice, we have found that failure to handle internal conflict effectively is as likely to be the cause of bad conflict-handling with others as is simply not having the interpersonal skills, conflict-handling tools, or proper formulation of what to say.

## CONFLICT SIDESTEPS

It's the subject of many movies: the pressures experienced by a child struggling with the well-intentioned dreams of parents ("Be a doctor!" "Go to law school!" "When you take over the family business . . .") and their own dream to get a PhD in archaeology, become an actor, or pursue trade school. Whether externally expressed or not, we all can relate to these tensions, either from our own experience or those of family and friends.

"Go to medical school to make your family proud" is the side that represents generosity, a desire to make your family proud, ambition, and a hope for the financial security that you never had growing up. It's the side that is loyal to the people you care most about in the world. But the side that says "Maybe you should take a year and pursue drama and music" is also real. And it deserves a voice.

The problem is that many times, we don't listen to all the sides. Or we code one side as "good" and the other as "bad" or "immoral" or "selfish" or "unrealistic." "Oh, this is just me being selfish and ungrateful," or "Pursuing drama and music is a pipe dream. I'll end up a busker in the subway if I don't go to law school."

Here's the problem with these one-line "excuses." It's not that they might not have a scintilla (or more) of truth to them. It's that they are often incomplete, one-sided, or dismissive of a very real, genuine, and, dare we say, entirely appropriate other side of you. And if you take the time to really look at that side of yourself, you often find that there is a much more accurate, fulsome, and compelling story to tell yourself about yourself. Owning that side doesn't make you bad, selfish, or disloyal. It just makes you who you are. The more you can find ways to put that complexity forward in your conversations and interactions with others, the less scary "conflict" becomes.

Why? Because the responses that typically "trigger" the silenced or shamed parts of ourselves might lose their sting. When we make this kind of internal shift, our assertive ability and capacity for handling differences increase. The first shift here is acknowledging and then tackling the internal negotiation within. That conversation with yourself might go something like this:

> Pursuing a personal career interest is not being selfish. It's giving myself a chance at being fulfilled and happy, a goal that I know matters to my parents. Moreover, equating taking a year to explore my passion to ending up a busker in a subway for the rest of my life is succumbing to unhelpful catastrophic thinking. It is detached from the self that I know will explore this responsibly and can pivot back to law school (or whatever) in a year.

With a shifted internal mindset like the one above, imagine how differently the conversation might go with a parent. Instead of silence, eye-rolling, or an escalatory fight, you might say:

> I want to make you proud by pursuing a legal career. And there are aspects of that career that are attractive to me too, including the financial security that I know we've never had as a family. At the same time, giving myself a chance to pursue a career in musical theater isn't so much being selfish as it is pursuing a real passion of mine. And that is important to me and I hope it's something you can respect even if you disagree.

In speaking aloud, with confidence and integrity and kindness, the truth of the various internal voices that might seem to be in tension, the anxiety and pressure of trying to silence one side in favor of the other is eliminated. And what emerges often is more inviting and certainly is more authentic than the contorted efforts to silence and minimize one voice to avoid tension or conflict with the other person in a relationship. This is how to negotiate disagreement without giving up or giving in, all while helping your internal selves—and your relationship with the other—come together in an otherwise conflicted world.

In our work, we've discovered that part of what makes engaging conflict with others hard is that we have not spent enough time examining our own internal conflicts and narratives. Failure to do this means one of two things: we avoid the conflict entirely, or we may end up raising the issue but find ourselves susceptible to either defensiveness or caving in.

These unresolved pains are deeply embedded within complex networks of brain cells. Neurons link fragments of past painful memories—formed when something or someone hurt us—to pathways associated with physical pain, ensuring we viscerally remember what caused us harm, thus increasing the chances we'll reflexively shield ourselves from future hurt. Or at least, that's the presumed intent of nature's design. From research studying memory formation and post-traumatic stress disorder, we now know that in moments of stress and trauma, the adrenaline rush we experience from our sympathetic (fight-or-flight) nervous system—also by design—has the added effect of supercharging our brain's ability to form lasting memories. This explains why years after surviving a devastating car accident, whenever Joel touched the steering wheel of a car his brain triggered threat-detecting pathways.

Or consider Thomas, the graduating college student who dutifully heads off to law school, suppressing his reservations. Three years and several hundred thousand dollars in debt later, the newly minted lawyer finds himself headed to a large corporate law firm, dreading his life, and bent on escape after paying back his school loans. Not exactly a great outcome.

But the result might not be better if instead Thomas, without doing the internal work, simply declares he is going to defer a year and apply to the Juilliard School, the prestigious institution for the performing arts, instead. First, he may be easily susceptible to a barrage of internal attacks. "You are selfish and ungrateful" will land more powerfully if he has not done the internal work to know that pursuing a dream for a year is neither selfish nor ungrateful nor a decision of a lifetime.

Alternately, though, he might be prone to defensiveness that doesn't acknowledge or verbalize the very real side of himself that wants to please, live up to expectations, and be a source of pride for the family. Plus, caving in or becoming defensive takes away the possibility of a real conversation around a genuine dilemma: there really are two sides there. And the biggest gift he might be able to give would be to involve his parents and family in a shared and vulnerable conversation around those sides.

Along with colleagues Toby Berkman, affiliated faculty at the Program on Negotiation at Harvard Law School, and Sara del Nido Budish, assistant director of the Harvard Negotiation and Mediation Clinical Program, Bob has broadly categorized three genres of negotiation within:

1.   Good + Good = Bad
2.   Good + Bad = Bad
3.   A → B = Bad

## 1. Good + Good = Bad

A common internal conflict arises in situations where two identities we value and aspire toward come into odds with each other in a specific context. Here are a few examples:

- You want to be a good teacher and responsible parent to your children; you also want to be their friend, liked, appreciated, and admired by them. Now that they are tweens, you often find yourself stuck between the two, confusing yourself and your child about the inconsistency and seeming randomness of decisions you make around them.
- You've always prided yourself on being willing to cross the political aisle and problem-solve with Democrats in your community who had different views on issues related to the public school

curriculum. But now some on the liberal-leaning side are calling your fellow council member and neighbor a bigot for refusing to endorse a multicultural curriculum you see as highly politicized. It's important for you to stick up for your fellow council member, especially in the face of outrageous name-calling; at the same time, you don't approve of your own side's call to raise the volume and go on the offensive with an "anti-woke" media campaign that calls some of the liberal-leaning members "socialists" and "communists." You feel stuck. Further engaging with Democrats engaged in the name-calling feels like betraying your well-intentioned friend whose views you agree with, but participating in your side's own "fight back" media relations strategy also feels wrong and unhelpful.

- You are a corporate executive running a large division within a huge national corporation. You care about being seen as a cooperative team player with fellow department heads across the company, but you also care about being seen as someone who goes to bat for your employees in your own division. Ordinarily, being someone who is a good team player and someone who cares about keeping one's staff happy and motivated, both objectively good qualities, don't pose a dilemma for you. But now the company is facing a financial crisis and needs to cut staff. You want to do your part and take a proportional share of the budget cuts in your division; on the other hand, your team is awesome, already overworked and desperately needs more, not fewer, resources. How do you manage these competing interests?

Each of these dilemmas can be analyzed entirely in analytic terms. But there is a risk to that. Because the situation is actually triggering or activating an internal conflict that speaks to a deeper identity-based concern, it's critical that you name what's going on within. Without the pausing and the naming, you may be apt to fall victim to a default behavioral pattern that may leave you feeling even more ambivalent, stuck, and just awful. Yielding to a default reaction misses the chance to examine the deeper internal conflict. One side "cedes" to the other, and we lose the chance to reframe the situation in ways that could integrate both of our "sides" and lead to more creative and mutually beneficial outcomes for everyone.

## 2. Good + Bad = Bad

The second internal conflict can be even more challenging for some. It's when we code one story about ourselves with a degree of moral approbation, judgment, or even shame. Several of the examples we've given you (i.e., Buttigieg's struggle to come out; Thomas's struggle between law school and Juilliard) typify this internal conflict. One identity gets tagged as "selfish" or "wrong" or "immoral" or "bad," while the other side is heralded in some way as what a "good person" or a "grateful family member" would do.

You want to be a good son, brother, sister, mother, aunt, worker, student, committee member. But you also . . .

. . . need a vacation.

. . . want to be an artist.

. . . are determined to get the piercings.

. . . really do think there is a concerted attack against Christians in this country.

. . . have some preferences for where to go on family vacation, even if you are the last unpartnered and childless adult in your large family and so are expected to be "more flexible."

You end up coding the "generous" instincts as "worthy" and "good" and code the others along a continuum from "selfish" or "irresponsible" to "immoral" or "wrong." The story of Pete Buttigieg is a classic example of the "worthy" versus "shameful" internal conflict struggle that, if not taken on internally, can result in both internal misery and a lack of authenticity in relationships. But these internal identity challenges come up all the time.

Bob recently served on a volunteer advisory board full of generous, kind, and soft-spoken persons. Because of his legal background and his expertise in negotiation and process design, he was quick to point out various ways in which the board was eschewing due diligence for the sake of efficiency and harmony. At first his suggestions to slow things down were welcome. But soon enough he sensed that other people were starting to see him less as a "helpful negotiation and legal expert" and more as a "nitpicking troublemaker with a law degree in tow." His first reaction in response to the change in tone was to hold back from speaking when something felt "off" to him. "Troublemaker" and "legalistic nitpicker" were the last things he wanted to be. If Bob weren't able to reframe the coding of this negatively-valenced identity, it would be tough for him to be the best board member he could be, even if it would avoid lots of conflict and make for more enjoyable meetings. By reframing the "troublemaker" side to a self-concept of "good trouble," Bob was able to voice both sides of himself and convey to his fellow board members the dangers of investing part of the organization's endowment in a strategy that had not been pressure-tested with constituents. Even though the process Bob advocated for slowed progress in the short term, the more consensus-based approach the organization ultimately adopted resulted in a major resetting of strategic goals that simply would not have been discussed without his "good trouble" contrarian approach in early conversations.

### 3. A → B = Bad

Another moment when we tend to experience internal conflict is at the intersection between our professional and personal identities. Let's look at what happened to Talia, the start-up founder, who faced the prospect of a big payday from the acquisition of her company. Near the close of an almost-triumphant negotiation, Talia suddenly demanded an additional $20 million, with a raft of new conditions. Was Talia just playing hardball with the buyer or was she stuck in a bad negotiation with herself?

So much of Talia's self-concept was connected to being an entrepreneur, a leader, a brilliant businessperson. She struggled to imagine a new story for herself, about who she was and who she would become (stay-at-home mom? philanthropist? amateur golfer?) once the sale was completed. Her failure to negotiate this inner conflict between transitioning identities blew up the entire deal. Two years after the failed acquisition, and with the benefit of maturity and a concerted effort to be more conflict resilient with her own internal conflicts, Talia was able to negotiate a deal nearly as good as the first, but this time without the internal *Sturm und Drang* and without blowing it up at the last minute stemming from her inability to confront her internal demons about transitioning into a new "self-identity."

Or consider Nick and his daughter Yaz. She had always been Daddy's little girl. And Nick loved it. But things started to change when she moved across the country for college. Or, to be more precise, when she returned home for the summer after her first year in college. At first Nick chalked the tension up to the expected clash that might ensue when a child returns home after their first year of freedom in college. Except the tension that emerged after Yaz's first year in college never really dissipated. In fact, in many ways it grew over time.

Now in her mid-twenties, halfway through medical school, and well beyond a late adolescent rebellious streak, Yaz's relationship with her dad remains off—sometimes distant and strained, often ritualized, and far from ideal for either of them. Have they drifted politically? Lost interest in each other? Just grown apart?

The truth is, part of what gets things stuck is that Nick insists on playing the part of dad to a ten-year-old girl whenever they get together. Yaz finds this maddening—not because she doesn't need the love, care, counsel, wisdom, and affection of her dad in her life. But she needs a dad who can play the role of dad to a young adult and aspiring professional, not to a ten-year-old girl.

In the fear of losing the special identity of dad to his child, Nick hasn't seen the possibility of a new, equally important, inviting, and more appropriate role of dad to an adult. And he is perplexed when the fatherly advice that enthralled Yaz as a little girl is rebuffed now.

There's a horizon-expanding opportunity for Nick to move from "beloved dad to a little girl" to the "beloved dad of an amazing young woman" he raised. But Nick doesn't see it this way. All he sees is loss and threat, and this causes him to double down on what he knows how to do—playing dad to a kid—and unwittingly further alienating himself from Yaz. By not facing the conflict within and the need to transition from one way of being dad to a new way, Nick ends up pushing away what he most wants.

But it's not like Yaz has no role in this. Yes, she is frustrated and annoyed by the infantile and condescending way her dad often treats her. Except when she isn't. Because she can admit to herself that there are moments when she purposefully plays the role of a ten-year-old girl to get the coddling and sweetness that she wants when she's most depleted and exhausted. Those increasingly rare moments are the ones that Nick holds on to and cherishes.

But in a very real way, the relationship is stuck and in a slow descent. Failure to negotiate and confront the internal conflict each of them is experiencing—the challenge of moving a relationship from a little-girl relationship with Dad to a grown-adult relationship with Dad—is putting the entire relationship at risk. Even though confronting the internal tension Nick feels directly and then jointly problem-solving would be strange, uncomfortable, and challenging, it also offers the best possibility for both Nick and Yaz to get the thing they most want and need: each other.

· · ·

The journey to handling our internal conflicts with resilience and integrity is within our reach. Whether you're a ruminator, prone to constant self-talk, or reluctant to spend huge amounts of time on self-reflection, a three-step approach—first introduced by Bob and his coauthors—makes managing the negotiation within a little easier and can offer personal and professional benefits in how you handle conflict and manage across-the-table negotiation. This approach is known as *mirror work*, *chair work*, and *table work*.

## MIRROR WORK

The negotiation within starts by taking a good look at ourselves in conflict. Start by thinking about a conflict of yours that is upcoming and haunting you or one that has happened in the past but still feels unresolved or upsetting. It will be especially helpful if you can identify a conflict that feels like it comes up in a number of contexts and where it's even hard for you to get started. Alternatively, find a context where, after the conflict occurs, you find yourself regretting either saying something or, just as likely, not saying something that mattered to you. If you have trouble coming up with a specific conflict with a specific person, perhaps consider an issue about which you feel strongly and about which you struggle to have productive conversations with others who see it differently.

Once you've identified an example, spend some time doing some careful looking in the mirror—some serious self-examination. This is where we invite you to go back and consider the answer to some key questions:

- What are some of the reasons why it is important for you to raise this opinion/issue/concern with the other person(s)?
- What are some of the reasons why you prefer to avoid it or are prone to avoid it?

As you list these reasons, consider the ways in which your reasons for wanting to raise this topic and your reasons for not wanting to raise it might fall into some kind of pattern that goes beyond this particular circumstance. For example, do you notice that:

- You tend to be silent when you feel that raising an issue would be seen as selfish?
- You are quieter in situations where there is a perceived power difference?
- You are more aggressive in situations where you feel something might be lost than in situations where something might be gained (called "loss aversion")?
- You tend to devalue sides of yourself that might be called "emotional" or "needy" and overvalue those sides that might be deemed "rational" or intellectually justifiable?
- You tend to prioritize sides of yourself that are protective of others and minimize or downplay your own needs/views?

As you do this work, try to name different "identities" or stories of self that come up for you. In the naming, do this without evaluation or judgment. Once you've done this, you might have named two, five, or even twenty competing "identities" or stories of self.

Consider Gustavo's dilemma. For several years he'd been serving on the vestry of his local parish, an Episcopal community that strove to be especially collaborative and democratic in its decision-making. Ten months after a new rector arrived, however, it became clear that the new priest, while verbally supporting the values of the community, preferred a more top-down and traditional decision-making structure. On various occasions, Gustavo had tentatively pushed back when he felt that his fellow vestry members, in an effort to make the new priest feel welcome, were more laissez-faire in allowing the newcomer to have her way.

But now the rector announced that a staff member was leaving and that she had identified a good replacement. Internally, Gustavo's jaw dropped. He appreciated that a new rector would expect a wide swath of deference in making hires for her staff. But shouldn't she have allowed for a more consultative and deliberative process before making the hire, especially given the nature and history of the community?

But Gustavo also found himself stuck on whether to raise the issue at all. As he worked with Bob to examine what was holding him back, he discovered various competing sides of himself in conflict. There was:

- The side that believed strongly that decision-making would be better and healthier when done through a more democratic and consultative process
- The side of him that didn't want to be disruptive and be seen as a troublemaker or rabble-rouser, especially in the context of a faith community
- The side of him that wanted to be liked both by the new rector and by the other vestry members, who seemed more ready to acquiesce to the pastor
- The side of him who felt some responsibility for the situation since he had sat on the committee that chose the new rector in the first place
- The side of him that had no objection to the newly-hired candidate but was just unhappy with the process
- And the side of him that knew that because of his own personal history with the church growing up, he tended to dig in and become incensed by any decisions from clergy that he experienced as hierarchal or from "on high."

After doing this work, Gustavo thought, "Wow! No wonder I feel stuck and conflicted here—both unable to speak and unable to let it go!" Indeed, if you engage the mirror work thoroughly and well, you'll find you are able to name sides of yourself that you've known all along, but also that you've never really honored with a name or a "side."

Once you've done this, spend time asking yourself: Are there certain of these identities that tend to get voiced while others get silenced, quieted down, or diminished? What patterns do you notice? For example, Gustavo observed that, in general, he found it easy to voice a concern or worry with others in the first instance but that when it wasn't met with immediate and substantial support, the side of himself that doubted his own feelings—and the side that didn't want to be a troublemaker—kicked into high gear, silencing all the other voices entirely. It was as if the "You might be wrong here" side and the "Don't make trouble" side had an absolute and immediate veto over all the other voices.

The truth is that all of us can be prone to a series of common moves to short-circuit the long—but worthwhile—project of mirror work. First is outright *denial*: "No, this side of me is really not relevant in this case."

Second, similar in outcome but different in nature, is *avoidance*: "I just don't want to think about this right now. Isn't there a quicker and better way to become more conflict resilient?" We get it. Quicker and better are always attractive and they sell. Who doesn't want the meal plan that gives you a flat tummy in ten days with little effort? But just like a flat tummy in ten days without much effort, quick and fast solutions to attain conflict resilience are hard to come by. At the same time, just like a good diet and fitness regimen, hard and concerted work over time will start to produce some discernible results in the short term if you are rigorous and follow through.

Third, and extremely pernicious, is *suppression*: "This side of me is just so awful. I need to keep it hidden, diminish it, make it go away. If anyone found out, I'd be completely unlikable." This one is really tough. In a way, it's a bit of what was going on with Gustavo. The worry of being seen as a troublemaker combined with uncertainty of actually being wrong felt so overwhelming to him that it suppressed all the sides that had an important contribution to make to the group. It's almost always the case, in our experience, that when someone is engaging in suppression, they have wandered away from accurate mirror work to something we call "circus mirrors."

Most of us remember those funny mirrors we might see at an amusement park, boardwalk, circus, or arcade. You stand in front of them and they make you look taller or shorter, rounder or longer in ways that make us giggle and often say, "Gross!" Particularly when it comes to suppression, we've found that distorted self-images, like circus mirrors, can easily replace the image we see of ourselves. We no longer see an objective view of ourselves that is grounded in reality. Because of our tendency to evaluate, judge, and criticize certain internal narratives and stories, we end up with a distorted self-image.

This is more consistent with what goes on in our brain than you might think. Research has shown that some parts of our brain (the parietal lobes, insula, somatosensory areas) responsible for how we feel our bodies (the sense called interoception) and how we map our bodies in space also naturally influence how we perceive ourselves, our sense of bodily self. For some of us, our brain-body map is more malleable, like putty, and therefore can tend to become quite distorted over time through various life experiences and the environments we exist in (e.g., the people around us with whom we compare ourselves). This has specifically been observed in people who are highly empathetic as well as people who suffer from conditions like body dysmorphia, anorexic-bulimic eating disorders, and body identity integrity disorder. The circus-mirror effect is quite real. And if we aren't aware of it, these warped self-images of ourselves, especially if they are distressing and extensively hardwired throughout our brain, are likely to supplant a more fulsome and accurate image of ourselves, replete with all of our real and sometimes competing identities. The circus-mirror effect consequently blinds us to the full range of possibilities that exist in the world:

> If I raise this and I'm wrong, folks will just see me as a complainer. Moreover, the side of me that thinks more transparency in decision-making is appropriate is probably wrong and misplaced. I'm the problematic team member who doesn't understand my role in the parish as I should. I need to shut it down and go with the flow.

In our work and research, we've found the biggest fuel for "circus mirrors" is *shame*. Among challenging emotions like self-doubt, guilt, and feelings of inadequacy, shame is an even more toxic emotion when not handled well within. Later we offer strategies for taming or pruning shame so that its role in our own internal story of self is measured, appropriate, and accurate. For now, suffice to say that the distortive circus mirrors can cause us to evaluate, silence, and judge some aspects of our personality that need some reality-checking.

Consider Sebastian's situation. By any personal or professional measure, Sebastian was a success. In his mid-forties, he had founded a very successful lobbying boutique in Nashville, married his college sweetheart, and boasted two great kids and a golden retriever. When Sebastian first reached out to Bob for counsel, Bob imagined it was going to be a standard-issue commercial mediation. But Bob was wrong.

Sebastian wanted help in his personal life. After her husband died, Donna, his mother-in-law, wanted to move in with him and his wife, Teresita. Sebastian was terrified. It was clear to him that if Donna moved in, his (largely happy) life as he knew it would be over. While he had a decent relationship with Donna, she had a terrifying hold on Teresita and held strong and unyielding views on every topic under the sun. And when Donna declared it, the available responses to her viewpoints were limited: wholehearted assent, uncomfortable silence, or full-on battle where her respect for you as a decent person hung in the balance.

Bob immediately knew that solving this was not just about finding the right words. Sebastian was a top-flight lobbyist—finding the right words to smooth-talk his way through some of the most awkward and challenging stances with legislative staff in the state capital was his specialty.

Through some of his mirror work, it became clear that Sebastian's first task was to deal with a challenging internal conflict. One side of him knew, deep in his bones, that expecting him to take in his mother-in-law with nary a conversation and as a matter of course was simply inappropriate and wrong. But another side of him felt that duty to family always came first; that in his wife's culture, creating an intergenerational household was much more common and expected than in his own, and that he wanted to do right by his family, his wife, and Donna.

Sebastian didn't want to abandon his mother-in-law; he wanted to ensure she was well cared for. But he also needed a solution that worked for himself, his wife, and their kids. From Bob's perspective it was clear that, with a bit of creativity, there were indeed options that could both protect Sebastian's family and ensure Donna received the care she needed.

When Bob tried to get him to see this, Sebastian countered with a carousel of objections about how he didn't understand their family and how what he really needed was help silencing the "selfish" side so he could deal with Donna day-to-day and find ways to manage her as the newest member of the household.

Bob wasn't persuaded. For Sebastian, feelings of guilt and shame were holding him back from giving voice to the otherwise legitimate side that wanted a conversation, voice, and vote around these issues. This is where "chair work" comes in.

## CHAIR WORK

With the various and often warring narratives and identities named, it's now time to give them a distinct and audible voice. This is chair work.

When we talk about "chair work," it's not a metaphor. It means what we call it. The idea here is that each of the "identities" or "narratives" you discovered during the mirror work stage is given a physical chair and an audible voice in a conversation between the selves. If you identify five different sides of yourself, we recommend you set up five chairs in a room. If two or three sides, then two or three chairs.

So, in Sebastian's case, Bob designated two chairs. One was the side that didn't want Donna to come live with him and that, at the very least, wanted to talk about other situations that could work. The other side was the side that felt that welcoming Donna into the home was the right and generous thing to do. Bob then invited Sebastian to jump from chair to chair and audibly engage the conversation between these two sides.

At first, this conversation was short-lived. As soon as the side that Sebastian coded "selfish" made its reasonable and persuasive case that there were lots of ways of caring for Donna and his entire family without having Donna move in, the side he coded "generous" responded, "No. It will be much harder for them. Do your duty and stand down." Suddenly the chair that wanted to find a collaborative and creative way forward fell silent. "What happened?" Bob asked.

"Well," he said, pointing to the empty chair of the "generous" side, "that side is just right. This side of me is just being an immature and selfish baby." It's in this chair work where conflict resilience gets tested in the fire. Bob decided to keep Sebastian in his "selfish" chair and asked, "How does it feel to be so easily dismissed by Sebastian's generous side?" Sebastian, in the "selfish" chair, said, "It doesn't feel good, but I know it's the right thing."

"Hmmm," Bob responded. "I'm not quite sure you've expressed a feeling here, so let me ask you again. At the moment when you get silenced by that generous side, what emotions come up for you?"

Silence.

A long silence.

Bob could see some tears starting to well up.

"I feel angry and sad and helpless. I feel like a really bad person. It reminds me of when I was a kid and my older sister was going through a rough time. My parents were focusing a lot of their attention on her and I was feeling, well, pretty alone. And so, at some point I asked my dad if he could go to a few of my baseball games in the summer. He said he'd try but also told me that my sister really needed a lot of attention right now and that it was all he could do to pay attention to her and stay afloat at work and that since things were going fine for me, I shouldn't be imposing more expectations on anyone in the family. I remember leaving that conversation feeling so ashamed of myself for not seeing how hard my parents were working just to keep the family going. And after the generous chair scolded me in this chair, I feel that shame all over again. It's as if I'm transported back to that moment— the self-absorbed boy worrying about whether my dad would show up for a Little League game while my whole family was in a free fall around me. That's why I just can't bring this up. It's too overwhelming for me."

"It is overwhelming," Bob replied. "And totally understandable as to why you are so stuck here. But what I don't believe is that you can't bring it up. That's why you hired me and I know you can do it. Here's what I'd like to do. I'd like to ask you to say where in this room is that little boy who had the gumption to ask his dad to attend some Little League games?"

"What do you mean?" Sebastian asked.

"Well, if you had to physically place that little boy who, many years ago, had the gumption to ask his dad to attend a few baseball games in this room, where would you put him right now?"

"This is weird," Sebastian murmured, "but I guess he'd be over there, near the door, ready to walk out just in case the answer was no."

"OK. Great," Bob said. "I want you to go over there and become that little boy who did stand up for himself in his family a long time ago. And I want you to coach the side of yourself now that doesn't think it can do that anymore in this family situation. I want to see what that little boy would say. Can you do that for me?"

"Um, OK. I still think this is weird," Sebastian replied as he cautiously got up and walked into the corner by the door.

"OK, Sebastian. I'm going to sit in the chair of 'adult' Sebastian. Now, you are that little boy giving advice to older Sebastian who can't do this. Go."

Suddenly, Sebastian-as-little-boy spoke with confidence and clarity to the empty chair, "Come on, Sebastian. How did you lose your gumption? You did such a good job asking Dad to come to the game. And even though he made you feel badly when you did ask, the fact is, he ultimately did come to a game, right? And, if you remember correctly, he even apologized for not being able to come to more games. And truth be told, I deserved to have some of Dad's attention even as he struggled through a rough time. Please show me that you can still stand up for yourself in this situation. Please. Do this for me."

"Cut," Bob said. "OK. So, what do you think?"

Sebastian just looked at Bob with a mistiness in his eyes as he walked back to his chair. "Yes. Yes. This 'selfish' chair isn't selfish after all. It's breathing life into the ten-year-old me who somehow learned to silence even some basic needs in service of the family."

Chair work is liberating and empowering—and sometimes overwhelming. Not every example is as emotionally dramatic as this. But the task of giving an audible voice to each of the "identities" and helping those identities listen to each other and be heard is a key step to building internal conflict resilience.

The beauty of chair work is that it is all about assertion without judgment or evaluation. It's about giving legitimate and authentic voice to the many sides of who we are. It's not about insistence, aggression, selfishness, domination, or being a troublemaker. It's simply about externalizing the internal conflict with an audible and authentic voice. And the process of doing that, believe it or not, empowers us and diminishes the anxiety of the conflict. It makes it manageable. It reminds us that as humans, we are nothing if not living contradictions and tensions. There is no shame in that.

While separating out the voices by putting them into individual chairs may seem hokey or gimmicky, our own experience is that the physicality of the exercise is part of what forces a reckoning that will set you up for the table work to follow.

In Sebastian's case, Bob was able to step in and force the "I need to raise this" side to have a bit more voice. But what do you do if you don't have a coach available at the moment that one of the chairs is falling comfortably into a pattern of silence, resignation, judgment, or circus-mirror distortion?

We have a few tips. First, while it's always nice to have a professional coach to help you along, a trusted friend or colleague with whom you can share the dilemma can often play the role of your coach. In fact, in some of the larger workshops on conflict resilience that Bob teaches, trusted colleagues are trained and drafted into the role of coach with great success. A common piece of feedback Bob often hears is, "The best part of the course was the chance to work with [Coach A] on my own dilemma." While disappointing for Bob that a witty quip during one of his lectures isn't the highlight, it's always gratifying to see the power of informal coaching work through a structured, step-by-step process.

But what about when you don't have access to even a trusted colleague or friend? In that case, here is some guidance we can offer to engage the chair work. First, we are serious about the advice of setting up physical chairs for this if you can. As we said, it may feel hokey or unnecessary, but trust us. The physicality of the chair experience is part of what fuels the "conversation" between the various sides of you. And if you are by yourself, no one will think anything of you getting up and moving from chair to chair as you have an audible conversation with yourself. This leads to the second piece of advice: the conversation between the sides should be audible.

We imagine you're thinking, "This feels weird. Why can't I just play this out in my head?" We agree it can feel weird. But with decades of experience under our belt and with science to support our experience, all we can say is that the quality of the learning is enhanced by both the physicality and the audibility of the voice. The more parts of our brain that come online, the more senses we engage. The more muscle movements and other sensations we can recruit during the chair work process, the more we can leverage the parts of our brain that are responsible for feeling strong emotions and a sense of purpose and meaning. The more moved we are, the more likely we are to record the experience in our brain and remember what that BBO, the bigger, better offer, feels like—asserting a side of ourselves that we don't usually give voice to rather than relying on our default reaction to protect ourselves and feel safe.

This reprograms and rewires our brain through a process neuroscientists call "neuroplasticity"—our brain's ability to change and adapt. Our brain is highly adaptive and flexible to new circumstances. These changes happen constantly, often without our conscious involvement, which can lead to some changes being maladaptive. These changes can be connectivity changes (altering what chemicals are secreted between synapses, which occurs with short-term memory and short-term motor skills), structural changes (altering the brain's physical shape, more responsible for long-term memory or long-term motor skills), and, most powerful, functional changes (where whole networks shift and change to favor different pathways). Through the process of learning and deliberate practice, the neurons naturally weaken less-used connections, and can form and strengthen the connections that we want. Researchers who study the effects of cognitive behavioral therapy (CBT) in stimulating the brain's more adaptive functional patterns that lead to lasting behavioral changes have found that the more parts of our brain we can engage (our senses, our muscle movements), the more types of structural and functional changes can be seen on brain scans, and the more likely these techniques can allow us to embody new patterns of behavior to better navigate our lives.

Think of it like a rehearsal. It doesn't help a violinist to practice the notes in their head as much as it does to actually practice playing the violin. Similarly, the process of chair work where you give audible voice and agency to each side or identity literally builds up the neural "muscles" for conflict resilience.

Third, in the moment that you feel a certain side of yourself—perhaps the one that tends to concede more quickly—acceding to a louder or more dominant side, we want to offer a few lines to keep the "quieter" or "shamed" or "negatively" coded side going. Specifically, lean into that quieter/more recessive side and start off by saying to yourself, "And yet—this is a side of me that is real and worthwhile because..." Then fill in the blank.

If that feels like a stretch you can say, "I'm not sure how much I like this side of me. And yet—I am duty-bound to represent it and explain why it deserves to be heard..." Then, represent!

One way that some of our chairs get silenced is because we are overwhelmed with feelings—sometimes powerful and frequently quite negative—that shove that "chair" or "identity" back into the closet. Those feelings may be stemming from a voice in another chair, perhaps one that we have yet to name, perhaps yelling at you and saying that "YOU are the problem," or "Go away," or "You'll have a chance to be heard later" (where *later* means at some indeterminate and undefined time that is a euphemism for *never*).

If thoughts like these come to your mind, we suggest that you name the feelings associated with them out loud. You might say, "When I sit in this chair, I feel some shame; at the same time, I also feel [FILL-IN-THE-BLANK]..." Then just say, "And yet—this is a part of me that is valuable and justified and deserves attention at times as well."

In Chapter 6, we will discuss the critical role of effective assertion on the path to conflict resilience. You'll also see that when we discuss assertion, we mean assertion about facts, ideas, perceptions, values, and beliefs as well as assertions about emotions and feelings. By using some of the prompts we suggest above, you can make sure that the chair work doesn't just fizzle out at the first sign that one of your more dominant or easily voiced chairs drowns out the side that feels more tender, harder to own, or more vulnerable.

Finally, when doing the chair work, the point is not to "resolve" the identities or have one win or be deemed more legitimate or the winner. The point is that all of these chairs—all of these identities—are worthy of getting a hearing and a voice at the table with the others. It does *not* mean that all the chairs need to be vindicated at the negotiation table. It's just that when we fail to even raise them or validate them to ourselves, we disserve everyone—ourselves, the other, and the value that wrestling with conflict in relationships and life offers us. Moreover, if we are coding internal conflict as bad, poisonous, or to be eliminated, how will we ever be resilient enough to handle the conflict that comes up in life with others?

When we shut down our own negotiations within, we cut off the possibility for connection with others because chances are the other person also has competing internal identities that are complicating and influencing the interaction we are having across the table with them. Shutting down some of our competing selves can often also disrespect our counterpart across the table. At the same time, we are left with painful internal conflict.

By giving voice, we invite voice. By bringing the internal conflict forward, we will feel uncomfortable, but the discomfort opens new possibilities. If our work with clients and our work studying brain science and health impacts has shown us anything, it's that the costs of internal conflicts—negotiations within ignored or handled badly—are often at least as high (if not higher) than any conflict across the table might be with our colleague, family member, or friend might be.

## TABLE WORK

Joel had decided. But now he needed to have a dreaded exchange with his mentor. For years, Joel was the de facto lieutenant to his mentor, tackling projects others recoiled from. But over time, Joel's mission and expertise—once a reflection of his mentor's vision—were now uniquely his own. Becoming more independent in his own career trajectory would mean moving away from his mentor's vision, and possibly losing some (if not all) of his support if the conversation were not handled adroitly. Whatever the outcome, Joel could no longer balance the workload of what had become two diverging ambitions without failing at both. Something needed to change, and his mentor was going to be unhappy about it.

To prepare for this conversation, Joel had tackled the mirror work and the chair work. He felt ready to have the frank discussion with his mentor who had been a true champion of his career for many years—a fact that Joel was deeply grateful for and which weighed on him as the scheduled time to meet with his mentor drew closer. A few minutes before the meeting, Joel started to get cold feet and sent an email to his administrative assistant, apologizing and saying he needed to reschedule the meeting.

Joel met up with Bob to vent his feelings later that day. When Bob asked him what happened, he admitted, "I fell apart. I felt so ready. But right when it was time to actually meet, I could already hear my mentor 'addressing' my concerns and reminding me how much I would be disappointing the values of the field of medicine if I didn't keep the status quo. I just backed down. It was like the hugeness of how much of a challenge it was going to be to navigate that negotiation—and survive—finally hit me."

The truth is that moving from chair work to table work is hard. It's also true that even if we prepare, it may not go as well as we hoped for or planned.

It's worth stating that even if your handling of the internal conflicts ended with chair work, we'd still consider it a victory. To name and clarify for yourself the reasons why you get caught up and stuck—that level of deeper understanding—shortens your recovery time; it helps you stop the spiraling.

At the same time, you didn't pick up this book just to become agonizingly self-aware. Nor did we write the book for that purpose. You want to produce different results and to engage the conflict and the challenge of it more directly and effectively.

When it comes to table work, we have lots of advice to offer in Chapter 6 on giving voice and assertion and in Chapter 7 on process design, but let's start to dig in here. Table work is the place where we initiate the hard work of representing ourselves in the real world, the hard work of bringing the internal conflict to the table with our counterparties—whether they be a fiancé, a boss, or the imposing members of the school board. Although there isn't an easy way to bring your full self to the table—your views, needs, doubts, and internal tensions—there are ways to increase the chances that you'll be able to do enough of that to invite a different, more authentic, and more productive negotiation or conversation.

The first step in table work is communicating effectively the desire and need for a new kind of conversation that is as assertive and clear as it is inviting. All too often, our experience is that someone who has spent hours, weeks, months doing the behind-the-scenes internal work is so anxious that they end up finding a narrow window of opportunity to raise the issue across the table and it ends up blowing up or, worse, being downplayed or ignored.

If the set of issues and concerns that you're raising with the other side has been on your mind for a long time before you had the courage and wherewithal to rephrase them, it may not be reasonable to expect that your counterpart is going to be prepared to handle it with aplomb and grace in the moment. We've seen the opposite problem come up just as frequently. In the process of signaling that you want to find time for a different kind of interaction, you telegraph a level of gravity and consternation that sends your counterpart into a spasm of anxiety and worry. What can it be that they want to discuss with me? How bad is this? Are they dying? Breaking up with me? Suing me? Quitting?

Consider a framing that might have worked for Joel by making the challenging meeting a little less overwhelming, obviating the last-minute urge to cancel:

> I know this month has been busy and it's been a bit of time since we last had a one-on-one check-in meeting, but I'm wondering if we can find a bit of time in the next week where I can share

some frustrations and worries I've been having with respect to my career and our work together. To be clear, this is not something that I want you to be fretting about. At the same time, it is important and it's been on my mind for a while as something I'd really be grateful to discuss with you. So it just felt right to find a time to talk it through with you rather than just let it marinate in my head without your input and wisdom. Would you be open to that?

The jackpot here is to signal a desire to have a different kind of conversation at the right time or place that is serious and important, but not overplayed. The best way to do this, in our experience, is to be direct and clear. Note also the transparency of the request and the positive role offered to Joel's mentor—a desire to hear his "input" and "wisdom." Such framing both conveys the importance of the conversation while providing an inviting frame for your interlocutor.

The next step in table work is *preparation*. As you get ready to meet, you already have the loads of preparation you did from the chair work. But chances are, you may not have spent a lot of time thinking deeply about your counterpart in the conversation or negotiation. Now is the time to do that.

As you begin this new way of interacting, spend time writing down answers to the following questions:

- What are their interests here? Specifically, what is important to them in terms of substance, in terms of relationship, and in terms of emotions that the conversation may bring up for them?
- What are some possible reactions they will have when you raise with them your own identities, needs, concerns, and interests?

We'd suggest you write these out. Then, for each of these responses, write down what you might say or do in response. Even better, write down several different possible responses so you can get a sense of the terrain available to you.

Prep work will help you be nimble when you meet with them. Admittedly, you won't be able to predict every single response. And you might be taken by surprise. But the goal here is *not* to script the conversation. When we are in conflict with each other, conversations are rarely linear. While Bob appreciates the thoroughness of a student or a client who scripts a negotiation as a way of preparing, he usually suggests that the script be thrown away. For navigating conflict, having a point-by-point Google map direction isn't as helpful as it is to have a general understanding of the topography and terrain complemented with some adaptable skills for navigating that terrain in the midst of unpredictability.

The final step in table work is for you to, at last, *show up with your whole self* to the literal or figurative table. In Chapter 7, we talk extensively about setting up process—designing an appropriate environment for handling conflict. We urge you to read that chapter before you begin the conversation or negotiation. But here we want to offer advice that is more tailored to ensuring that your internal "chairs" get voiced in the conversation. You might begin by thanking your counterpart(s) for being willing to participate in a new, different kind of conversation.

You'll probably be feeling anxious and worried—both about how well you will do and how they will react. The best way to handle that? Acknowledge it—to them and to yourself. We've found that it can help just to say, "Hey, this is a bit new for me. I might be less articulate than I'd prefer. I know it might be new for you too. So, I hope we can each extend some grace to each other."

While it will not always be possible, we believe that direct engagement of conflict and differences is best done in person. And when that doesn't work, real-time videoconferencing is second best. This is because, as you speak, you want as much information as possible about how the other side is reacting. When you announce your anxiety and worry and ask for grace, does their face soften and do they lean in? Or do they look like they might be vexed? Troubled? Confused? If you're on the phone—or even videoconferencing—you might lose some of this vital feedback. That feedback is critical for how to proceed.

Beware to avoid a common pitfall! Your counterpart looks startled, confused, worried, or maybe a bit miffed by your new approach. Knocked off balance by this, you might be prone to either back down or bulldoze through so that you can go home and write in your journal that you did it. Avoid these rookie errors if you can. Remember, the goal isn't just to say, "At least I tried!" It's actually to create the conditions that make engaging the conflict in a real genuine conversation as likely and productive as possible. That means that when you notice a reaction of potential annoyance, vexation, consternation, or concern, the best thing to do is to pause, observe, and name what you see. You might even wonder aloud to them an emotion you think their facial expression might be communicating, and ask them to "say more" or to elaborate and respond to your observation.

Emotions come from the brain and the brain is complicated—it's almost impossible to know with 100 percent certainty what the other person is feeling, no matter what their physical expressions or actions, so approach this with humility and a generous curiosity. What might this look like? It can be as simple as, "Lindsey, I'm getting the sense you're worried." Or, "Before I go on, I sense some annoyance. I definitely want to hear it if it's there. Let me know." Or, "Gosh, Abdullah, before I go on let me check what's your reaction to what I've said so far?" In Chapter 5 we discuss why skilled deep listening is crucial to conflict resilience and how to consistently excel at it.

Even if the instinct in the moment might be to ignore the other person's reaction for fear that it will distract from your agenda, in most cases, ignoring your intuition about what might be going on for them is a mistake. It's better to attend to it early on so that if you proceed through the conflict or negotiation, they are as able as possible to participate fully. The goal, after all, is to get "buy-in" for engaging the conversation from your counterpart. So skipping the step of getting their assent to the conversation ends up being a mistake, even if it feels more efficient or "on point" in the moment. To be clear, the actual phraseology of what this might sound like will differ depending on the kind of relationship you have. Is it professional? Personal? Do you tend to be jokesters with each other? Or is yours one of those friendships that always go deep? Or maybe you've never had a serious conversation about anything with this person? Regardless of the usual approach, the goal is to clearly signal that this conversation will be meaningfully different and to do so in a way that attracts their attention, but not a sense of undue anxiety or panic.

Embracing the negotiation within—turning inward to recognize, name, hold, and give voice to our many (often contradictory) identities and desires—lays the groundwork for developing conflict resilience. Navigating these conflicted inner selves and the narratives that accompany them can present a formidable challenge. However, by practicing mirror work, chair work, and table work, we not only gain insight into how to engage our inner conflicts, but also discover effective strategies for handling the conflicts that arise in our various interpersonal connections. Our ability to sit with and grow from conflict, especially across lines of difference, fundamentally depends on our willingness to engage authentically with the perspectives of others. And to do so with this deeper level of genuine vulnerability.

To be clear, this hard internal work is not about becoming the bravest, most heroic person in the face of conflict. It's about becoming the person who can say, "Right now, I'm not feeling brave. This side of me is scared..." Then still say, "And yet..."

Part 2

# EXPLORE
# (AND BE BRAVE)

# Chapter 5

# CULTIVATING GENUINE CURIOSITY

## The Power of Deep Listening

On the first day of Bob's law school negotiation class, Bob invites students to draw "negotiation self-portraits" on large pieces of flip-chart paper, depicting their perceived strengths and weaknesses as a negotiator. Often, students draw themselves with oversized ears and then, when introducing themselves, explain that the large ears represent the fact that they are "great listeners."

Weeks later, on the last day of class, Bob asks the students to redraw themselves on flip-chart paper, depicting once again their perceived strengths and weaknesses in light of dozens of hours of class. Often, the same students draw themselves with very small ears, sheepishly explaining that they now realize that they aren't the great listeners they thought they were and that listening is a skill they still desperately need to work on.

You might interpret this shift over a semesters-long intensive course as a warning to avoid Bob's negotiation class because it worsens one's listening skills! But (hopefully) a more accurate view is that spending many hours in an intensive negotiation class makes students realize both how challenging it is to be an effective listener and how critical the skill is to being a great negotiator and to managing conflict with aplomb.

We've rarely encountered someone who disagrees with us that listening is an important skill for managing conflict, being a great negotiator, or succeeding as a leader. But despite the nearly universal enthusiastic head nod to listening in general, we frequently encounter real resistance to deep and extended listening when it comes to putting the aspirational into day-to-day practice. Some of the most common objections to deep listening are:

- If I listen too much, they will think I agree with them and I don't agree with them;
- Deep listening is too time-consuming and inefficient, I need to get my point across and move on;
- Deep listening is just tiring, and I don't have the emotional bandwidth for it;
- If I listen to them too much, I might be persuaded and then I will be less able to achieve my objectives.

Still others may regard listening in conflict as simply a necessary and annoying speed bump, a required toll that forces you to slow down before you can make your own argument or render your own viewpoint. For those who view listening with this lens, they typically deliver the right "words" to signal that they are active listening without doing the deep work, and they end up being accused of insincerity or condescension.

We are sympathetic to the objections above and to the tendency to see listening as nothing more than a "check-the-box" performance you must complete before you can get on to "delivering your message" or your perspective. But even as we appreciate this viewpoint, we have some bad news: if you really do see listening as a "step" or "thing to do" before you say your viewpoint, your verdict, or why they are wrong, then—sorry—perhaps you actually *are* being condescending.

This is one of the reasons why deep listening is so hard. We often think of sharing our own views, feelings, and opinions as "being vulnerable." And of course, there is indeed vulnerability in this, as you no doubt sensed through the table work we discussed in Chapter 4. But it turns out that "deep listening" is perhaps the most vulnerable thing we can do with others with whom we disagree. That's because deep listening is only genuine when we are truly open to the possibility that our viewpoint, perspective, or story isn't necessarily wholly correct, 100% true, or completely right. Or, at the very least, that our view may not be the *only* legitimate way of seeing a situation. And for many of us, when it comes to the toughest and most polarizing issues, letting go of certainty and leaning into the curiosity is profoundly scary, destabilizing, and yes, vulnerable.

Bob experienced this firsthand when delivering remarks to a large group of Roman Catholic clergy in September 2022 in Washington, D.C. In introducing the importance of conflict resilience for an increasingly polarized American Catholic Church, Bob stressed the imperative of becoming a truly "listening Church." Until Bob's talk halfway through the conference, there seemed to be widespread enthusiasm from many on the importance of listening in matters related to church teaching on controversial issues. But Bob's insistence that deep listening required a genuine shift away from certainty toward curiosity—toward the possibility that you might not hold the whole story or truth—landed like a lead balloon with some in the crowd. During a Q&A after his remarks, a prominent church leader stood up and said, "But Professor Bordone, aren't there some things that are just false and therefore need to be corrected and *not* listened to?"

This is a good and fair question and perhaps one you often feel in moments of conflict with friends and family around deeply polarizing issues. In this chapter, we invite you to shift some commonly held assumptions about deep listening and its relevance to conflict resilience and negotiation. We also share with you the component pieces of deep listening and some hacks for how to stick with deep listening even when everything in our brain and in our heart wants to return us to the five Fs: *fight, flight, freeze, fawn,* or *fester.* We hope at the end you'll appreciate that deep listening isn't an abdication of your viewpoint, nor is it an affirmation of the "rightness" or "truth" of the other's perspective. But it is an openness to the possibility that you're missing something—that there is some piece or angle of what they are saying that adds a more complicated and nuanced piece to the original conclusions and story you had in your head about the "what" and the "why" of their stance. Also, paradoxically, we hope you'll see that deep listening can give you what you need to be strategically persuasive when it comes time to assert your viewpoint, a topic we take up in Chapter 6.

## ASSUMPTIONS THAT UNDERMINE DEEP LISTENING

Whatever they may be, we all come to negotiations and conflict situations with our own assumptions about what it means to listen. For some of us, we assume that listening is only for those who are weak or that it conveys a lack of control. We might hold the assumption that "I won't persuade them by listening—I need to make arguments." Or we may struggle with the assumption that listening conveys agreement, which is a huge threat when you absolutely do not agree. Or we reflexively assume that we are listening because the other person has a problem or an issue that they want us to fix—that they are asking us for our assessment of the situation and how to figure it out; this often comes with the uncontrollable urge to want to suggest potential solutions. This last assumption is one that Joel has always had to wrestle with.

Many years ago, Joel's close friend Ryan called him up on the phone. He had just been through a breakup and was at a total loss about how things went awry in the relationship. Ryan confided, "It's like I know that no 'great' relationship ends up in a breakup, but I just can't help thinking about all the 'what-ifs' that might have led us to resolve the issues we were going through."

"Well," Joel interjected, "one way you can start to get out of your head is to do a visualization exercise where you imagine that each thought is a leaf in a river or a balloon that you release into the air, letting each thought go nonjudgmentally. It might make it easier not to get so stuck on any single thought."

Ryan, without skipping a beat, continued, "Yeah, I could see that being helpful. But really, it feels like it's this lack of closure that really upsets me."

Joel beamed. "Oh! Actually, one strategy to help for that is to write a letter to the other person (that you don't plan on sending, of course) where you get to air out everything that you feel you didn't have a chance to say. You can even play out a totally fictional response and write back to yourself what you imagine they might have said. Although it's not based totally in reality, it allows you an opportunity to feel some closure."

Ryan's voice thinned slightly. "It's bad . . . I mean, I've barely even slept these last few nights . . ."

And just as Joel began to launch into advice about taking melatonin to help with sleep, Ryan snapped back: "Joel, I know you're trying to help. But I don't need strategies right now. Honestly, I just need someone to listen. That's it. That's what I need."

This was a hard perspective for Joel to grasp. He was perplexed. For Joel, strategies and fixing things as soon as they come up is where his mind goes to first—problem appears, you fix it, repeat. Similarly, it's what he assumed anyone else with a problem would want. But he was lucky that his friend interrupted him and said something. Joel genuinely had no idea that people existed in the world who might not actually want solutions to their problems—at least not immediately. It didn't make any sense to him at the time, but it challenged his usual notion about what people wanted in conversation. To this day, he still has to deliberately pause and resist the urge to jump right in with potential solutions when someone presents a dilemma, conflict, or problem to him. He has to remind himself to first ask what the other person needs from his listening at that time.

So, if you are anything like Joel—and we know many of you are—you are not alone! If holding any (or all) of the aforementioned limiting assumptions about listening sounds like you, then the work this chapter provides is going to challenge and enrich you. The antidote to unhelpful assumptions such as these isn't so much to have no assumptions about the role of listening in conflict and negotiation (a nearly impossible task), but rather to negotiate with yourself to adopt a more accurate and helpful set of assumptions.

For example, *"If I listen carefully and deeply with genuine curiosity, I may learn useful information that will help me in my own efforts to be persuasive and effectively assertive."*

Perhaps more than any other, this attitudinal shift can motivate you away from one of the five F responses and toward deep listening. The shift requires you to let go of the notion that you know how the other person thinks, what matters to them, and what motivates them. This shift is incredibly hard to do for a bunch of reasons.

Consider a controversial public issue about which you feel strongly. Perhaps it's your view on abortion, immigration, Supreme Court term limits, or the Israel-Palestine conflict. Now think about someone who holds the opposite view on the issue. If you're like most people, you instantly conjure the image of a full-fledged person, complete with gender, age, race, maybe even clothing (!), and a life story that fits your stereotype of people who hold that opposite viewpoint. Your brain's ability to envision a full-fledged person based simply on the prompt we gave you—to think of someone who has the opposite viewpoint you do on an issue about which you feel strongly—is amazing, isn't it? If you are preparing for a debate with such a person, it might even be helpful to do this as part of your preparation. And, to give you credit, the image you conjured up and the story you told has some basis in reality— the lived truth of your experience, what mass media has told us about "those people," and even what general demographic trends and tendencies may tell us about people who hold a certain viewpoint on a well-known controversial issue. It's a testimony to the wonder of the human mind that we can conjure up a person and the basic contours of their life story based on a label such as "pro-life" or "woke" or "evangelical" or "coastal liberal" or "Gen Zer."

The truth is, when it comes to conflict resilience, the image you conjured up can also be deeply unhelpful if not sabotaging. Why? Because it tends to kill our curiosity by putting a caricatured story on a much more complex real-life person based on a single view they hold in contravention to your own. And if you are preparing to engage an actual person in a hard conversation or a negotiation where you are trying to influence them rather than show the savvy of your arguments, the tendency to conjure up a cartoon character of a human being can be self-defeating and dangerous. This "fill in the blanks with our stereotype" bias—also known as *implicit bias*—kills our curiosity and blunts our ability to listen well. Even more consequentially, it reduces our chances of being persuasive or expressing empathy or finding common ground. When our goal is simply connecting or deepening a relationship or finding a way forward despite the disagreement, our fabricated story of "them" short-circuits the process. It's as if we've written their script before we get to the conversation. That means we're not ready so much for a conversation as a performance.

Some years ago, Bob had the chance to witness one of his dispute-resolution colleagues in a challenging conversation with an Israeli settler who believed that it was appropriate for Israel to annex the entire West Bank. The interviewer was an exquisite listener—patient, full of curious open-ended questions, deeply empathic, even in moments when Bob knew that the interviewer viscerally disagreed with the perspective of the settler. The interviewer would deftly reflect back not only the substance but also the emotion behind what the settler was expressing. Between delicately measured pauses woven into his gentle yet persistent questioning, his body language consistently communicated that he was sharply focused on what the settler was saying and the depth of the settler's feeling and conviction on the issue. The sense that the interviewer saw the settler and no one else in the entire room was palpable. Throughout, the settler's tone was bellicose, and his positions seemed completely impervious to persuasion. "Right-wing extremist" came to Bob's mind as the engagement went on. He was glad he was not the one in the conversation.

Then, suddenly, a magical moment, thanks to the incredible deep listening of Bob's colleague. The Israeli settler declared in a calm but certain tone, "You know, what really matters here is simply that people acknowledge the historic claim of the Jewish people to this land. That they acknowledge that this land belongs to us, the chosen people of God. That's what matters to me. If people could acknowledge that, I certainly can acknowledge that perhaps, at this moment in the scope of human history and for various geopolitical and security reasons, it might not be the time for Jewish people to live on, possess, and occupy this land. I mean, we have lived here and then not lived here for centuries. What's important is the establishment of our right, not current tenancy right now."

Bob's mouth dropped. The patient listening ultimately revealed not so much a softening of opinion but rather the basis of the true interest of this settler. The settler was less interested in occupying the land now or ousting Palestinians from their current home than he was concerned with the acknowledgment of a historical (and, in his mind, divine) reality. To be clear, we get that if you are on the opposite side of the issue here, the statement of the Israeli settler is unlikely to be seen as a "concession" or move toward "reasonableness." But if you are trying to understand how to move forward on a seemingly intractable problem that an hour earlier had been framed entirely in zero-sum terms—whether you are a diplomat, peacemaker, mediator, facilitator, or a human who must coexist with other humans—this incredible piece of information opens a new door of possibility toward a détente across difference in the current moment.

The deep listening had led to an unexpected opening—a deal might be possible by acknowledging Israel's historic sovereignty of land but using a time preference, perhaps even one set for centuries and not just years—as a way to create some value between opposed parties in this moment. Deep listening helped identify the underlying concern of the Israeli settler while also revealing a common source of value creation present in many negotiations—the possibility of making a pie-expanding trade based on time preferences. In negotiation, making trades based on differences in time preferences can be a real source of mutual value creation. The simplest example is a loan. You may be willing to lend me $5,000 now in exchange for $5,000 plus interest in two years. To use another example: Imagine two siblings fighting over who gets ownership of their parents' most valuable Fabergé egg after their death. The siblings won't have to battle each other to their own death when—after sufficient deep listening—one ultimately says, "I just need to have the ownership to sell this and fund my retirement," and the other says, "I just want the egg on my shelf to remind me of Mom and Dad." The difference in time preference allows the former to sell the egg to the Museum of Fine Arts now, leaving a "life estate" to the sibling who wants to enjoy the egg while she is still alive. While the sale happens in the present, the egg goes to the museum at the death of the sibling who wants to enjoy it in their living room while they are alive.

Only the deep listening can break an impasse that seems intractable—whether on the global or the local scale.

## LISTEN . . . TO SEE

If you're like many of the executives, clients, patients, or other perfectly sensible humans we work with, you may be thinking, "OK. Thanks for these stories. But I've spent so much time with my impossibly ignorant brother-in-law, and I really and truly do know what he's thinking and why he's thinking it. So there is *nothing* new to learn here. Indulging him with listening will make him think that his [racist, anti-American, sexist, ageist, anti-Semitic, anti-Muslim, fill-in-the-blank] attitude is OK. And it's not. There is nothing new to learn here, and it's exhausting to sit through. I'm not going to endure the abuse and legitimize his views."

First, let us be clear: We *do* get it. And we agree, at least partially. It *is* exhausting to listen deeply. Also, to be honest, it takes an emotional toll on the listener whether we find the thoughts of the other person offensive or even if we're listening from a place of solidarity and compassion for their experience. So we don't want to downplay that reality.

But we don't want to let you off the hook either. While we're not prepared to accept the idea that you truly know your brother-in-law's heart, for the sake of argument we'll concede that point for the moment. Even in the truly imaginary situation where you could read the other's heart, wholly and fully, listening is a valuable and essential conflict resilience skill when we're trying to deal with the most consequential and divisive differences with others. Why? Because quite apart from anything we might learn about them or the situation or the context, deep listening meets a key interest of theirs—which is to *feel heard*. We have never met any human being who didn't have an interest in feeling heard. And we know that when someone feels heard, it increases the likelihood that they will reciprocate and give you a chance to share your perspective (covered in the next chapter).

The fundamental human interest in *feeling heard* not only matters in terms of increasing the likelihood that they will reciprocate and listen to you. It can even have tangible impacts on the bottom line and for what happens "next" in a conflict or working toward a deal or agreement. Consider the work of psychology researchers Drs. Gregory Lester and Susan Smith in the medical malpractice context. These researchers aimed to understand whether the way a physician talks and listens, combined with how patients perceive the outcome of their treatment, influences the likelihood of initiating a malpractice suit. For this they conducted an experiment involving 160 adult participants. In this research, participants watched a videotaped scenario of a physician-patient interaction. These were not just any interactions. The interactions varied, depicting either positive or negative communication behaviors by the physician. Each participant was also told that the case they watched had one of four different outcomes: either everything went well, there was a poor outcome that was not the physician's fault, a poor outcome for uncertain reasons, or a poor outcome that was squarely the physician's fault. Afterward, participants were asked to rate their litigious feelings—in other words, how likely they might be to sue.

As you might expect, when the physician showcased negative communication behaviors like barely listening to the patient, participants felt a stronger urge to litigate. Also, the more the participant perceived that the bad medical outcome was the physician's fault, the higher their litigious intent. But here's what was unexpected: in the cases where the physician was not skilled at listening and communication, participants felt just as much of a desire to sue when the doctor was perceived as at fault as when the poor outcome happened for uncertain reasons. Based on these results (and if you want to avoid legitimate financial damages in the future), we should probably revise the expression "It's not what you say, it's how you say it" to "It's not what you say—or even do—it's how you listen."

Quite apart from the value of making a counterpart feel heard and seen, recent research by Dr. Guy Itzchakov, associate professor in the Department of Human Services at the University of Haifa and director of the Interpersonal Listening and Social Influence Lab, has demonstrated empirically that when a conversation partner conveys high-quality listening—characterized by *focused attention, understanding,* and *positive intentions*—speakers end up feeling more socially comfortable and connected to the listener in a way that softens their polarized views, reducing the extreme of their attitude. This research shows that high-quality listening—even without making *any* counterarguments of your own—has the effect of reducing extreme thinking and facilitating depolarization. Talk about listening as a stealth tool for persuasion!

The benefits also extend beyond the dialectical. Listening has long been recognized for its psychological and emotional benefits, but recent research has shed light on its potential physical health-related advantages as well. Joel has conducted a study demonstrating that listening can have a profound impact on cognitive resilience.

His research has shown that having a listener available most or all of the time can boost global cognition, which encompasses various cognitive abilities such as executive function, problem-solving, decision-making, judgment, and logical memory.

As part of his clinical and scientific work, Joel has reviewed the cases of thousands of individuals to determine the complete health of their brains. This is incredibly challenging work, requiring a review of every sliver of information available of each person's life story. But one specific pearl of information, if available, typically makes his task instantly easier: their social history—more specifically their social life, whether they were part of a closely knit social group or worked in a field where they were in frequent contact with supportive listeners or were surrounded by friends and family who clearly knew them well. For these lucky people, chances are that their memory and thinking skills were well preserved despite whatever disease-related changes may have been occurring in their brains. As demonstrated in one of his studies examining the MRI brain scans of over 2,000 people, the ready presence of a listener can make a person's brain functioning appear as though it is four years younger than that of someone who does not have people available to listen to them whenever they're needed. The findings in this study are particularly relevant for middle-aged adults who may be vulnerable to cognitive decline. By creating a situation where we are surrounded by more deep listeners and engaging as a deep listener for others at work and at home, we can potentially improve our cognitive function and slow down the cognitive aging process in our brains by more than four years (actually, 4.25 years to be exact).

The health-related benefits of deep listening are likely linked to the social and emotional connections it fosters. When we deeply listen to others, we create stronger bonds and establish trust, which can reduce stress, anxiety, and feelings of isolation. These positive emotional outcomes, in turn, can contribute to improved cognitive function, mental health, and overall physical health. Additionally, the process of deep listening itself requires the use of various cognitive skills, such as attention, memory, and comprehension.

Think back to a time when someone mentioned that you were a great listener for them. Can you recall what parts of your brain you might have been engaging throughout your dialogue? Perhaps your brain was particularly good at consistently bringing your attention back to what was being said. Perhaps you did a great job of remembering what they said and were able to call back specific words they used to describe how they were feeling. Or, maybe—like piecing together a complex puzzle—you were able to bring elements of what they said all throughout into a cohesive revelation that they hadn't thought of before that allowed them a rich new understanding of themselves and their situation. Your brain was likely fully active and engaged, functioning at the level of (dare we say) a social genius. By consistently practicing deep listening, individuals are essentially exercising their cognitive muscles with high-intensity, high-return compound movements, leading to amped-up improvements in mental acuity and resilience. Instead of "no pain, no gain," it's "all brain, all gain."

But what about listening to someone spew on a "hot-button" topic for you—abortion, securing the border, climate change, voting rights, religious freedom, trans rights, or the Second Amendment, for example? You may be thinking back to a time when an extended family member or a coworker described their view on a touchy subject and, the further it was from your own point of view, you likely recall how it raised your blood pressure, made your face flush, and made your heart pound with anger, fear, or despair. How could deep listening to someone when you literally feel your muscles tense up and your blood pressure rise possibly be good for your health?

To restate what we've said before—listening to viewpoints that you feel are prejudiced, bigoted, wrongheaded, or deeply divergent from your own values and worldview is hard. The physiological stress response, when repeated over and over, can lead to increased risk of many illnesses and even death due to how it affects your immune system, systemic injury from chronic inflammatory responses, and many microscopic insults to the blood vessels throughout your body, including your brain. It's also less about the fact that you're experiencing a stressor, and more about your perception of that stress—whether you see it as harmful and out of your control, or you see it as a challenge from which you can grow.

Conflict resilience is *not* comfortable. One of the premises of our entire project is that part of why we are less and less conflict resilient as individuals, a society, and a culture is that we prioritize comfort and feelings of psychological safety or calm over the disruption that being in conversation with others with opposing viewpoints brings. But to yield the long-term gains of improved relationships, better-functioning organizations, and a healthier society, we need to work through the discomfort. Hard and sometimes exhausting work is part of most things that are valuable. Whether it's the challenge of a morning workout to keep physically fit or the decades-long battle involved in confronting and working through trauma, or the years of discipline and late-night study that catapult you to admission at your dream college, the dividends come only for those willing to put in the effort.

And so, yes, deep listening calls for courage—and discomfort. Here we want to emphasize again the difference between feeling awkward, anxious, and uncomfortable (something we urge) and the abuse and damage that would come from exposing yourself to a situation where you'd be retraumatized (something we urge you to avoid). While it's not always easy to know where this line should be drawn, we simply want to state clearly: there are limits to conflict resilience. And these limits are deeply personal, relating to one's past experiences and trauma history, as we discuss in more detail in Chapter 8. But for now, we distinguish feelings of displeasure from subjecting yourself to trauma here. And you should as well.

When you're brave enough to engage with others around a sensitive topic that heightens your anxiety and discomfort, the quality of the listening matters all the more. In their 2020 study, Guy Itzchakov and Netta Weinstein aimed to better understand the impact of high-quality listening—again, characterized as attentive, empathic, and nonjudgmental—on the psychological needs and self-esteem of speakers discussing prejudiced attitudes. Across two experiments they recruited hundreds of undergraduate students as participants. Each participant was in a quiet room with a test administrator and was handed a questionnaire with the following paragraph:

> I would like you to take a couple of minutes to think about a specific bias that you may feel or may have felt. Most people will have felt some sort of bias during their lives. This bias can be towards any group of people, for example, older people, people of color, the opposite gender, or people from different socioeconomic status. In the box below, please write about this bias, how you were feeling, and what your overall experience was.

After they finished their written response, they received the following instruction by the test administrator:

> I would now like you to describe the bias you just wrote about to me. Everything we talk about here is confidential and will not be recorded. When you are ready, please begin.

Each participant spoke about their own prejudiced attitudes to the test administrator for about eight to ten minutes (most used the full ten). What they did not know was that they had each been randomly assigned to a test administrator who was either a trained higher-quality listener or a lower-quality listener.

Why were the researchers specifically interested in listening's impact on self-esteem and feelings of autonomy? Well, let's first get real about the power dynamics at play when we're navigating tough conversations, especially those that can potentially shake how we feel about our identity, our views, our values, our selves—our self-esteem. Prior studies have confirmed the notion that when we disclose information about ourselves to someone who then disagrees, we tend to shut down and become incredibly defensive, usually out of fear of rejection because, let's face it, no one wants their sense of worth to take a hit. When someone we're talking to pushes back, what happens? Our walls go up and we dig our heels in, doubling down on our views if we feel threatened—the so-called "backlash effect." The backlash effect occurs when individuals respond to opposition by becoming more entrenched in their original views. This defensive reaction often leads to a reinforcement of their beliefs and a stronger resistance to change, even in the face of contradictory evidence.

Now, here's where it gets complicated but also incredibly promising: dialogue in conflict can be both a risk and a resource. When someone agrees with your prejudiced viewpoint, sure, it shields your self-esteem, but it also reinforces your prejudice at the cost of connection and even personal growth. Deep listening done well, however, has nothing to do with agreement. To the contrary, it means making someone feel heard without agreeing or affirming your assent or their accuracy in any way. By first making your conversational counterpart feel seen and heard, it becomes easier for you to raise different or conflicting viewpoints. This approach shifts the dynamic away from an experience of confrontation and toward an engaged, collaborative discussion aimed at jointly exploring new insights and generating potential solutions.

So, what did the researchers find in the study on listening to prejudiced attitudes? Their data showed that when you're heard by a higher-quality listener—an attentive, empathic, and nonjudgmental listener—your sense of autonomy, connection, and self-esteem shoots through the roof. And, specifically, in a conversation that could otherwise threaten a person's self-esteem, speakers who felt genuinely heard experienced a boost in their sense of autonomy and, through that, a boost in their self-esteem. This wasn't a one-off either; the results were consistent across participants from Israel and the United Kingdom, which suggests that this is a universal phenomenon, not just a cultural or situational quirk.

High-quality deep listening doesn't just make you feel heard; it empowers you, nourishes your self-worth, and makes tackling difficult conversations much easier. As a deep listener, you gain an invaluable superpower that can transform not only the quality of the interaction and your capacity to sit and be present for it, but also the well-being of the person speaking and possibly their ability to be a better listener for you and others. Never underestimate the power of high-quality listening, especially when navigating challenging, emotionally charged dialogues.

If you're sitting there thinking, "Yeah, but if my opponent is spewing on and on about some bigoted topic, the last thing I want to do is enhance their self-worth!" we get this understandable reaction. At the same time, whether my purpose is to have them hear my ideas, to understand them better, or to frame my arguments in ways that are most persuasive to them, threatening their identity and self-worth is hardly a way forward. The act of honoring the person, hearing their story and perspective, and treating them with dignity is the most likely way to increase the chances they will listen to and respect you. In the moment when you want to retort, attack, or walk away, we empathize with your resistance to enhance their sense of self-worth. But that is precisely where being able to play the long game makes the difference between real leadership and effective persuasion versus simply playing their game back—two people speaking, no people listening. As Tim Wilson, one of the founders of Seeds of Peace, the summer leadership and dialogue program we referenced in Chapter 2, always says, "God gave you two ears and one mouth for a reason."

Our decision to highlight both the humanistic and economic value of listening is very intentional: the more you appreciate what you stand to gain from listening, the more your brain's reward-reinforcement systems (including the BBO—the bigger, better offer) kicks in to motivate you to invest the time and energy to hone this skill. Clinical psychologist and neuroscientist Dr. Helen Weng and others used functional magnetic resonance imaging (fMRI) scans to examine training-induced changes in the brain's responses to social situations that required a more altruistic or compassionate response, like listening. They found that greater practice and repetition in prosocial behaviors increased the engagement of brain systems involved in social cognition and emotion regulation (including the inferior parietal cortex and the dorsolateral prefrontal cortex) and increased functional connectivity between these same brain regions involved in social cognition and emotion regulation with the nucleus accumbens, a brain region involved heavily in reward processing.

Think of how many times people wait in long lines outside in freezing weather to be the first to get a new Apple device or to get tickets to a once-in-a-lifetime concert. Or the lengths that reality TV show contestants will go to to win a prize. We become remarkably talented at enduring difficulty or delaying pleasure when we can reorient our brains to focus on the specificity and size of a reward that's waiting for us. Thus, the more aware you are of the manifold rewards of deep listening, the more motivated you are to listen, the more likely you are to get that reward for deep listening, the more motivated your brain will be to listen the next time, and so on, like a deep-listening flywheel. Being aware of the material and relational benefits of listening will build your resilience to sit through and with the discomfort when you are in the heat of the hard conversation or conflict. As one of Bob's coaching clients recently shared with him, "The more I do this deep-listening thing, the more I realize that the *fear and anxiety* of listening is far worse than whatever discomfort or challenge I feel when I'm actually doing it. And afterward, I always feel like I am surprised to learn something about the other person, even when it's not always good. So I guess I just need to set my mind to engaging these tough conversations with my listening hat on rather than fret, wait, worry, or fight."

If you're still unpersuaded about the value of deep listening, try this exercise: Think of a time you were in a conversation with someone about something that mattered to you when you felt the other person wasn't really listening. What behaviors were they exhibiting? Write them out. Now find a friend or colleague and ask them to spend three minutes with you where you are trying to talk to them about something important and where they are exhibiting the behaviors that you experienced as "not listening" or "bad listening." When you're done, write down what the experience was like for you. Did it make you want to engage with your "friend as bad listener" more? Did you find them more persuasive? More influential? More trustworthy?

We're pretty certain you are glad the annoying exercise is over. And if that is how you are feeling, encode this experience in your memory. It's the lived experience of being on the other side of a conversation without deep listening. And it's typically corrosive to our ability to persuade, build trust, reach agreement, have our perspective understood, and be conflict resilient.

## WHAT IS "DEEP LISTENING"?

So, what do we mean by "deep listening"? At this point in our journey together, it won't surprise you to know it's a lot more than a set of behaviors or just sitting there quietly, although deep listening does involve a set of behaviors that include—but are not limited to—sitting there quietly at times. Deep listening is both a *stance* and a set of *acts or behaviors*.

## ADOPTING A LISTENING STANCE

If any listening behavior is going to work and be more than just a "speed bump" to get over (because leadership gurus talk about the importance of listening all the time), it must start with the self. Part of that involves adopting a healthy set of assumptions that make exerting the effort and time for deep listening seem worth the investment. But let's face it: Listening takes a huge amount of courage and vulnerability. It involves subjecting yourself, at best, to viewpoints that you might disagree with on an intellectual basis and, at worst, to ideas and proposals that could and would harm you if enacted. And listening is often not an equal-opportunity endeavor.

If you are a Jewish Israeli, listening to someone make a case against the legitimacy of your country or call you a colonizer may not feel like an academic or intellectual exercise. It's much more likely to strike you as something deeply personal, gut-wrenching, and perhaps even hateful. Similarly, if you are a Palestinian, being told that you have no claim to the home your grandmother was forced out of in 1948, when she was a child, and that you were never really a "people" anyway will likely evoke profound pain, requiring immense courage and resilience to endure.

The same can be said for so many conflicts across lines of difference: the queer person listening to arguments suggesting that marriage equality might lead to the breakdown of the "family" or the end of Western civilization; the older adult at the dinner table engaging in a conversation where their own family says that "all elderly people" should be required to take a cognitive test to run for office and should be ashamed of the legacy of hate their generation left behind; the person of color hearing that racism is "over" and it's time to move on; or the person who values safety and self-reliance being told that firearms should be banned. If what's being talked about affects you or people you love in real and immediate ways, listening is personal. It can feel as if your very identity, legitimacy, and worth are under assault. That's because the ideas being expressed on the other side, if fully realized, might actually cost you your identity, legitimacy, worth, career, family, or even liberty. This is where conflict resilience comes in.

We acknowledge just how challenging and unequal listening can be in hard contexts. Yet we argue that it is still the *best way* to ensure that our institutions, relationships, and society remain as robust and healthy as possible. We see it as the only way to avoid the kind of disintegration that will ultimately yield to disconnection and violence.

Needless to say, it will be virtually impossible to enact any sincere or legitimate behavior of deep listening without the hard internal work and preparation we discussed in Part 1 (e.g., training yourself to be aware when you're about to go into one of the five Fs, naming emotions that are coming up and other techniques to reduce the intensity of the emotions, and reappraising the situation and how it may be irritating core parts of your history or identity). This kind of shift in stance allows you to suspend, at least for the purposes of the conversation, the notion that the other person is bad, stupid, shortsighted, racist, anti-Muslim, anti-Semitic, unpatriotic, ageist, privileged, etc. The examples above go to the heart of identity.

But adopting a genuinely curious listening stance to colleagues in a workplace who insist that remote work will permanently ruin the sense of cohesion in the office or that workers under the age of thirty are entitled and lazy offers similar kinds of challenges.

Besides simply willing yourself into a stance of curiosity on the ephemeral hope that maybe you will learn something new or at least make them feel heard, here are two hacks that we have found can work effectively for internal mind shifts to help you enact deep-listening behaviors:

1.  Change your task
2.  Build an internal lockbox

## 1. Change Your Task

If your curiosity is gone, consider mentally shifting what your task is. Instead of thinking, "I need to engage in deep listening," you might do the following:

- Imagine that you are writing this person's five-hundred-page biography. To make it rich and juicy—a *New York Times* bestseller—you need to deeply understand everything about them.
- Imagine that you are in a class where your grade is based entirely on whether you can deeply reflect the "what" and the "why" of how the person feels the way they do.
- Imagine yourself as someone like Oprah Winfrey—a talk-show host with a special skill for getting guests to open up and "tell all" about their life, in a nonthreatening and inviting way.

These "hacks" may seem silly, but trust us, they are often fabulously effective. When we reimagine in our mind what our purpose is in the conversation and shift it to something that can feel fun or that helps us channel our efforts to succeed in a different direction or role, the shift can lead to unexpected and authentic curiosity. Both the content and the tone of our listening changes. It may seem magical, but it often works.

## 2. Build an Internal Lockbox

Let's imagine the hack above isn't cutting it. You find yourself too hurt, angry, offended, or upset to be in a listening stance. If that's the case, have a quick internal conversation with your multiple selves. There is a side of you saying, "I can't stand another second of this. I need to respond (or exit the conversation)." But then there is another side that may be saying, "I am here for a reason. [I want to build the relationship. I want to know how best to persuade. I want to help them see me better and more clearly, etc.] And this is the side—even if it is only a very small side—that knows that I need to understand more, stay engaged, be curious, if I am to achieve this purpose." Once you name those two sides, create a lockbox in your mind and say to yourself:

I am going to gently place the enraged/angry/"need to respond right now" side of me into this lockbox for the next ten minutes and indulge the "I am here for a reason and will be curious" side. I will then come back to the "here is my response" side and make sure it gets represented in this conversation.

This internal hack—moving from either/or to both/and—can powerfully affect your ability to stay in the game and enact the behaviors of deep listening in a way that will be sincere, authentic, and real. This kind of internal stance work is why we call the listening needed to be conflict resilient "deep listening." It is so much more than enacting a set of behaviors that may look like active listening (similar to what you might expect to see in an instructional video or a conflict resolution class) but will come across as fake, rehearsed, or strained in real life.

Perhaps the only thing worse than not listening well is enacting listening behaviors that are insincere and performative. When you do that, you move from being argumentative or avoidant to being condescending and arrogant—not really an improvement. And, truth is, most people can see right through this.

Our brain is naturally wired to expertly detect insincere behaviors. To constantly pick up on clues of insincerity, your brain combines various elements of social cognition—visual perspective-taking, theory of mind, moral judgments, detection of the intent to deceive—through our frontal lobe, limbic system, and an area of the brain that serves as an information hub known as the left temporoparietal junction (an area of the brain approximately above your left ear). It's possible that our brains evolved to do this because it violates the social norm of truthfulness and may ultimately help protect ourselves and others. In fact, it takes significant injury to the brain, such as from a neuro-degenerative disease like Alzheimer's disease or frontotemporal lobar degeneration, for that ability to dampen. So, be sure that you are doing whatever it takes so that your deep listening is as sincere as possible, such as changing your task or using an internal lockbox, because your counterpart's brain will know the truth and it will definitely matter.

## ADOPTING DEEP-LISTENING BEHAVIORS

Most of us have heard of "active listening." Active listening got its name to underscore the point that it involves active and engaged behavior—that it is more than simply sitting there quietly while someone else talks. We have opted to call conflict-resilient listening *deep listening* for several important reasons, even though we would agree that *deep listening* involves behaviors like active listening that are more than just sitting there quietly or occasionally nodding your head. Again, the first reason why we call for deep listening is the substantial and hard "stance" work that is *prerequisite* to the actions. Deep listening is so much more than the "actions." It's our experience that enacting the specific behaviors of active listening without first taking on the internal stance described above is likely to come across as condescending, false, and performative. In many respects, then, it is the opposite of deep. And it can be so ineffective that it can give listening an undeserved bad reputation.

But the second reason why we use the term "deep listening" is that we believe this kind of listening requires *both* active behaviors *and* periods of passive silence and pauses. It also involves—as much as the logistics of a situation enable—nonverbal behaviors that can make another feel heard.

Broadly, we break deep-listening behaviors into three distinct skill sets:

1. Reflecting back
2. Open-ended inquiry
3. Mindful silence and focused nonverbal attention

Let's take each in turn.

## 1. Reflecting Back

In literature on effective listening behaviors, "reflecting back" is often characterized as paraphrasing, summarizing, repeating, or even parroting back. In our view, each of these characterizations has some merit to it and also leaves something to be desired.

The goal of *reflecting back* is to make sure that you have captured the main arguments, "facts," content, or substantive points of the person on the other side of the conflict or negotiation. In this sense, it is akin to paraphrasing. But it is more than just capturing—as accurately and non-judgmentally as possible—the main arguments or substantive points.

*Reflecting back* also involves acknowledging the *emotional* content or spirit of the person on the other side of the conflict or negotiation as a way of demonstrating not only that you have captured the substantive information, but also that you are connecting with them on a human level.

We want to be clear here. By reflecting back the emotional content, we do not mean to suggest that you might, should, or ought to also *feel* those same emotions yourself. Nor does reflecting back their feelings mean that you think the emotions coming at you are appropriate or justified, or even that you agree that they are emotions that a so-called "reasonable" person might feel. The purpose of reflecting the emotional content back is simply to connect and make the other person feel seen. Meeting this basic human need is *not* a concession. It is simply part of what it means to build trust and establish a necessary (but by no means sufficient) aspect of a workable relationship across lines of difference.

When it comes to deep listening, be sure to avoid what we call "selective reflection" of the other's points. For example, your counterpart has given you six reasons why they believe legalizing sex work is a good idea. In reflecting back what you heard, you repeat Ideas 1, 2, and 6, and you purposefully ignore Ideas 3 and 4 because they don't advance the narrative you'd like to create when it's your time to advocate; then you twist Idea 5 in your favor even though you're reasonably certain that what you're reflecting back is *not* what they intended.

Selective reflecting to manipulate or twist what you've heard in your favor tends to fail not only as a deep-listening move, but also from a strategic negotiation perspective. It tends to diminish trust and damage the relationship, making it less likely that your counterpart will be persuaded, share more information about how they see the situation, concede a point, want to continue the conversation, or back down.

Here's what reflecting back done well (by Carrie below) might look like:

**Miranda:** Carrie, you wouldn't believe what I was reading about earlier. It's infuriating how resistant some people are to repatriating museum collections. Rich Western museums run by colonizer European countries need to send those stolen items back to the places from which they were stolen! This shouldn't even be controversial. The people opposing this are so wrongheaded, so complicit in the sins of their forebears, and frankly, so arrogant.

**Carrie:** Wow, Miranda! You clearly feel very strongly about this! [REFLECTING BACK EMOTION]

**Miranda:** I do. It's disgusting and infuriating.

**Carrie:** Part of what is driving the disgust and fury for you, if I understand it, is you see those who are against repatriating artifacts as coming from a place of privilege, that there is a real blind spot in terms of understanding even the basis by which they first came to have these ill-gotten goods. For you, you can't even see how there could be a legitimate other viewpoint on this. That's why, for you, the inaction from museum leadership amounts to complicity, to perpetuating the colonialism of their ancestors. [REFLECTING BACK THE MAIN IDEAS, CONTENT, ARGUMENTS]

**Miranda:** Yes, that's exactly what I'm saying! When you look at these museum collections, what you're really seeing is a sanitized version of colonialism. It's like Colonialism 2.0. I mean, how did they get most of these artifacts? They were taken, often following plunder or massacre, sometimes under pressure, or just by outright theft! Museums serve as these "innocent" containers that silently perpetuate colonial crimes.

**Carrie:** Hmm, so you feel that museums aren't just passive holders of items that were obtained through illegitimate means; they're an extension of colonialism in the present day. They often house artifacts acquired under questionable circumstances, perpetuating the story of the colonizers rather than the colonized. From your perspective, they don't really tell the full story of how the items were acquired. [REFLECTING BACK CONTENT]

**Miranda:** Yes. But it's not "questionable." My point is that there is no question that these artifacts need to be returned. Period. These museum collections are filled with stolen goods. It's just so unethical. These are stolen goods we're talking about! The only right thing to do is to return these artifacts to their rightful communities where they have real historical and cultural value.

**Carrie:** So for you, there is a clear-cut decision here and it's maddening to you to see it otherwise. These artifacts are basically stolen property and should be returned to their communities of origin, where they hold more than just aesthetic value. [REFLECTING BOTH EMOTION AND CONTENT]

**Miranda:** Absolutely!

*END SCENE*

This exchange may seem straightforward, but if Carrie deeply disagreed with Miranda, she likely needed to also manage her own emotions while reflecting back, paraphrasing the meaning of what Miranda was saying so that she felt truly heard without endorsing Miranda's view. One challenge to paying close attention to an opposing viewpoint is a kind of "limbic irritability," where your brain's limbic system, like the hot eye of a stove, may already have some heat from the stress of your week, an emotionally charged videoconference a few minutes before, or whatever's been going on in your life. Maybe you also didn't get much sleep last night. And now, it doesn't take very much additional heat on top of that for your limbic system to be white hot. It can almost feel raw and tender, and you need a longer while to let that warmth steadily cool down.

Limbic irritability refers to this heightened sensitive state of emotional reactivity, where even small stressors can trigger intense feelings. This happens because the limbic system—connected structures in the brain, including the amygdala, that play a key role in a wide range of emotional processes—is involved in detecting novelty and unexpected events, especially potentially harmful threats that might be worth acting on quickly to survive.

When the limbic system becomes hyperactive, it can make it difficult to stay calm and composed. And after such hyperactivity, the limbic system has a "cool-off" period, like how the eye of a stove that's been on for hours takes time to cool down once the stove is turned off. If you keep turning the stove back on before it fully cools, however, not only does the burner stay warmer longer, but it also takes less time to get extremely hot. Similarly, each additional trigger or stressor can extend your limbic system's cool-off period, making it harder to recover and easier to activate again. Additionally, the prefrontal cortex, which plays a role in regulating your responses and sustaining your attention, may become less effective in managing this heightened activity, leading to even greater reactivity.

Being aware of your "limbic irritability" can help you recognize when it's harder to listen and reflect back effectively. It's reasonable to acknowledge you need to take a break and revisit the conversation later, when your limbic system is less irritable. This way, the odds will be in your favor that you'll be effective at deep listening without the distraction of intense emotions overwhelming your mind and body.

## 2. Open-Ended Inquiry (or channeling your inner seven-year-old but with the right tone)

A key deep-listening skill and one that is very connected to curiosity is open-ended inquiry. When we say "open-ended," we mean asking genuine and curious questions that do not yield to either a "yes" or "no" answer or an "either/or" response. Open-ended questions in deep listening force the person on the other side to elaborate with a response that is more than one or two words. This is part of what makes it so useful in a difficult dialogue or a stuck negotiation. The open-ended nature of the question forces them to give some serious thought to why they said what they said. Their response gives you added insight to the "thinking" or "reasoning" behind their conclusion. In the toughest of dialogues or negotiations, where emotions are running high and patience is running thin, an open-ended question is almost like a Jedi mind trick—it's an ultimate stealth weapon for inviting deeper thinking and learning instead of pouring more emotional fuel onto the fire.

Open-ended inquiry can look like the following:

- "Say more about..."
- "Help me understand..."
- "Please elaborate..."
- "What thoughts do you have on..."

In theory, asking open-ended questions should be relatively easy and straightforward. In truth, it is extremely challenging for a host of reasons.

The biggest reason why open-ended inquiry is tough relates to our internal mindset. For much of the time when we find ourselves in conflict, we aren't all that interested in having the other side "say more" or help us understand. We either want to escape the argument, win the argument, or just close our ears and fold our arms.

There isn't an "easy" fix for this, but there is a hack that we have discovered that can boost our curiosity. Quite simply, it's an invitation to imagine that you have returned to your seven-year-old self. Not in all respects, but in one related specifically to the curiosity that most seven-year-old children seem to have. If you are like us, you were an absolute question box as a kid: "But why do I have to wear my jacket?" or "Why are we going to church?" or "Why do I have to be nice to my nasty and selfish cousin who is a brat?"

Kids have an insatiable appetite for asking "why" questions. While you probably don't want to adopt the whiny tone of your seven-year-old self, reclaiming the seven-year-old's insatiable curiosity can be helpful when it comes to open-ended inquiry, which leads to a genuine tone shift, a new set of questions, and, frankly, a bit of self-entertainment!

When it comes to open-ended inquiry, there are several common pitfalls that need to be avoided. First, it's not uncommon when we ask an open-ended question, as opposed to a "yes or no" or "either/or" question, that our query is followed by what may feel like an exceptionally long and awkward silence. In truth, the silence is typically no more than five to maybe ten seconds (at most), but it can feel like an eternity. Because silence in a conflict can feel awkward, we often follow up our very skillful open-ended question with a "yes or no" or "either/or" before the other side can respond.

Here's an example:

**Dash:** What do you think would be a good resolution to the Israeli-Palestinian crisis? [WONDERFUL, OPEN-ENDED QUESTION]

*[Two seconds of silence elapses that feels like an eternity to Dash]*

**Dash:** Should Israel just pull out of the occupied territories? [YES OR NO QUESTION THAT PROVIDES AN EASY ESCAPE FOR THE CONVERSATIONAL COUNTERPART]

**Mallory:** No.

**Dash:** OK, so what do you think should be the way forward? [GREAT OPEN-ENDED QUESTION, A NICE RECOVERY]

*[Silence for five seconds]*

**Dash:** Should the Israelis just continue to plod along "as is" or do you think they should work toward a two-state solution? [UNFORTUNATE EITHER/OR QUESTION RUINING THE OPEN-ENDED INQUIRY]

When we start to move from closed to open-ended questions, there are often awkward pauses on the other end. Why? Because people simply are not accustomed to open-ended questions. That is why open-ended inquiry is so powerful in negotiation and conflict situations. It is disarming and surprising—in good and unexpected ways. Open-ended questions invite the other side to think expansively and share more fully. Open-ended questions force a real self-reflection from the responder—and this is exactly the kind of information you want in a negotiation or conflict—the highest-quality, most well-considered, deepest, and most honest response. But that means you can't thwart your own effort to get that information by following up a fantastic open-ended question with a closed dead-end follow-up seconds later. Lean into the silence—another important conflict resilience tool.

Two quick hacks for resisting the temptation to follow up open-ended inquiry with a closed question:

- *The Seven-Second Rule:* Whenever you ask an open-ended question, pause for a minimum of seven seconds, no matter how uncomfortable these moments make us. Years ago, Bob had a wonderfully earnest student who seemed incapable of sitting in silence. Midway through the semester, Bob told the student, "Sagar—your goal for the rest of the semester is, in every single simulation, to ask one open-ended question and then pause for seven seconds or until your counterpart responds, whichever comes first." It was a tough ask for Sagar. But by the end of the semester, he had transformed from someone whom many perceived as sweet but insecure into a trusted and valued colleague.

- *The Do-Over:* Whenever you inadvertently mess up (and you will mess up—we all do) and ask a closed question, interrupt yourself and just say, "No, I want to ask the question differently . . ." Then ask an open-ended question instead. This sounds simple, but in practice it can feel awkward. Awkward or not, though, the "do-over" works. More than that, people on the other side of the conversation notice and appreciate the move because they see you are making more space for them, that you are less interested in "trapping them" than in hearing and understanding them. Freeing your negotiation or conflict counterpart from the chains of "yes/no" or "either/or" builds relational capital and gets you a more informed and fulsome response. It conveys respect—that you want to hear their unvarnished and full answer, not box them into a multiple-choice trap.

### 3. Mindful Silence and Focused Nonverbal Attention

*Mindful silence.* A silent pause is different from sitting there passively while the other person rambles on and on indefinitely. It's also different from the kind of silence you might show while attending the symphony or while listening to a lecture. Rather, mindful silence is an intentional and focused slowing down of the pace of the conversation, allowing for a short pause before either reflecting back information or emotions or asking an open-ended question.

Consider the experience of Dr. Rochelle Walensky, the former director of the Centers for Disease Control and Prevention (CDC). Dr. Walensky had spent many years working on HIV research before ascending to the top job at the CDC. In an interview from the podcast *In the Bubble* shortly after being named head of the agency, Walensky said:

> When you give a new HIV diagnosis to somebody, the next thing you do is wait and you don't speak again until they speak. And that gives you a sense of what it is that's hurting them the most. What are they worried about? Are they worried about their job or are they worried about their safety? Or are they worried about their children. . . . What is it that's there? And that's usually the next thing that comes out. . . . What is it that's worrying you the most?

This purposeful silence or pause is critical to what it means to be a deep listener. Leaning into the silence and waiting. It slows the pace down and communicates care and concern. It's also an invitation to your counterpart to reflect before responding, which short-circuits the point/counterpoint escalation that characterizes so many polarizing and unproductive conflicts, the kind of squabbles and shouting matches we often see on cable news. And yet, mindful silence can be quite challenging for us to do. A 2019 study published in the *Journal of Internal Medicine* by Dr. Naykky Ospina and her colleagues at the University of Florida reported that in the doctor's office, when a patient starts describing their condition, 69 percent of doctors give a patient just eighteen seconds before interrupting. This results in the true reason for a patient's visit never being elicited in about 77 percent of cases. This clearly is not quality health care—or deep listening.

More recently, Professor Jared Curhan and his team at the MIT Sloan School of Management published a study in the *Journal of Applied Psychology* supporting the importance of silence in negotiation. Their results found that "instructing negotiators to use silence is more effective for value creation than instructing them to problem solve." Curhan's research suggests that silent pauses often stimulate creative thinking. In addition to the creativity, these mindful pauses convey to the speaker that you are really considering what they said. The pause also acts as a circuit breaker to prevent the kind of tit-for-tat escalation that turns a disagreement into an escalatory and unproductive fight.

*Focused nonverbal attention.* The groundbreaking Broadway musical *How to Dance in Ohio* is based on a true story about the experience of autistic teenagers preparing for a Friday night prom, starring a cast of teenage actors living with autism spectrum disorder. In the production, Tommy, a warm and funny high school senior, feels deeply for others internally, but has a disconnect when it comes to communicating his curiosity and care to others. This is an experience that Joel, who also identifies as neurodivergent, can relate with as a common challenge to navigating social relationships as well. Tommy sings about having been coached to furrow his brow as a way to communicate his curiosity to others. The moment in the show when he awkwardly crinkles his brow in a strained and rehearsed way is at once heartbreaking and endearing. Audiences typically break out in an empathic and somewhat guilty laugh at this exaggerated and pantomimed gesture of empathy. He is focused, interested, and he cares. But his default nonverbal cues unintentionally convey detachment while his staged brow-furrowing inadvertently falls flat too. It's a poignant moment in the show: Tommy is learning both to appreciate the importance of conveying care and concern on his face as well as to understand that just feeling whatever he is internally isn't enough to sustain a conversation, never mind a relationship. Also, it is heartbreaking for the audience to see the lesson he's taken—that an exaggerated furrowing of the brow is the thing that might help build the connection. Still, for Tommy, it's progress.

As the audience feels a wave of emotion and empathy for Tommy at this moment, we are also reminded of something that many of us know intuitively but can forget at times, namely, the role of nonverbal cues and behaviors in influencing whether someone feels heard and feels seen. The lesson Tommy takes—that nonverbal cues communicate listening (or its opposite)—is one that is real for all of us. Of course, the answer to conveying interest and empathy is rarely an exaggerated furrowing of our brow. Plus, due to all sorts of cultural and contextual factors, including but not limited to the neurodiversity of human beings, not all people register nonverbal cues the way you may expect they might. That said, research has demonstrated that nonverbal cues are critical in the listening enterprise. Nonverbal cues can communicate care and concern. They can also convey genuine interest and engagement.

Effective nonverbal deep-listening behaviors might include making steady eye contact (but not awkward and intense staring), facing your body toward the speaker (whenever possible), leaning in, and perhaps using softer facial expressions that communicate, "I'm here with you."

This nonverbal immediacy can act as a bridge of interpersonal warmth, creating a new, more genuine, and open connection between speaker and listener where there is a shared feeling of closeness and, scariest of all, mutual vulnerability. These are signs of what researchers call "person-centeredness," a quality that serves up a megadose of empathy and validates the emotional state and lived experience of the speaker.

Lastly, we can't overlook how crucial it is to have a nonjudgmental stance as part of this collection of nonverbal behaviors. This is a genuine disposition that sets aside preconceptions, affirms the speaker's intrinsic worth, and accepts their freedom to express themselves, notably without needing to endorse or agree on the substance of what's said.

## DEEP LISTENING BEFORE EFFECTIVE ASSERTION

Cultivating deep listening—both the internal stance and the behavioral skills—is critical to conflict resilience, to effective negotiation, and to leadership. It produces better substantive outcomes, but also fosters stronger connections while enhancing your overall quality of life. Great listening—whether you are on the listening side or the "receiving" side—also has medically documented benefits for our physical, mental, and social well-being throughout our lives.

To be conflict resilient, developing the internal stance and the behavioral skill of deep listening is essential. Deep listening will help you handle conflict more adroitly, enable you to create more sustainable relationships, and help you achieve more value-creating and satisfying outcomes in your negotiations.

Deep listening alone is only one part of conflict resilience. In the next chapter, we'll explore how to effectively assert yourself in these situations to create a powerful connection and unlock new possibilities. It builds upon the internal mirror, chair, and table work we've introduced in Chapter 4, providing you more specific language and tools to join with the deep-listening skills here.

Chapter 6

# GIVING VOICE

## Effective Assertion as a Catalyst of Connection and Possibility

Bob still cannot forget the dreaded Macy's "take 25% off everything in the store" coupon. It had fine print in a barely readable font listing about fifty major "exclusions" from fragrances to Tommy Hilfiger and Polo-branded merchandise to "doorbuster" special deals. The mere thought of this coupon conjures up anxiety for Bob that goes all the way back to his childhood. Bob has a distinct childhood memory of being with his mom, going up to a Macy's cash register with purchase in hand and the dreaded coupon. Then the scanner denies the discount. What happens next is the stuff of sketch comedy:

**Cashier:** I'm sorry, ma'am, but the coupon doesn't apply because this item is already on sale at thirty percent off.

**Mrs. Bordone:** Try again, please.

*Cashier reluctantly indulges the request.*

**Cashier:** I'm sorry, this item doesn't work for the coupon.

**Mrs. Bordone:** Well, it says twenty-five percent off everything in the store. And I am a Macy's cardholder.

**Cashier:** Well, it doesn't apply. This is an excluded item.

**Mrs. Bordone:** Well then, the coupon is a lie because it says twenty-five percent off *everything* in the store. You need to take the twenty-five percent off.

**Cashier:** I'm sorry, ma'am, this is the price. It's an excluded item because it is already on a Doorbuster Special. Do you want the item or not?

**Mrs. Bordone (in a loud and insistent voice):** Yes, I want the item. I want the item with the thirty percent off and then the twenty-five percent coupon.

**Cashier:** As I said, the coupon doesn't apply.

**Mrs. Bordone:** Call the manager then, because this says twenty-five percent off *everything* in the store.

At this point, you can imagine adolescent Bob doing everything he can to resist his urge to escape the scene yelling, "I am *not* with this woman!"

The conversation between Bob and his mom afterward is even more cringey.

"Mom, that was embarrassing! There is an exclusion in small print!"

"Bobby, if you don't stand up for yourself, they'll take advantage of you! And you see, I won. I got it. Your father wouldn't have stood up for himself and he would have paid the extra money. You need to learn to stand up for yourself!"

Although it is true that Bob's mother achieved an outcome that was positive for her, the zero-sum, scorched-earth, transactional nature of her exchange is an example of what not to do when the stakes are anything more than a one-off transaction where you care neither about the relationship nor the optics of the exchange. Yes, you may "win" in a single transactional situation by mercilessly steamrolling your way through it, but the majority of conflicts and negotiations that you'll encounter in your life—especially the ones that matter—are not one-offs and require a very different approach.

One of the reasons why so many of us stumble in our efforts at assertiveness in conflict is that we misunderstand what assertiveness is. For some, the kinds of stubborn insistence—the doubling down, raising of voices, rallying of arguments, and digging in—are the marks of what it means to be appropriately assertive and a great negotiator. And for those who agree that this is how a great negotiator behaves, you may aspire to be the real-life version of the movie character who pounds the table, takes no prisoners, and only offers the tiniest of concessions in exchange for massive gives from the other side. On the other hand, if this is your idea of what great negotiators need to do, but you can't imagine acting like this yourself because you consider such behaviors harsh, rude, brash, or inappropriate, you're likely to think, "I'm a terrible negotiator," or "I need to avoid conflict at all costs because I'm just not the type of person to make a fuss."

The real issue, however, isn't your ability to be a conflict-resilient negotiator. The problem lies in the distorted notion of what effective assertion means—a notion that has become increasingly dominant in our culture and is echoed not just in TV and movies, but also in politics, school board meetings, and, regrettably, even within our families with growing frequency.

But here's the rub. Even if Bob's mother might have been objectively wrong about whether the coupon with dozens of exclusions should be honored and perhaps embarrassing in her approach with the Macy's sales clerk, there was an important truth and life lesson to what she said: Indeed, being assertive about one's needs, interests, perspective, and feelings *is* a critical skill for leadership, negotiation, and life. Finding an appropriate way to advocate for and assert your perspective is essential for thriving and surviving in a world full of differences and conflict. All too often we discount or even disregard the costs of avoiding, being silent, or not speaking. Some of the common excuses:

"It's not worth my time."

"This is more important to them than it is to me."

"Maybe I'm wrong anyway."

"They have all the power anyway, so I'll lose."

"That's OK. I really don't want to make a scene."

"I can deal with this better than they can."

"I'm not cut out for this."

We walk away, stay silent, and grumble. But there is still something on the inside that is nagging us and keeping us awake at night. In a transactional negotiation, maybe we just continue to have a bitter aftertaste, knowing that if we pushed a bit harder, we could have persuaded the seller to take $20,000 off the house or gotten the refund that we know we deserved.

In other situations, the feeling may be different. Perhaps we feel like we sold out someone we care about because we didn't stand up for them in a conversation with colleagues. Or maybe, by not speaking our mind, we find ourselves reevaluating the closeness we feel to someone or our ability to connect with them and consciously or subconsciously ratchet the value of the relationship downward. By not sharing how we feel, we end up sabotaging ourselves, cutting off the possibility of something deeper or more generative with this person out of fear that asserting our feelings authentically will push them away rather than draw us closer. What's worse, the other person doesn't even know that something they did or said has affected the relationship so badly. Yes, they may have asserted a viewpoint that upset or offended us. But our decision to not raise it with them cuts off the chance for a constructive conversation, a deepening of the relationship, and perhaps a chance for an apology or expression of regret. We fail to appreciate the value that effective assertion can provide and we miscalculate the costs that aggression or avoidance imposes on us in terms of disappointing outcomes, broken relationships, increased anxiety, and reduced overall happiness.

At least part of the reason why we tend to avoid or assert poorly is the tendency to misidentify what needs to be asserted, or to do it in a way that backfires, damages relationships, and leaves everyone, from strangers to significant others, feeling awful and, if we're not careful, estranged.

In this chapter, we break open the power of *effective assertion* in conflict, which requires an important shift in mindset from certainty to curiosity. We also discuss different types of assertion and explain the important distinction between asserting your interests and your positions. In the process, we'll show why *effective assertion* is so necessary to conflict resilience and how, when done well, it can bring as much value to our negotiations, our conflicts, our organizations, and our civic engagements as it does joy to our relationships with family, friends, and, yes, even current and future lovers!

Indulge us for a moment in an exercise we conduct with our students when teaching conflict resilience:

Count the number of times the letter *F* appears in the ALL-CAPS sentence below. When you are reasonably certain you have counted correctly, make a mental note of your tally and turn the page.

THOSE OF US WHO FOCUS

ON ISSUES OF FAIRNESS TOO

OFTEN

EFFECT

AGREEMENT

BY GIVING IN

INSTEAD OF FIRST USING OUR

POWERS OF PERSUASION TO

EFFECT

A FAIR OUTCOME THAT WILL

FULLY SATISFY ALL OF OUR

LEGITIMATE INTERESTS.

Now that you've turned the page, how many Fs did you count? More than 13? Fewer than 10? If you are like most people, your count is likely to be between 10 and 13 Fs. But the correct answer is 16. That's right—there are 16 Fs in the sentence on the last page!

Don't get upset with yourself, though. Fewer than 10 percent of people count accurately and get it right.

The purpose of this exercise isn't to assess your counting skills; it's to drive home an important point. Almost everyone gets this objective and verifiable exercise wrong. Imagine how off the mark we can be when we encounter a much more complex, nuanced, and messy situation than counting the number of times the letter *F* is printed on a piece of paper. In conflicts, particularly moments of deep disagreement about what's right, true, fair, or accurate, we humans tend to plunge into them with the understandable notion that we are fair-minded, thorough, objective, and fact-driven. Therefore, we are undoubtedly right, and they are irrefutably wrong.

*If you go in with the purpose of showing someone you are right and they are wrong, however, you are likely to get yourself into trouble.* The reason is that all of us—even the most objectively careful, evidence-based, and factually devoted among us—are susceptible to partisan perceptions.

Yes, we can hear you now, perhaps putting this book down with a bit of frustration and aggravation. Our advice here can be very hard to swallow. It is hard even for us at times. You might be thinking, "This is ridiculous! I am not going to normalize or legitimize the possibility that..."

- A presidential election was/was not stolen
- Health care is/is not a human right
- Climate change is/is not real
- Europeans do/do not pay their fair share of NATO defense costs
- Vaccines are/are not safe and effective
- Donald Trump is/is not responsible for the violence on January 6
- Abortion is/is not murder

Regardless of your stance on these issues, it can be extremely challenging in a conversation to consider letting go of something you believe to be an incontrovertible fact. So, let us be clear. We are *not* saying that you need to let go of your belief about the information. But you need to let go of certainty—either about the situation or about how the other person understands the situation—and do the very hard work of believing you may be wrong, misinformed, or just partially informed.

This internal shift matters for a few reasons.

First, without it, a genuine conversation is not possible. And saying you want one can even be condescending and insincere. A conversation without some real curiosity on your end precludes listening for anything more than proving your counterpart wrong. And that's not an invitation that anyone on the other side is particularly keen to join. That's just an invitation to a debate. Only curiosity about something (virtually anything!) the other person has to say can create conditions for a genuine dialogue or conversation. That's at least partly why—despite what might feel counterintuitive for a book about conflict and negotiation—we have sequenced our chapter on listening before our chapter on assertion.

Second, the internal work of opening ourselves up to the idea that we do not know the entire story shifts the *way in which we assert*. It allows us to say, "There are some things that I feel pretty strongly that I know, and there are some things that I probably don't know or would like to learn and know more about." That stance allows for a confident assertion on issues and subjects you know something about while working symbiotically with listening to express a desire to learn more about what you might be missing or don't know. That kind of assertion is easier for anyone on the receiving end.

There is nothing weak, wishy-washy, or contingent about this kind of assertion. It allows you to be clear about what you know and why. At the same time, it also allows you to signal that you do not think the other side is, in general, a bad, irrational, stupid, or ill-informed person—just that your understanding of how they see an issue does not add up, compute, or make full (or perhaps any) sense to you, and you genuinely, kindly, and affirmatively want to understand why it adds up, computes, or makes sense to them.

Simply put, asserting the idea that your view represents objective and complete truth is almost certain to backfire. But beginning assertion from a place of examining how you see something and with evidence supporting it, while knowing there are others who may have different evidence and different ways of thinking, opens space for real engagement and connection.

Once you've done the hard internal work of allowing the possibility that there is something about an issue or perspective that you don't yet know, you're in a much better place to be effectively assertive about the way you see things, why it is your perspective, and why it matters. And all of this will land differently from an assertive stance that declares your view to be true and the others to be false, invalid, or misdirected.

To be effectively assertive does not mean putting the relationship at risk; nor does it mean being belligerent, insistent, or loud. Done well, assertion creates an opportunity for better substantive outcomes, more trust, deeper connection, and more resilient relationships, organizations, and communities.

## INTERESTS ARE MORE IMPORTANT THAN POSITIONS

Before we discuss what *effective assertion* looks like "at the table" with others, let's consider a few scenarios that illustrate the difference between negotiating from a position versus negotiating from an interest.

- With an offer in hand to be the general counsel of a progressive nonprofit based in Chicago, Tania approached Bob for negotiation coaching. A good lawyer, Tania arrived prepared with a list of prioritized "requirements":
  - Minimum salary of $325,000
  - 4 weeks of paid vacation

- Immediate vesting of 401(k) benefits
- Generous expense budget
- A personal assistant
- Latitude from the board for a staff reorganization within 2 years

"Where do I begin?" Tania asked.

- Reggie was exasperated by a repeated and upsetting interaction with his business partner Esther. They work with clients to help create their online social media presence; business was flourishing. But every time Reggie and Esther had a bit of downtime, Esther complained about how Reggie made decisions about how to spend money, calling him "feckless" and "irresponsible." What was supposed to be fun social time often ended up ending in constant fights, with the two of them sulking and shutting down afterward. Reggie wanted to get Esther to stop the criticism and trust him once and for all.

- "Frightened, paralyzed, angry, and stuck." That's how Muna characterized visiting family in Arizona over the holidays. "I don't want to discuss all the ways I disagree with my family on every single issue. Most of the time, I'm just as happy to be quiet, eat pie, and play pickleball," Muna confessed. "But there are a few items that cut to my soul, particularly the way my family members talk about undocumented persons. I have many friends at home in Miami who are undocumented and so sitting there as my family mischaracterizes these people eats at my soul. By the end of my visit, I feel as if I can barely breathe. I can't wait to get out of there."

All of these dilemmas are similar insofar as they represent a challenge of assertion. But from an analytical perspective, they also have meaningful differences that have consequences for conflict-resilient assertion in practice.

In their bestselling book *Getting to Yes: Negotiating Agreement Without Giving In*, published decades ago, Roger Fisher, William Ury, and Bruce Patton discuss the importance of moving from positions to interests to achieve mutual gains or integrative outcomes in negotiation. Virtually every negotiation book since then has emphasized this critical positions-to-interests shift as an essential part of its prescriptive advice. We are no exception.

Simple in concept yet hard to implement in practice, moving from positions to underlying interests is one of the key skills for effective negotiators and those who strive toward conflict resilience in their lives. As Bob has told his law students for years, "If the only thing you learn in this entire course is how to move yourself and your negotiation counterpart from positions to interests, the return on your investment personally and professionally will be off the charts."

So, what is the difference between a position and an interest? Put simply, "positions" are what someone says they want in a negotiation. For instance, Tanya's *position* includes a minimum salary of at least $325,000, four weeks of paid vacation, and immediate vesting of retirement benefits provided by her future employer. Her *interests*, however, are the underlying needs, concerns, goals, desires, and fears that lie behind or underneath the "position." For example, the interests that drive her position of a salary of $325,000 may be manifold:

- Fair pay appropriate for the relevant market
- Need to pay her daughter's private school tuition
- Need to make monthly mortgage payments and have some reserve funds for a family vacation
- Need to help out her mom, who is retired and living on a fixed income
- Status appropriate to her new role
- Desire to feel valued and important

When it comes to asserting, Tania should prepare by understanding the underlying interests that matter to her and not just her position of, in this case, wanting at least $325,000. When parties in a negotiation get stuck on positions, the negotiation can often be an unproductive battle of wills. Even worse, value-creating options that could possibly meet the interests of all parties are sacrificed for a middle-ground set of compromises that satisfy no one at all.

For example, if part of the reason why Tania needs the $325,000 is for money for private school tuition, mortgage payments, and a vacation, it may be that her future employer has a board member who might be willing to offer a time-share vacation plan to Tania's family for a week every summer. Or perhaps the nonprofit has a deal with a local bank that can refinance the mortgage at a lower rate. Or maybe the nonprofit has an interest in not setting a precedent for a very high salary but would be willing to pay Tania a lower salary and make direct tuition payments for her daughter. These are simple examples. But the more nuanced Tania and her future employer can be in articulating interests instead of just positions, the more space that opens for creative solutions that optimize outcomes and create value, not just split a fixed pie. And typically, moving from positions to interests avoids middle-ground compromises that leave everyone less satisfied than they could have been if the focus had been on meeting the underlying interests of the parties. If Tania is concerned about tuition payments and the board of the nonprofit wants to avoid a precedent of a very high salary for its new CEO, splitting the difference with a number between their initial offer of $225,000 and her demand for $325,000 may meet neither of their interests as well as the $225,000 salary and a direct tuition payment of $30,000 to the private school that her daughter plans to attend.

The value of preparation that focuses on interests instead of positions is that it allows you to assert what's really important to you, minimizing logjams and eliminating conflicts that aren't really there.

When it comes to negotiations—whether over the terms of a job contract, the sale of a house, or an international military defense alliance—relying on positions creates many unnecessary perils. First, it often reinforces the unhelpful and fundamentally false sense that the parties are fundamentally opposed: I want to be paid more and you want to pay me less. I support the transportation funding bill; you oppose it. I support a free trade agreement; you want to impose high tariffs. On the surface, the opposed positions might be true. But it creates a false binary that misses an opportunity for joint gain and value creation. When we dig under the positions to get at the underlying interests, we may discover much that is shared or simply differing and noncompeting.

Second, it's typically easier for parties to share interests in a negotiation than positions. If you are someone who struggles with assertion, you're likely to find it much easier to say, "It's important for me to earn a fair salary commensurate with market practice and one that will ensure I can support my child's tuition, our living costs, and other family obligations" than it is to say, "I need $325,000 a year, take it or leave it." And, of course, the former framing opens us to so many more creative possibilities for the parties to discuss at the same time it makes it harder for the other party to just respond with "We only have $225,000, sorry."

One of the biggest value-adds we provide in our consulting practice is helping parties identify the underlying interests behind their positions. Almost without exception, they find sharing interests easier to do and more authentic than simply doubling down or giving in. And in almost every case, parties discover that a negotiation based on interests transforms a zero-sum battle of haggling into an opportunity to create value, minimize concession-making, and make everyone better off.

Even for those who might still struggle in asserting their interests, it's still better to be asserting the thing that really matters most instead of a long list of positions that get parties stuck and are just a proxy for what really matters.

## ASSERTING FEELINGS

In many classic negotiations, like Tania's compensation package with her employers, the positions-to-interests move unlocks a world of possibility. At first glance, the conflict between Reggie and Esther may seem similar. Reggie's interest is to get Esther to trust him and stop bugging him about how he spends firm money. Esther, on the other hand, has a different view about responsible budgeting and the appropriate way for allocating financial resources. The substantive dispute between the two is how to work out these differences. At one level, it seems that a conversation about each of their respective interests on budgeting and financial decision-making would help them identify a suitable way forward. But there is likely more going on here that a simple analysis of substantive interests might miss.

When Bob first started working with Reggie, he asked Reggie to write out a typical script between the two of them:

**Esther:** So, Reggie, I noticed that you purchased some new artwork for the waiting area in our lobby. I don't remember talking about that with you and it seems a bit much, especially in light of the steep increase in rental payments we have to make for our office space.

**Reggie:** It's totally fine. And yes, I got these great paintings at an art show two weeks ago. They're by an up-and-coming artist, so it's a great investment too.

**Esther:** Well, I thought we were just making the lobby look nice, not making investments in art. I wish you'd be more careful with the way you spend discretionary money.

**Reggie:** OK. To be honest, I think you're overreacting. This is a fantastic piece by a great artist, and it will enhance the lobby space and our image with clients. I wish you'd stop pestering me about spending money and finances. I know what I'm doing and it's annoying.

**Esther:** Well, it's annoying to me when you spend thousands of dollars on things we don't need without consultation . . .

What's going on here?

Obviously neither Reggie nor Esther is doing much deep listening. The result is that this conversation is escalating quickly and getting defensive. And, from an assertion perspective, it might seem that Reggie is holding his own. He is explaining his reasons why purchasing the artwork is a good business decision, a good investment, and makes all-around sense. But all he is getting is opposition and criticism.

Even though Reggie came to Bob for help on "asserting his viewpoint more persuasively," it soon became evident that this looping conversation was nosediving in two ways. First, Reggie really did need the advice on listening from Chapter 5. But second, he was enacting a common mistake that we've seen in our work in hundreds of contexts through the years. Though reasonably effective at asserting his interests, criteria, and decision-making rationale, he was failing at asserting the *feelings* that came up for him whenever Esther switched the track of the conversation to the topics of spending and budgets. And it was very clear to Bob that the assertiveness challenge for Reggie was around asserting *feelings*, not *facts*.

The breakthrough realization occurred after Bob saw the transcript and asked Reggie, "When Esther does this to you, how do you feel?"

"Frustrated and annoyed," he replied.

"What else?" Bob asked.

"Oh. I dunno. Just like she should respect me more."

"OK, so you feel a bit disrespected."

"Yeah, I guess."

"And what else?"

"Um, I don't know."

LONG PAUSE

"You know, I feel a lot of shame. I feel infantilized and condescended to and just completely like a stupid little boy."

Bob leaned in. "Say more about that, Reggie, if you're willing."

What followed was a tender, sad, and emotional story. It turned out that whenever Esther brought up the issue of budget or spending, it was as if Reggie were transported to his boyhood family of origin. He recounted the searing experience of being the target of constant criticism from his parents about his spending habits with scolding entreaties to "be more like your older brother." The very mention of spending and budget by Esther triggered a well of overwhelming negative feelings for Reggie, feelings of shame, defensiveness, incompetence, and inferiority that went back to a childhood of always feeling like he didn't measure up to his "responsible" and thrifty older brother. Behaviorally, this tended to make Reggie respond to the sense of shame and embarrassment with highly defensive and even antagonistic responses. In those moments with Esther, he felt as if he were a little boy being chastised by his parents for not being more like his role-model brother.

Diagnostically, there was something very important for Reggie to assert—but it wasn't an argument about the merits or demerits of his approach to budgeting, buying art, or spending money. Rather, it was asserting the *feelings* that came up for him when Esther brought up this conversation.

If Reggie and Esther were ever to have an actual and productive conversation about the way they wanted to handle expenses and budgeting, they would first need to figure out how Esther could bring up her genuine concerns in a way that did not send Reggie through a time warp twenty years into the past. When Bob asked Reggie, "Do you think Esther has any idea this is happening when she brings this up?" he said, "Of course not! I'm not sure I even did until you asked me to 'say more.' But this wave of emotions, especially of shame and inferiority, do flood me in those moments." "And do you think if you shared this with her that she'd use it against you?" "No, definitely not. Part of what is so hard for me is that I generally love working with Esther. It's just that these issues around spending money tend to get us so bollixed up. I often worry they will be the downfall of our collaboration. That's why I'm here paying you. If we can figure this out, we'd be better than ever!"

Only when Reggie found a way to assert the *emotions* that came up for him when Esther criticized his spending decisions could he have any hope for a productive discussion around budgeting.

Imagine how different this assertion might be:

**Reggie:** Esther, I was wondering if you and I could talk a bit about some of the times we disagree on spending and finance issues and, in particular, some of the things that often go on for me that I think contribute to why things escalate and we get stuck.

**Esther:** Um. OK. This feels weird. Are you finally willing to admit that you just spend money irresponsibly?

**Reggie:** Well, I wanted to talk less about the merits of your views on this and just more on how I experience the conversations. I know this will be a bit strange. I also think it is important and that it might help us both have better conversations about this in the future.

**Esther:** Sure. Yes. I'm all for that.

**Reggie:** OK. Thanks. What I wanted to share with you is the strong set of emotions that overwhelm me when you bring up a critique, question, or observation about my spending. I am pretty confident that you are coming from a genuine place of concern and frustration with me. I've felt that. And yet, when

I hear this from you, I get stuck. I'm unable to acknowledge what's going on with you. Instead, I find myself feeling strong emotions of shame, guilt, defensiveness, and insecurity. And I think this dynamic is what ends up contributing to the breakdown between us.

**Esther:** Well, I think you're overreacting. I clearly don't mean to make you feel shame.

**Reggie:** Yes, I know that. But that is what I feel. And the reason why, I think, is that it sends me back to my childhood and, specifically, to my parents' constant criticism of me for being financially irresponsible in comparison to my brother. To this day, every time I buy something new—even if it's reasonable—I hear them say, "Oh, there goes Reggie. Spending like money grows on trees." I know you don't intend to bring up these strong emotions in me, but that is what is happening on the inside. And so, on the outside, I end up getting defensive, and, frankly, sometimes downright mean, and we just have an unproductive squabble. I thought it was important to share this with you.

**Esther:** Well, I definitely don't mean to do that to you. I'm sorry about that. But we do need to find some way to talk about budget and finances, so I don't know what to do . . .

**Reggie:** I agree that we have to talk about this and there has to be a way for you to raise your concerns. And that's what I want to talk about—some way that not only allows you to bring this up so that I can hear it, but also in a way that doesn't trigger the emotional cascade internally. I think if we can figure this out, we'll be able to have more productive conversations about your concerns. I'm not sure we'll always agree on the merits, but I do think I can learn more about your concerns in a way that doesn't just make me stop listening and shut down. I really want to figure out how we can tackle this together. What do you think?

**Esther:** Of course, Reggie. Thanks for raising this. I'm sure it's hard for you to feel like you are time-warped into a childhood drama and, like you, I care about having productive conversations together about this instead of the same old fight.

In our work and experience, Reggie's assertion challenge is not unique. We have found that for as often as parties are asserting positions when they should instead be asserting interests, there are times when they are asserting *interests*, *facts*, or *arguments* when they should instead be asserting their *feelings*.

One of the surest signs that someone doesn't understand how to handle conflict is when they urge, "Stick to the facts and be rational." Or "Keep the feelings out of it." The truth is, sometimes we can't get to a useful or productive conversation about substantive interests until we discuss the feelings. Sometimes we can't even really discover all of our interests until we work through the mess of the feelings. Pretending feelings are irrelevant, not there, or "not appropriate" ignores the reality of what is making a particular conflict hard to engage. Being conflict resilient means having the courage to tread new ground in our differences with others. It invites a rawness and a vulnerability that also opens up new space for connection, possibility, and transformation.

Our emotional responses to stressors might seem like the natural ebb and flow of life—sometimes we feel overwhelmed, sometimes we take things in stride. But beneath these responses lie intricate neural patterns and molecular reactions that can shape our health. Researchers, including psychologist Sarah Master and her team at UCLA, have tried to understand how coping by acknowledging and expressing emotion plays a role in our neurobiological responses.

A term used often in this work is *EAC*—Emotional Approach Coping. In this method, a person confronted with stress not only leans into emotions, processes them, and expresses them, but also does so with conscious intention. The EAC approach has three key steps: *identification of emotions, processing those emotions*, and *expressing those emotions*—all done with conscious intention.

*Identification* means developing an awareness of a full range of feelings that you may be experiencing in a given moment. For example, you might be highly aware of being angry but conscious intention makes you also aware that you feel lonely, worried, sad, and confused at the same time. *Processing* entails using mindful awareness or meta-cognition to help identify the cause and source of those emotions. Processing can look like talking about feelings or writing in a journal. For example, in a conflict over abortion rights, if your counterpart says, "You have no idea what you're talking about," you may become aware of both anger and self-doubt. The cause is partly what the counterpart said to you, but processing invites you to go deeper and become aware that, in general, when you're accused of not having expertise or knowledge, self-doubt bubbles up, causing you to either cave or shut down. The processing of the emotions allows you to identify patterns across a lifetime of experience. In addition, seeing the pattern makes it easier for you to have more autonomy over how you chose to respond to those emotions. Finally, *expressing* involves making the conscious decision to share the full range of your emotions, whether with the counterpart or in some other way.

Master's team had an intriguing hypothesis that people who lean into this EAC method might show brain activity that is often seen in people who are motivated to acknowledge and approach stress, rather than avoid it, and which is generally associated with better physical and mental health. Compared to those who do not use EAC, they also hypothesized that those who do might demonstrate healthier responses on a molecular level, especially concerning measures of inflammation and stress. To unpack this, forty-six participants were asked about their emotional processing and expression habits when faced with stress. The study then mapped their brain patterns using a brain-wave test called electroencephalography (EEG). A subset of these individuals also had their oral fluids tested for certain stress and inflammation markers before and after being exposed to a laboratory-induced stressor.

The results of the study offer a window into the nuanced interplay between communicating our emotions and our physiology. People who more often expressed their emotions displayed more left-sided frontal EEG asymmetry. Individuals who are more motivated to confront stress directly have often been found to have this kind of brain activity. Moreover, those who leaned into EAC, especially the emotional processing, had a reduced inflammatory response to stress. In such individuals, levels of a molecule linked to inflammation and cell death (TNF-$\alpha$) were lower compared to those who did not use EAC. Overall, the left-sided frontal EEG asymmetry was linked to markers of the body's inflammatory stress response, suggesting that people who were more EAC-oriented were generally better shielded against the potentially harmful effects of stress—before, during, and even after stressful events.

The bottom line is that the way we approach our emotions, especially during times of stress, is intertwined with our neurobiology, potentially sculpting our neural patterns and physiological reactions. It reminds us that truly understanding our emotions is a journey that goes beyond the mind, reaching deep into the very molecules that constitute our being.

That said, we would be remiss if we gave the impression that asserting feelings is a panacea. We often turn to our closest allies, our partners, or counselors during times of stress. In moments of duress, asserting our emotions and seeking comfort might seem instinctive. But does the act of emotional expression always offer relief? Does the support from a loved one always yield the comfort or breakthroughs we hope for? A study led by Heidi Kane, associate professor of behavioral and brain sciences at University of Texas at Dallas, examined these intricate emotional dynamics, revealing unexpected insights.

Couples were brought into a lab, with one partner chosen to undertake a stressful task. Some participants were allowed to express their feelings about the task, while others kept their feelings bottled up. Similarly, some received supportive messages from their partners, acting as a surrogate for real-world support, while others went without. Those participants high in EAC, the individuals who typically lean into their emotions and assert them, showed a surprising reaction. When they expressed their feelings to their partners, their stress indicators, like cortisol and salivary alpha-amylase, skyrocketed. Moreover, they ruminated more on the stressful task afterward. Fortunately, when their partners offered support, the cortisol levels seemed to settle. Meanwhile, as you might expect, those low in EAC (the folks who aren't as accustomed to asserting their emotions) experienced the opposite. Upon expressing their feelings, their stress markers dipped and they felt fewer negative emotions.

But here's a twist: the influence of partner support added a complex layer. Although partner support reduced the negative emotions for those high in EAC, it *increased* negative emotions for those low in EAC.

What does this mean? Emotional dynamics are deeply personal, and asserting emotions does not work for everyone all the time and in all contexts. One size does not fit all. For some, leaning into emotions and expressing them, especially without the cushion of support, can exacerbate stress. For others, the mere act of sharing provides solace.

However, rather than simply accepting that it's personal, there are steps you can take to navigate these dynamics more effectively:

1. *Know Your Style:* Reflect on the specific scenarios where your tendency for EAC is high or low. Understanding your tendencies can help you anticipate how you might react and better prepare for specific conflict situations.

2. *Communicate Needs:* If you are high in EAC, let your counterpart (or other ideal supportive person in your life) know that you may need reassurance and support after expressing your emotions. Conversely, if you are low in EAC, communicate that you might need space after sharing to process your feelings independently.

3. *Practice Self-Compassion:* Whatever your style, practice self-compassion. Accept that it's OK to feel stressed—the goal is to gradually improve how you manage your emotions, not to avoid feeling emotions or to always remain perfectly rational.

4. *Seek Professional Guidance:* If you find it challenging to navigate these dynamics, consider seeking support from a therapist or counselor who can provide personalized strategies to help you manage stress and emotional expression.

These complex dynamics underscore the nuanced nature of human emotions and how we relate with one another. Your well-being depends not only on whether you express or suppress emotions, but also on your coping styles and the presence of supportive counterparts. By understanding your EAC tendencies and clearly communicating your needs, you can navigate emotional expression more effectively across various conflict situations and likely strengthen your relationships.

Overall, in building capacity for conflict resilience, the wisdom of moving from positions to interests applies as much as ever. But so too does the important work of identifying the emotions that conflict brings up for you and finding ways—especially ways that are unique to you and your situation in the moment—to assert those feelings with authenticity and integrity.

## SPEAK YOUR TRUTH AS YOUR PERSPECTIVE AND YOURS ALONE

The stories of southern governors busing unwitting migrants to northern cities and dumping them at random landmarks or in front of city halls in northern cities cut to Muna's soul. For her, the inhumanity of it was too much to bear. Her roommate and best friend from college was undocumented and she had a firsthand account of the fear and intimidation that thousands face when they flee their homeland to come to the U.S. for safety, protection, and a better life. She also had a lively, if secondhand, sense of the enormous courage that taking such a journey requires.

As a result, visiting her family in Arizona for the holidays always felt challenging; Muna loved her family. But her family stood on the opposite side of the political spectrum when it came to U.S. immigration policy. For Muna's parents and siblings, undocumented persons were illegal immigrants who often took jobs from those who came to the States legally and whose presence hurt low-wage workers in the U.S. If these people refused to come to the U.S. legally, they needed to be sent back to deter others from coming to the U.S. outside a legal process. Practically no tactic, including coerced busing to northern cities and family separation, was outside her family's list of "acceptable measures of law enforcement." From her family's perspective, enforcing the law was an act of justice and integrity, not one of cruelty. Only Muna's willingness to bite her tongue, breathe deeply, and say something placating to bring tempers down kept the family from descending into chaos at times.

But not this year. This year, Muna was determined to find a way to speak her mind to her family to show them how wrongheaded and even inhumane their thinking was on this issue. She wanted to preserve the relationship with her family. But not at the expense of losing her soul.

"Facts are facts," she declared, "and I have to get these otherwise good people out of their media bubble and their parochial thinking."

This time, Muna was ready for the showdown.

Even if Muna's "hot button" issue or her opinion on it isn't similar to your own, most of us can relate her predicament to one we've been in. Someone in your life—a colleague, a fellow board member, a life-long friend—persists in a belief or a viewpoint that you see as somewhere between wrongheaded and deranged; you've endured it for a while, perhaps changing the topic, joining where you could find a shared point of agreement or offering an alternate opinion without really digging in. But as time goes on, you feel something important is being lost. In the case of someone with whom you have a light or impermanent touchpoint, you might let it go and perhaps just let the relationship fade. But in the case of enduring friendships, close work colleagues, or family, you are more and more stuck. It gets harder the more personal it is: your daughter insists on having your grandson vaccinated while you are convinced that vaccines are unnecessary and dangerous; your spouse is so committed to supporting public schools that they are ready to send your son to the most abysmal school in a nearly failing public school district rather than spend the money you've both been saving to send him to a high-quality private academy with values aligned with your own; your sister—wise and rational in most respects—refuses to join the rest of the family on your annual vacation in Florida because of the issues she has with the state's "don't say gay" policy and its controversial approach to teaching American history.

As in Tania's and Reggie's examples, each of the above contexts is an opportunity for effective assertion in the context of conflict resilience. But unlike Tania and Reggie, the assertion called for in such situations is categorically different in form and requires a different type of preparation. While it is easy to see Muna's assertion example as like Tania's (i.e., my substantive interest is to persuade family members that I am right and they are wrong) or Reggie's (I need to let them know of my passion, fury, anger, and worry), the nature of the issue and the context for Muna taps into something deeper and unique, making this type of assertion particularly challenging to do well. Unlike assertion relating to a substantive interest or an emotion, the challenge here is how to assert something that you are persuaded is true and correct when you are almost 100 percent certain the others in the conversation will always see it quite differently. From a purely analytic perspective, it's unlikely and hardly defensible in a basic negotiation like Tania's for the other party to counter her by saying, "It is not in your substantive interest to get a fair salary." That person may disagree with you about what the fair salary is, but a conversation about whether a "fair salary" is or is not in Tania's interest crosses the line into absurdity. Similarly, it's one thing for Esther to say, "Some people would not feel shame in a situation like this, Reggie." It's quite another for her to say, "I disagree. You do not feel shame, Reggie." The latter response, again, is somewhere between absurd and offensive.

But for Muna, the very nature of the thing she needs to assert about—what is the best immigration policy and what is an appropriate way to enforce it—is one that feels objectively clear, perhaps even with moral and ethical red lines that feel nonnegotiable. And yet, what's complicated is that there is an almost certain chance that her counterpart will disagree and see the ethics and morality very differently. This difference might call into question more than just, "How can we live with the discomfort of our disagreement?" but also, "Do we each see the other as a good person?" or "Are you really a member of this family?" or "How can you be a patriotic American who supports democracy and liberty with a view like that?"

When Muna says, "It is wrong for governors of southern states to bus migrants to New York or Los Angeles or Chicago," her relatives will surely disagree by saying some version of "No, it is perfectly appropriate," or maybe even "It's the best strategy to solve this problem."

How can Muna—or any of us—effectively assert a position that feels absolutely true to her, knowing that her family members hold an opposing view that may alter the story she tells about who they are, their values, and even whether they are a good person?

## ASSERTION IN PRACTICE

Luckily, there are practical "at the table" guidelines that can increase your chances of success and help you assert yourself more effectively. However, asserting deeply held beliefs and viewpoints tied to core aspects of identity remains one of the toughest challenges. Whether you're advocating for your interests in a business negotiation, expressing vulnerable emotions that might cause distress, or standing up for beliefs central to your identity, here are some practical steps that can guide you:

1. Listen deeply *first* to assert strategically
2. Assert fully—your data, reasoning, and conclusion
3. Avoid absolutes and sweeping generalizations

### 1. Listen Deeply *First* to Assert Strategically

As part of the corporate reorg, Kit's Commercial Marketing division was going to merge with his colleague Tabitha's Content Creation division. Both Kit and Tabitha were vying to head what would become a single, newly merged group. At a weekly all-hands meeting with their boss, Tabitha pointedly asked Kit, "It's clear you want to be the leader of the combined group after our reorg. What makes you think this role should go to you?"

Having already thought through the reasons why he should be group leader, Kit responded with his strongest and most persuasive case of why he was uniquely situated to lead the combined group going forward. On the rational merits, Kit had good reasons and facts. And he delivered his reasons in a clear and confident tone.

What could be wrong with this?

Perhaps nothing.

On the other hand, *assertion is most effective when it follows deep listening and is tailored to what is learned from that listening.*

Embedded in Tabitha's question is so much more than an inquiry about the rational reasons behind Kit's case. Does she want to undermine him? Make her own case? Perhaps she is worried about the challenges of working under him rather than as a lateral colleague? Maybe she just wants to make sure she'll still have the autonomy she needs to do her job? Or that she'll be able to finish her projects and protect her team? Perhaps she doesn't actually want to lead the team; she's just curious whether she prefers the familiar choice of Kit taking on the leadership role or if she'd rather the company conduct an external search. By immediately launching into his response, Kit loses an important opportunity for what we call *targeted assertion:* this is assertion that is aimed at the real concerns, worries, and interests of the person on the other side.

Imagine if Kit just said, "Tabitha, yes, I'd love to lead the new division and it sounds as if you have some thoughts. Or maybe even concerns on this? As you think about who should lead this, what qualities do you think matter and how can I be best responsive to what is behind your question?"

Here Kit is direct at the same time he is curious. He demonstrates a willingness to answer Tabitha's question but is seeking useful information that will allow him to be truly responsive to whatever concerns, interests, or worries she may have.

*Targeted assertion* is powerful because it is responsive to the needs, interests, and concerns of the person with whom you are in conflict. Rather than assume what you think is or should be meaningful or persuasive, by listening first, you learn what really matters so you can make a more thoughtful effort at assertion.

The other advantage to listening first is that it slows down the interaction—whether it's a brewing conflict or disagreement or just a tension point—allowing for a more mindful consideration of whatever information you are providing and reducing the likelihood of a tit-for-tat escalation that can turn assertiveness into aggression.

As discussed in Chapter 3, slowing down the action in a conflict situation and allowing for reflection can help move the focus of brain activity from the threat-detecting limbic system of the brain to the more deliberative and self-regulating systems based in frontal-lobe brain networks.

Similarly, listening first to better understand the emotional valence of what your counterpart is perceiving about the situation can strengthen your assertion and doubly serve as a catalyst to also strengthen the relationship between the two of you. Imagine if Kit had listened to Tabitha's concerns and she had shared that she was frustrated about all the changes going on so quickly and how she had been feeling so powerless in shaping the future of the newly merged division. Kit could respond, "It makes sense that you would feel both frustrated and powerless. I've had similar feelings as well about the process behind the reorg, which is also why I feel so motivated to lead the new division and really establish a greater sense of direction and consistency for the team."

This may seem like such a simple statement, but beyond Kit reasserting his interests, what is also happening beneath the surface of this verbal acknowledgment of Tabitha's feelings? Researcher Alisa Yu and her colleagues studied the dynamics of workplace emotions to discover how such acknowledgments might build interpersonal trust among colleagues.

Her team examined these dynamics through the lens of "Costly Signaling Theory." It's the idea that some actions, though they might seem trivial, send strong signals about a person's motivations and intentions. The act of verbally acknowledging someone's emotions, as Yu and her team hypothesized, might be one such "costly signal." It suggests that the recognizer is willing to go the extra mile, to spend personal resources, to understand and support the individual expressing the emotion. Over the span of six studies, the researchers found consistent evidence supporting their hypothesis. When someone acknowledged the emotions of another, it was perceived as a significant gesture, signaling genuine effort and understanding. This, in turn, amplified feelings of trust between the two individuals.

But here's where it gets even juicier. The act of acknowledging negative emotions was seen as more "costly" than acknowledging positive ones. In essence, noting someone's distress or frustration carried more weight and built more trust than recognizing their happiness or excitement. But be careful and be sure to apply deep listening as intentionally as possible too. The studies showed that getting it wrong could have varied outcomes. Although mislabeling negative emotions as positive didn't have the same trust-building effect, don't fear getting it wrong too much—misidentifying someone's positive emotions as negative still led to building more trust than not recognizing the emotions at all. These findings reveal a subtle connection between emotion, language, and trust in our personal and professional relationships. Recognizing and expressing others' feelings, especially during difficult times, can strengthen bonds and build trust.

Part of the goal of *targeted assertion* is to be able to make one's point in a way that enhances the chances it will be heard and received positively to prevent a "fight" escalation, or any other default reaction among the five Fs. The other goal is to enhance the level of trust and connection in the relationship. When assertion is responsive to the expressed needs of the person with whom you're speaking, it is way more likely to be received positively even if it doesn't lead them to agree with your view of the situation.

## 2. Assert Fully—Your Data, Reasoning, and Conclusion

- "I think you're just wrong about this."
- "In my view, climate change is beyond human control, a natural phenomenon that no one can stop, start, or change."
- "She needs to be held accountable."

- "Your decision to pursue this in court is a big mistake."
- "I really think I'm being undercompensated for my work here."
- "This book is just awful."
- "The United States is weaker and more unstable now than it was four years ago."

On their own, each of the statements above is a fight waiting to happen—or an invitation to connect around a shared viewpoint—depending on whether the conversational counterpart agrees or disagrees with the speaker. Assertive statements like those above seem to be all around us, whether they are about banal topics—"This ice cream is delicious!"—or consequential ones: "There is no way I will ever agree to the notion that the government erasing college debt is a good idea!" These assertions can be problematic not because of the specific opinion that they might represent, but because they are offered as definitive conclusions—the endpoints of a thought process. Yet, if you listen carefully, you'll note that most assertive statements are nothing more than a conclusion conveyed without data or support.

The truth is that any assessment, conclusion, feeling, or observation we may make about a situation, a relationship, an event, or an organization is formed within the constraints of (1) what is possible for any human being to observe and notice, (2) the meaning they make about what they observe, and (3) the conclusions they draw from the mental interaction between observation and meaning-making. It is critical to note that as humans, the limits of what we can observe and notice are *substantial*. Even as our most objective and thorough selves, we humans miss most of what is happening around us. As much as we'd like to believe we have exceptional powers of observation, we are not comic book superheroes and so we are necessarily subject to both partial *and* partisan perceptions. Our perceptions are *partial* because we humans are simply not capable of noticing and observing *everything* in our purview at a given time, no matter how hard we try. And our perceptions are *partisan* or biased because what we do notice or perceive tends to be influenced by preexisting notions in our mind about what is important, relevant, or interesting to us.

For example, we invite you to look around the space you're in right now. Make a list of all the things around you that are the color blue.

Take a good thirty seconds to do this.

When you are done, close your eyes and then call out (or make a mental note of) everything around you that is the color GREEN.

Now, as you open your eyes and without looking around you, call out everything around you that is BLUE.

If you are like most people, your list of items that are BLUE is significantly longer than the list of what is green. Moreover, it's our guess you recalled the blue items much more quickly. The reason is obvious. We invited you to spend thirty or more seconds observing all the things around you that were blue before asking you to close your eyes. So it's natural that if you did a good job following our instructions, your list of blue-colored items would be lengthy. But that doesn't mean that the green items weren't also there. It's just that we didn't draw your attention to them. This doesn't make you awful at observation. It just highlights the fact that we are more likely to notice and observe information that is important to us or whose salience has been raised for us in some way and to dismiss information that is less interesting, relevant, or valuable. This is a critical driver for why we are all prone to partial and partisan perceptions.

Researchers Chris Argyris and Don Schön and their colleagues at Action Design developed a tool called the Ladder of Inference to help individuals improve their ability to assert more constructively in conflict situations by working their way up the rungs of the ladder as they assert themselves, sharing what led up to the conclusion they've derived at the top of the ladder. The steps of the ladder are the following from top to bottom:

**"The Ladder of Inference."**

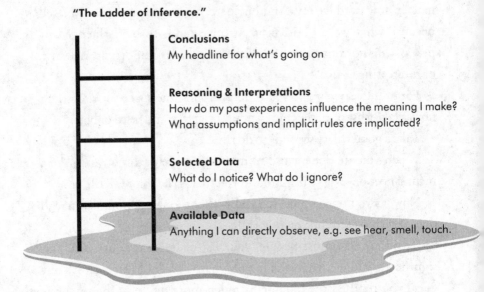

**Conclusions**
My headline for what's going on

**Reasoning & Interpretations**
How do my past experiences influence the meaning I make?
What assumptions and implicit rules are implicated?

**Selected Data**
What do I notice? What do I ignore?

**Available Data**
Anything I can directly observe, e.g. see hear, smell, touch.

For most of us, we tend to speak and assert ourselves from the top of the ladder without giving others the opportunity to understand how we got there, which would likely allow for much more informative dialogue marked by some mutual learning as the parties "worked each other's ladders," exploring the observed data and reasoning that each used to support their conclusions.

In most complex and controversial situations that lead to conflict, there is a vast array of inputs—an ocean of information. The ocean is so overwhelmingly huge that it is simply impossible for humans to notice and observe everything going on in a particular space at the same time. This is the "available data" that is at the bottom of the ladder. And we are all swimming in oceans of data that are too wide and deep—well beyond our capacity to capture fully.

Even worse, our brain's spotlight of attention is much narrower than you might assume, so we tend to only notice things that are salient or interesting to us, particularly those pieces of information or data that support our previously-held viewpoint (confirmation bias), that might be relevant to what's on our mind, or that strike us as useful for a specific interaction. This is the next rung on the ladder, the "Selected Data: What do I notice? What do I ignore?"

Also, we tend to miss or at times even ignore things that we deem unimportant, not relevant to us, or simply not on our radar. This is not necessarily because we are purposefully manipulating or actively trying to see things the wrong way. It's just a function of the collision between human limitation and individual interest. Examples of this are manifold in our day-to-day world. Because Bob has often taught young adults in their early to mid-twenties in a large lecture hall, he notices from the front of the room how on the first day of class there is a nontrivial number of students who are scanning their classmates across the lecture hall, scoping out who might be attractive and then scanning to see if they're wearing a wedding ring. Others, perhaps those already with wedding rings, aren't spending much time glancing at the hands of their classmates. The reality of a wedding ring is still there, but their brains are not clocking that particular feature of their classmates because it's unlikely to be registering with them as interesting or relevant information to their already happily coupled selves at that moment. They have a current mate.

Though this is a silly example, the point is that in just about any given context or conflict situation, we tend to notice details that give us useful information about a situation or the other person. We notice what seems important, relevant, or interesting to us. Even worse, as we mentioned before, because of the psychological heuristic termed confirmation bias, we are more likely to notice the data that supports our own view of the situation. And we tend to ignore, dismiss, or downplay data that is inconsistent with or that undermines our own preexisting perception.

Once we have selected a bit of data, we are quick to fill in blanks to tell a fuller story about the person, issue, organization, or situation—or all of the above. And the story we tell is typically based on our own history, past experience, and implicit and explicit beliefs. And, like it or not, these beliefs are full of bias.

Consider an example. What immediately comes to your mind if . . .

I tell you I am religious?
I tell you I am vegetarian?
I tell you I am a sport hunter?
I tell you I own a golden retriever?
I tell you I own a Chihuahua?
I tell you I am American?
I tell you I am Syrian?

Our guess is that each descriptor above conjures up an image of a specific kind of person—based on a single data point. The image or story in your head right now for each of these persons is based on your history and experience in the world—assumptions we have perhaps about religious people we know, or about religious figures like the pope or the archbishop of Canterbury, or stereotypes in the media, or maybe our own experience being a person of faith. Similarly, our image of an American and our image of a Syrian might be based on images from popular media, our lived experience, or what we know about the Syrian Civil War, for example. And to be clear, given your very specific lived experience, the images you have of the religious person, the vegetarian, the sport hunter, the golden retriever or Chihuahua owner, the American, or the Syrian are valid to you. They are based on something real in your lived experience.

But of course, whatever image or story that came to your mind, this is your own reasoning and interpretation of data and not the *only* way to paint the picture of any person. In fact, there is no reason to believe that the image that came to your mind has any more validity or objective truth than the one that might come up in the mind of someone reading this book next to you, apart from the fact that your image is based on your own experience. Anyone who is being honest with themselves must admit that their image is not necessarily a bad one or wrong, it's just not necessarily the whole truth or a full and accurate picture. It is a product of the stew in which we were raised and live—a complex amalgam of family, culture, school, nationality, economic background, and personal experience.

The observation that a simple adjective can conjure up a whole set of assumptions is an important one when it comes to being effectively assertive in conflict and negotiation. To get through the world, we tend to speak and think in simplified terms. We are apt to share only the top rung of the Ladder of Inference—our conclusion or our short headline about what is going on. For example, "The United States is a beacon of freedom and democracy," or "The United States perpetuates the legacy of colonialism, war, and cultural appropriation."

But to be effective in your assertion, you need to do more than just share your headline. *You need to share the data you observed in the universe along with the reasoning or meaning you made of it and then how that led to the conclusion you have drawn from the data and meaning-making.* This is what we mean when we say "assert fully."

In a heated conflict, we tend to assert little more than our top-of-the-ladder conclusions. We start and end with a declaration. We plant our flag in the conversation and then prepare to defend it against the world. This increasingly common kind of assertion leads to polarization, balkanization, unnecessary alienation, starved relationships, and less common ground. Importantly, it also misses out on the learning and surprise that can come from hearing others' conclusions, reasoning, and data. Instead of fostering a culture of constructive disagreement through meaningful dialogue, it merely intensifies demonization and dehumanization. The benefits of diversity and difference fade as we fall back into the five Fs.

When we can "work the ladder" in our assertion, we increase the likelihood of promoting a more generative and open learning conversation with those with whom we find ourselves in conflict. Even if there is little chance of changing our conclusion or persuading our counterpart to change theirs, the very act of sharing the data we observed and the reasoning we used to put a narrative onto that data helps clarify our own thinking and helps us identify with greater precision the fuller story behind the disagreement we seem to have with each other. Almost always, this promotes a salubrious humanization and empathy for the other person. Also, at times it can help each of us get a fuller picture of the messiness of the reality of the situation. Even better, it sometimes helps parties forge a way forward by identifying opportunities for collaboration and joint work even if conclusions remain as different as ever. Ultimately, this approach to assertion is what helps us come together in a conflicted world. It is what helps us negotiate disagreement without giving up or giving in.

If you are prone to an evidence- or data-based approach to decision-making and seeing the world, you are likely to find the Ladder of Inference an extremely attractive way to assert. But if you tend to reach conclusions from a more intuitive or "inner gut" sort of way, you might be quite turned off by the approach. "What happens if I don't have specific data to support my viewpoint?" In his struggle to define hard-core pornography in his 1964 concurring opinion in *Jacobellis v. Ohio*, Justice Potter Stewart simply said, "I know it when I see it."

If you are an "I know it when I see it" kind of person, we feel your struggle with this tool. The Ladder of Inference isn't always a perfect solution for building the skill of effective assertion. We don't want to diminish or downplay the value of intuition, one's gut sense of what's right or true. Anyone who has ever fallen head-over-heels in love can appreciate that sometimes there is something ephemeral and intangible—more a vibe than a piece of admissible evidence—that defies the logic of the Ladder of Inference. But this doesn't diminish the value of the tool. Whenever we are ready to assert something— "You're wrong!" or "They're criminals" or "The mainstream media is completely woke"—it's critical to take a step back and ask ourselves: Where is this conclusion coming from? What have we observed? What story have we put on it? And if it's less about specific observations in the world, we might ask ourselves, "What from our inner intuitive sense is guiding this conclusion?" Even sharing that intuitive or gut sense and where it comes from is a more edifying and productive way to assert than simply doubling down on your conclusion over and over again.

### 3. Avoid Absolutes and Sweeping Generalizations

One of the biggest "assertion" traps, especially as things get heated in a fight or conflict, is the allure of a generalization. Note: What we really wanted to say above is, "generalizations *always* backfire . . ." but then we thought the better of it!

In the heat of a fight, generalizations about the other person can often fly off the tongue:

*"Why are you always so quick to think this is part of a vast right-wing conspiracy?"*

*"Why do you see every idea we have about what your major should be as an attempt at control?"*

Using *always*, *never*, and similar all-encompassing globalizations tends to backfire in negotiation and other contentious contexts where conflicting views and experience are in play. Yet they are so tempting to use.

What's wrong with them?

First, sweeping generalizations tend to distract from the substance of our argument, making it harder for the person on the receiving end of the comment to discern the merit of what you are sharing. Instead of a serious conversation on the merits of immigration policy, or what's troubling about your parents' counsel, or a potentially poisonous dynamic that is occurring in your organization, a sweeping generalization ends up spinning the conversation into one about characterizing another's essence or being. And it invites snarky responses rather than thoughtfulness from the recipient of the generalization.

"What can I say? Since the election of Richard Nixon, conservative Republicans are always racist, sexist, and homophobic" is apt to elicit a defensive response, perhaps backed by a slew of examples when the general statement was untrue: "It was conservative Republican Ronald

Reagan who nominated the first woman to the Supreme Court and Republican George H. W. Bush who nominated the second African American ever to that same court" would be an unsurprising retort to the above all-encompassing example. The use of the word *always* ends up sending the conversation off course and onto a factual tangent that, in most cases, misses the meat of what might otherwise be a useful discussion that addresses the heart of what the real issues might be in each situation.

Stating that your spouse "never cooks or does the dishes" distracts from the real issue and invites a fight, overshadowing the more critical and truthful value of your message: you are frustrated that they rarely help with cooking or doing the dishes. In most cases, the issue isn't whether your spouse has *ever* offered to do the dishes or cook you a meal. Rather, it's about the meaning behind your observation that a specific task or set of tasks in the house tends to fall to one person and what that says about the relationship, about the allocation of duties in the house, and about your mutual expectations and hopes for each other. The real conflict—and the harder conversation—is about the meaning-making that is involved in the "doing of the dishes" and less about whether one spouse has ever (or never) done them. But when we hurl the generalization "You *never* do the dishes unless I ask you," the real conversation that requires true conflict resilience—the one about vulnerabilities, emotions, insecurities, and meaning-making— gets brushed under the rug in exchange for a backward-looking fact-checking investigation about dishwashing behaviors over the past few months of the relationship. Sweeping generalizations often shut down the possibility for a hard conversation requiring conflict resilience. Instead, such generalizations invite a predictable script of accusations and denials that are well-scripted if not also deeply dissatisfying. They rarely leave anyone feeling good even if they have the benefit of leading to a predictable outcome of exhaustion and dismay on all sides.

A more effective approach to assertion would sound like, "I've often observed that I end up doing the dishes and cooking unless I ask for help. I wonder if we can talk about this, and how it has made me feel. I'm honestly curious to learn more about how you see the situation."

An opening like this would likely be experienced as disorienting or maybe even stilted by a counterpart unaccustomed to this shift in language and tone. Yet it's likely to at least make the other person pause and, assuming they are reasonably invested in the relationship, give a nod of assent despite lingering skepticism.

You might need to continue with, "I think talking about this might be awkward and somewhat uncomfortable for me—and maybe for you too. At the same time, I realize that this dynamic has made me wonder about how we allocate chores and wanting to find a way to talk it through with you. When might be a good time for me to share more and also to hear your reaction to this?"

Similarly, imagine saying, "I often feel that Republicans' policy preferences are racist, sexist, and xenophobic. I know these are strong charges and I have some reasons why I've come to think this. I'm curious, first, what is your reaction to what I'm saying and, second, if I can share some more about how I've come to see things this way?"

We are *not* saying that our recharacterization is going to increase consensus or agreement on the issue, although we don't put that result outside of what's possible. But what we *are* saying is that by avoiding a sweeping generalization, you can proceed more deeply and constructively into a genuine exploration of the conflict and differences that you have with your counterpart. This approach requires real conflict resilience in a way that spewing absolutes and sweeping generalization doesn't.

Speaking to specific examples and broadening the nature of the conversation requires resilience, because engaging the deeper issues makes us vulnerable to the possibility of more hurt. What if you learn that the other person in the relationship really does take you for granted and doesn't care about how you see it? That would likely be worse than the performative, fact-based debate of who does the dishes when. At the same time, the new approach also opens us up to the possibility of more genuine connection, understanding, and, in many cases, joint problem-solving. The more effective framing of your assertion will almost certainly require more vulnerability, more discomfort, and more courage than the tit-for-tat fight (or dismissive eye roll) that an "always" or "never" statement brings.

## PUTTING IT ALL TOGETHER: LISTENING AND ASSERTION

In *Beyond Winning: Negotiating to Create Value in Deals and Disputes*, Robert H. Mnookin and his colleagues discuss what they coin as a tension between empathy and assertiveness. In Mnookin's view, negotiators need to somehow balance or trade off on the advantages of empathy and the requirement to assert one's needs to get what they want. At one level, we are sympathetic to the notion that there might be a tension between empathy and assertion in negotiation and conflict resolution. But in our view, the tension is illusory and unreal. Or perhaps more accurately stated, at times you might feel that empathy and assertion are at odds with each other and yet that's unlikely to be the case when you take the time to reflect, prepare, and be more mindful in your approach to conflict, negotiation, and difference. Much like the coordination of movements between opposing muscles so you can lift a table, carry a baby, or dance, to be truly conflict resilient, skills of patient, generous, and open deep listening come together in harmony with an ability for assertion through balanced integration, not opposing tension.

At any given moment in a conflict, listening, asserting, or both might feel nearly impossible. And for each of us, we may have some natural strengths and challenges for one or both of these skills. For most of us, our ability to listen and to assert is a complex combination of innate personality, upbringing, and context. Given that avoidance, canceling, and escape have become so easy and commonly pain-free (at least in the moment we experience the choice between entering the conflict or escaping), the invitation to build skills of deep listening and effective assertion can feel far from inviting. In those moments, everything in our brains goads us on toward the escape hatch. Yet to halt the deterioration of our society and to capitalize on the possibilities of vibrant and diverse organizations and families, it is incumbent on us to do the hard and uncomfortable work of both listening and sharing our own perspective.

There exists a fundamental principle for performers in the vulnerable space of improv and theater: "See and be seen." For Joel and other people like him who have a natural bias to avoid conflict or who tend to worry about whether they're being too aggressive in disagreement, it's a mantra and a guiding star. "See and be seen" serves as a poignant reminder of our innate human desire for connection and recognition. It's not just about the spotlight on the stage, but the profound interplay of giving and receiving genuine attention, of truly being present. This is where the magic of true collaboration and connection unfolds. Practically speaking, think about it—you're onstage, and if you're not "seen," both in the real sense and in that deeper, metaphorical sense, you fade into the background, hiding or holding back from allowing yourself the hard job of being "seen." Then, what happens to your piece of the story? Lost. Even more, you risk the *authenticity* of your own voice being lost. On the flip side, if you're not "seeing," if you're not locking into that connection with your fellow performers, the narrative, the very people you're there for—the audience—well, you're not really there at all either, are you? You lose the chance to truly connect with the story, the meaning, and the people who come, in their own quest, to both see and be seen. It's in this dynamic of seeing and being seen that we find the heart of not just theater, but human connection.

Combining deep listening and effective assertion at times when you find yourself in deep conflict will not be comfortable. It will entail really deploying the "brain hacks" throughout this book as well as the internal reflective interventions and behavior skills in these pages. This hard but important work won't always lend itself to elegant solutions or resolution—though it often will. What listening and assertion offer for sure is something priceless: increased connection, reduced polarization, a complexifying of our own and others' stories, and an increase in trust. Through the discomfort of disagreement, conflict-resilient brain hacks, and ensuing behaviors, we open the space for greater personal satisfaction with improved relationships, less antipathy and insecurity, and more authenticity.

Our journey so far has brought us from plumbing the depths of self—exploring our own internal conflicts and multiple conflicting identities—through to better articulating and understanding the interpersonal skills and behaviors that empower us in conflict and how we can improve them through increased self-awareness and practice. In the chapters ahead, we expand our lens beyond behavioral interpersonal skills and toward what's required to be an architect of at-the-table processes and organizational-systems design that will enable conflict resilience to flourish and become hardwired in our families, workplaces, and civil society. We also tackle the delicate question of assessing when the conflict-resilient move might actually be to disengage from a specific conversation, avoid certain topics, or, in more serious cases, consider exiting the relationship entirely.

Part 3

# COMMIT
# (AND OWN THE CONFLICT)

Chapter 7

# SETTING THE TABLE

Design a Conflict-Resilient Process

It had been an exhilarating but exhausting day for Bob and his team of instructors. They'd been working with a diverse group of teenagers to help them build conflict resilience skills in a weeklong program. Now, on the second day at 11 p.m., the teaching team's planning meeting for the next day was just wrapping up when they were interrupted by a loud knocking on the hotel door. It was the program director, with a look of consternation and dread on his face.

"What's wrong?" Bob asked.

"There's been a serious argument in the auditorium that almost came to blows. Can you come downstairs? We need your help!"

What transpired in the hours after class time was at once equally heartwarming and heartbreaking. Instead of participating in the scheduled evening social time of trivia and dancing, some of the workshop participants were inspired by the skills they were learning during the day. They decided to try their hand at their own informal dialogue on the topic of gender-affirming care for children and adolescents. But the dialogue broke down when several pro-transgender workshop participants labeled group participants who supported legislation that banned adolescent gender-affirming care as "bullies" and "fascists." As you can imagine, those on the receiving end didn't take these labels too well.

In their eagerness to practice the skills, the teens completely ignored the role that an intentional and carefully designed process can play not only in helping create conditions that support conflict resilience, but also in promoting behaviors designed to encourage wiser decisions and negotiations that will create more value for everyone involved.

The enthusiastic teens rushed headlong from class to dinner to an unstructured conversation about a divisive and hot topic among them, one that also hewed closely to divides in their politics, faith, understandings about the state of medical science, and geographic place of origin.

In this chapter, we offer insight and prescription about how to make conflict resilience possible in your conversations, your negotiations, and your organization by focusing on the role that intentional process design and container-building plays in creating an optimal environment for nurturing conflict resilience. Along the way, we share examples and stories from the world of international diplomacy, business, nonprofits, and individual one-on-one encounters.

## SKILLS ARE NOT ENOUGH

Bob is, admittedly, a slow learner. After nearly a decade of teaching negotiation and conflict resolution skills to hundreds of Harvard Law School students, executives, government officials, and nongovernmental organization (NGO) leaders, he started to lose heart. While there were countless stories of personal transformation and empowerment, he also saw the limits of workshops focused exclusively on individual interpersonal skills.

In many cases, the barrier to deploying the skills existed because parties had failed to do the internal work that we covered in Chapter 3. Skills development was necessary but not sufficient for effective conflict management or negotiation. Doing the internal work around managing one's negotiations within and understanding one's conflict tolerance were as important as learning the skills of deep listening and effective assertion.

But in other cases, the barrier to effective conflict resilience was less about a failure to do the hard internal work or a lack of individual interpersonal skill and more related to the problems with the environmental or organizational context that made it much harder to deploy conflict resilience to success. Whether in the workplace, school, church, or home, Bob realized that without a supportive and intentionally designed conflict-resilient process, it was much tougher—maybe even nearly impossible—for parties to be conflict resilient.

What was missing in so many situations was a process that provided the right conditions that would enable hard conversations, authentic differences, and genuine information exchange to occur. Although it was still possible to be conflict resilient and brave in the absence of a supportive process in some cases, it was much harder to do so.

Bob decided to team up with the late Harvard Law School professor Frank E. A. Sander, one of the founders of the Program on Negotiation at the law school, to offer an experimental reading group in an emerging and nascent area of legal academia called "dispute systems design." Within several years, Bob had started a full-fledged clinic at Harvard Law focusing on the intentional design of processes and systems that would support conflict-resilient practice and the management and resolution of conflict. By 2013, along with Frank Sander and colleagues Nancy Rogers and Craig McEwen, Bob had coauthored the first law school textbook on designing dispute resolution processes and systems.

In the years since, we have come to see that if we want to nurture conflict-resilient behavior in families, organizations, and our country, we also need to do the hard work of designing processes that can support and hold healthy conflict well.

Indeed, one of the challenges of our times has been that so many of the technological structures that have grown in the years since 2013 undermine and discourage conflict-resilient behavior. Whatever the social media platform, if you want to go viral, you say something outrageous and offensive; you don't establish and invite listening and engagement.

But it's not just technology that is undermining process; it's also the increasingly frenzied pace of life—a sense that we need to produce tangible and measurable results as soon as possible or else.

Then there are certain organizational or family cultures that impede our resilience in a more focused and contextual way. Recall a series of tragic crashes in 2018 and 2019 of new Boeing 737 MAX aircraft, which led to the grounding of all of them worldwide in 2019. It seemed as though these issues were resolved until a massive hole opened on the side of a Boeing plane flown by Alaska Airlines in February 2024, exposing deep-rooted cultural and operational problems within the company. These issues reverberated throughout Boeing, contributing to ongoing delays and technical failures in its Starliner space program. Problems such as software glitches and unanticipated communication issues left the spacecraft unable to properly dock with the International Space Station, resulting in a mission failure that stranded two American astronauts in space into 2025, many months past their original return date. Concerns about Boeing were so serious that in September 2024, NASA officials decided that the astronauts would return to Earth on a spacecraft designed by competitor SpaceX instead of Boeing's own Starliner series. The cultural problems at Boeing were so severe that they led to a broad management shakeup, including the chair of the board deciding not to seek reelection and the CEO announcing his resignation for the end of the year.

Once you scratch the surface of these disasters, you realize that Boeing had created a culture of humiliation and fear that made it extremely difficult for an employee who saw problems with the design of the 737 MAX aircraft to voice those concerns and not be ridiculed publicly. Even before the 2024 revelations, Ed Pierson, a senior manager at a Boeing 737 factory in Seattle, had extensively detailed how this culture of fear and recrimination caused him to go all the way to the top manager of the factory, only to be ignored. Ultimately, he went public about the issues of safety and the punishing environment for dissent. But at that point, it was too late. The accidents had already happened, costing hundreds of lives and grounding the Boeing 737 MAX fleet.

Was the failure here a product of bad engineering, science, or quality control? On the one hand, you can say yes—there were mistakes in all these areas.

But perhaps the ultimate cause of these failures was bad process and a lack of conflict resilience. Why? Because many of the doubts about the engineering, science, and quality issues were already identified, named, and even raised before the accidents occurred. It's just that there wasn't a process in place that allowed these concerns to get voiced and heard, addressed, solved, and dealt with.

Designing process and building a conflict-resilient culture takes intention and time. It's not cost-free. But whatever the costs of good process and a conflict-resilient culture, it's hard to argue that it's not a worthwhile investment.

## PROCESS ENEMIES

So, if process is so critical, what's so tough about getting this right? Here are the three most common barriers we see:

1. False urgency
2. Overwhelm
3. "One size fits all" thinking

### 1. False Urgency

The tension between the new principal and a group of long-serving faculty at one of the state's most high-performing public high schools had been brewing for months. The principal was recruited specifically for her success in diversifying and strengthening curriculum, improving discipline, and increasing teacher accountability. With the support of the superintendent, the principal spent the better part of her first semester announcing and trying to implement—despite fierce resistance—a slew of changes. Following the principal's announcement that a new assistant principal would be recruited from outside the ranks of the current faculty, the tension between school leadership and long-term faculty came to a head. The insurgent faculty demanded the immediate resignation of the principal. When the superintendent's office suggested face-to-face mediation, the parties agreed to a single one-hour sit-down insisting that "if things couldn't be worked out in that amount of time," they would need to "escalate to the press," as "students couldn't afford to suffer from a subpar learning environment for another day."

Most of us have experienced tense situations where we reach a breaking point and feel pressured to drive to a conclusion. However, from the standpoint of meeting both parties' short- and long-term interests and addressing the issues dividing the principal and the teachers, a single one-hour meeting was destined to fail. Worse still, scheduling the meeting under the pressure of an unreasonable deadline with no time for preparation or cooling off almost ensured failure, regardless of the negotiators' skill. As a mediator in this situation, you would be wise to propose a series of two-to-three-hour meetings, with the expectation of making some progress before committing to additional sessions.

We are sympathetic to the mental, emotional, and even physical exhaustion that conflict and bottled-up tension drive. Even in a negotiation driving a happy deal between entrepreneurs forging a joint venture together, the desire to drive an outcome any way you can and as quickly as possible is powerful. In a deal situation, that desire to "close the deal" can be exacerbated by the creation of some kind of deadline imposed by one of the parties. Yet, whether in a conflict situation like the one between the principal and her staff or a deal-making situation to get going on the joint venture, false urgency can often mean that careful process questions get ignored as parties rush into the details to be discussed, negotiated, or fought. But plunging headlong because of a false sense of urgency often contributes to breakdown or a failure to create as much value as might be possible.

Joel resonates with the challenges born of a false sense of urgency. They can often make his heart rate increase. He's been in them many times before—sometimes with family drama, sometimes with co-workers who disagree with the direction leadership is moving their organization, and other times with hospital staff about a "challenging" patient or family that is refusing a medical recommendation. Perhaps you've been in situations like this too. It's the "solve this interpersonal conflict for me immediately" situation that usually presents as "Please talk some sense into them!"

Joel once received a frantic call from his mother that opened with her pleading, "You need to speak with your sister, she's going to cancel her wedding. Please, talk some sense into her!" In the background, he heard his sister yelling, "No I'm not! Don't listen to her!" After ending the conversation with his mother, Joel called his sister and asked a few questions to better understand what had happened. He quickly discovered that she didn't want to cancel her wedding at all. In fact, she specifically wanted a small, intimate wedding ceremony with twenty close family and friends. Meanwhile, their mother insisted on a "small, intimate" ceremony with three hundred people! Hence their lively disagreement. Joel proposed a series of conversations—a mix of one-on-ones with each of them, a few discussions with his sister and her fiancé, some with the parents on both sides, and a few between Joel, his sister, and their mother.

Joel's sister replied bluntly, "Oh, gosh. The venue I want is willing to hold the date, but only until the end of the day, and there's a long waiting list. There's no time for all that . . . Please, talk some sense into Mom!"

For Joel, this was maddening. His internal voice almost exploded: "Do you really think I can solve this disagreement between the two of you in less than five minutes?"

This was a test of Joel's own conflict resilience. He had to pause to try to understand what was driving both his sister and his mother beneath the surface. Was one of them trying to force a decision to get her way, or were they both simply seeking a quick solution to end the discomfort of their disagreement? Neither approach was wise, as this conflict had escalated quickly and carried a lot of emotion and history.

At the same time, Joel empathizes with their underlying sense of urgency.

Here's the thing: you want solutions—and you want them now. This desire to resolve tension is natural. The desire to close the deal and celebrate is equally alluring. When we feel any discomfort with unresolved tension or the negotiation still in play, our brain is typically wired to drive our attention to whatever it will take to immediately resolve what's in dispute. Whenever we're not feeling mentally or physically great, our attention becomes laser-focused on eliminating the issue while our frontal-lobe systems that help us to deliberate and self-regulate tend to go offline, leaving us much more disinhibited and impulsive. Our brain reinforces these patterns of behavior by rewarding us immediately with dopamine and serotonin, so we feel less bad and so we're more likely to do it again in a future situation that is similar. This, combined with deep brain networks that initiate danger-averting actions (e.g., dodging an oncoming car), can trigger a strong urge to act immediately. This sensation can make you feel an intense drive to skip the thoughtful planning process and dive right in, mistakenly believing you can wing it or avoid the issue to temporarily alleviate discomfort (at least temporarily).

Having evolved to survive harsh environments with limited access to food, our brains are also prone to be drawn toward solutions that are as energy-efficient as possible. The more effortless, the fewer calories expended, the better for survival. This often amounts to having an embedded desire to want things done for us or to us. In the world of mediation, there are now automated sites where each side in a conflict can submit offers and counteroffers and artificial intelligence (AI) then helps the parties come up with a middle-ground solution without any discomfort, hard thinking, or use of time.

The challenge, however, is that for some of the most complex, nuanced, emotional, and partisan issues of our day—whether in our politics, workplace, or family—the path to working through them requires hard work, patience, and discomfort. That is, it requires conflict resilience.

Consider that a common piece of feedback we hear at the end of a conflict management workshop is, "Wow. I just love this stuff. But I'm worried. It seems as if it takes so much time and so much setup. I'm not sure I have the bandwidth for this."

It's hard to disagree that this work is time-consuming. And it can be tiring. But once you consider the costs of conflict unaddressed in terms of lower morale, bad feeling, employee turnover, burnout, and hurt relationships, it becomes clear that the investment is more than worth it by any measure.

Negotiation stories of breakthrough and unlikely agreements that make the national media usually do little more than outline the terms of agreement; at times, to make the story more interesting, perhaps there is a bit about the personality of the negotiator—their tenacity, creativity, planning, or wit. Perhaps there is something about the "right under the deadline" nature of the agreement and last-minute brinksmanship.

But you know what rarely gets a lot of attention? The painstaking process-design work that makes these agreements possible.

Rose Gottemoeller is a longtime senior U.S. diplomat who has spent a life doing stints at the State Department and in academia. She was the chief U.S. negotiator and assistant secretary of state for nuclear disarmament in negotiations with Russia that led to the New START Treaty under the Obama administration.

Bob once had the honor of hosting her in his negotiation class as a capstone speaker at Harvard Law School.

When it was time for the Q&A, a student who had been skeptical of all the "process talk" in the class over the course of the semester raised his hand.

With a touch of condescension and arrogance in his voice, he queried, "Madame Secretary, how much time did your negotiators spend on *process* issues before you dove into the substance of these negotiations?"

Gottemoeller replied, "Well, I have to say, these were incredibly efficient negotiations. We hardly spent any time on process at all."

The student started to smile; Bob's heart began to sink. Gottemoeller's answer was undermining a key lesson of the class.

The assistant secretary of state continued: "Yes. We completed our process-design work in record time—just six months of talks."

Bob glanced at the student, who flipped from gloating to crestfallen.

Despite having brains wired in ways that want us to believe otherwise, the slow and deliberate work of designing the right process *does* matter. But the tractor-beam force pushing us to breeze by process to dive into the issues or press for a quick resolution is hard to fight. And we get it!

*"We're only here for an hour. Let's see if we can get some alignment on our differences on how to address the crisis at our southern border."*

*"The VP is expecting our recommendations by Monday morning. Where do we each stand?"*

*"Now that we've introduced ourselves, let's dig in. What is on your mind that brought you to the focus group today?"*

Urgency culture has its draws.

It's just that most contexts where folks have different experiences, varying opinions, strong feelings, or creative energy aren't truly emergencies in need of an immediate answer. Taking the right amount of time to set up a series of facilitated meetings with the principal over a period of weeks is unlikely to profoundly make the educational situation for students worse than escalating it to a public relations nightmare. Slowing down the enthusiasm behind a joint venture with one of your customers is unlikely to ruin your business model unless your product is first-to-market and a competitor is breathing down your neck.

Yet it's hard to move away from a culture that reinforces the expectation that gratification should be immediate. Often, a false urgency to get things done—whether self-imposed or driven by external forces—trips us up, especially when differing or conflicting opinions and approaches come into play.

## 2. Overwhelm

Fighting the hardwired feeling of urgency to get immediate relief with little effort would be hard enough. Add to that the reality that process design can feel overwhelming. There are so many choices, so many pitfalls, and so many decisions that it's easy to say, "Given all of these challenges, maybe I'm just as well off by plunging into the details and hoping for the best." Trust us. That approach often ends up being the famous last words that lead to disaster.

### 3. "One Size Fits All" Thinking

While we admit cultural and contextual variation, we also believe that so many of the ideas, goals, and skills in this book have universal application. But when you are trying to build a process that encourages people to share their differences and that allows conflicts to surface and be handled well, it's simply the case that there isn't a universal or one-size-fits-all process.

The complications involved in bringing stakeholders together to agree upon a five-year strategic plan for a nonprofit will look very different from the stresses that might come up in a conversation you need to have with your best friend from high school about how your increasingly divergent views of what it means to be a Christian are inexorably driving you both apart. And you'll need an entirely different approach when you're negotiating a settlement between a surviving spouse and a large company whose negligence resulted in the untimely death of a beloved mother, daughter, wife, and friend.

One thing we want to emphasize—whether you are trying to build conflict resilience in your workplace, in your home, in your church, or with your significant other—process matters. It's not just for a formal workplace or negotiations at the United Nations.

So, let's dive into the "how-to" of process design.

## FIT THE FORUM TO THE FUSS

In 1994, the late Harvard law professor Frank E. A. Sander and Northwestern Law School professor Stephen Goldberg penned a short article called "Fitting the Forum to the Fuss." The basic premise was that lawyers, mediators, and other dispute resolvers should work to design dispute resolution processes appropriate for the kind of "fuss" or "conflict" in need of resolving. This article—and the phrase "fitting the forum to the fuss"—became widely known in scholarly and academic circles in the world of alternative dispute resolution. Sadly, despite its powerful ideas, the piece remains largely obscure in the practical day-to-day world.

So, here is a simple way into process design. Start by asking yourself a key question: *What is the purpose or product of the meeting, conversation, negotiation, or dialogue?*

In moments of extreme polarization, as we are seeing in our current culture, sometimes the purpose is simply to bring people in a room together and create a space where folks can speak authentically with each other across lines of difference and feel that they can be seen and heard. In such situations, agreement, a shared set of next steps, persuasion, or a signed agreement isn't the goal; the goal is simply to facilitate a genuine and difficult dialogue across lines of difference.

Other times, perhaps the goal of a meeting is to brainstorm ideas for how to build team camaraderie in the second quarter of the year or to decide who should be the outside speaker for the annual firm retreat. Still other times, the goal might be to negotiate the terms of a joint venture or to agree upon where you, your siblings, and your families will vacation together for the upcoming summer.

The purpose of the engagement drives how you set up the space.

So does the context.

For example, negotiating the terms of the joint venture between two companies is going to drive a very different process than negotiating whether you and your siblings will vacation at Walt Disney World, in London, or at a dude ranch in Montana. But both are negotiations where folks may have strong views and even stronger feelings. The difference here is the nature of the relationship and context.

So, in addition to thinking through the purpose of the conversation, you should also ask yourself: *What is the context?*

Considering the context means figuring out the relationship that the parties have, and the nature of the feelings involved. These answers will drive the level of detail and formality that your process might have. In general, though, it's our view that it's better to err on the side of formality than informality when it comes to process design.

In our work we've observed two key contexts where process is most likely to fall to the wayside. And, arguably, they are the contexts where forgoing process considerations can have the highest cost.

*Friends and Family.* First is the context of friendships and personal relationships. Understandably, there can be an assumption that if you need a formal process to work things out with friends and family, then maybe these people aren't as close to you as you think. The truth is, nothing could be further from the truth. Even if you're engaging a bunch of friends on where to go to dinner on a Friday night, if you have a sense that your buddies have different preferences on venue, budget, preferred food, and noise levels, putting some order on the conversation—even if it feels geeky and weird—can help you land on the best possible outcome and ensure over time that the group doesn't just default to the preferences of the richest, loudest, or most assertive in ways that take a toll on the relationships between the parties.

One of the most rewarding—and challenging—contexts in which we facilitate and mediate is in the family context, perhaps around dividing an estate among warring siblings or around deciding whether to withdraw a parent's life-sustaining medical care in exchange for comfort-oriented palliative care at the end of life. In most of these cases, there are histories of hurt, bad communication, misunderstanding, and missed opportunities in play. Sometimes, things aren't that bad. But there are almost always hidden tensions, sore points, and perhaps a resentment here or there. Almost without exception, the lack of any recognizable process exacerbates the latent negative feeling, making it tougher to work out differences on the substance and to maintain and honor the relationship as well.

*Pressure and Crisis.* The second context where even process-minded people throw process out the window is in times of extreme pressure and crisis. Again, this is understandable. If there is an intense deadline to get the new aircraft to the airline and onto the tarmac; if billions of dollars and many years have been spent; if another delay is going to perhaps result in a serious blow to reputation and the bottom line—this is no time to bring in the process police! Though our example is extreme, we contend that it's also worthy of taking note. The extra time to ensure that there is a process that enables and empowers dissenting voices, that is thorough, that creates psychological safety, is exactly what is needed in a time of crisis to reach a good decision. And, as you'll see, a process can be designed with the urgency of decision-making in mind.

## A PURPOSE-DRIVEN PROCESS

When it comes to working with others through conflict or negotiating through a deal or dispute, especially when the purpose or product of the engagement isn't clear, a key place to begin is by asking the deceptively simple question: What is *your* purpose?

This is one of our favorite questions because it can be deployed to good use in virtually any context. At the most existential and macro level, it's a way to wake up in the morning: "What is your purpose?" "Well, to live joyfully, be productive, spread kindness." At the most micro level, it's a question we often ask in a negotiation coaching session with respect to a single phrase that someone might use with the opposing party. "What was your purpose when you said to your negotiation counterpart, 'Your idea will never work'?"

Before bringing anyone to a table for a negotiation, a difficult conversation, or a dialogue across lines of difference, it's key to have a crisp answer to the question, "What is your purpose?"

Bob was recently working with a national church organization that wanted to address toxic polarization both within the church and within the broader U.S. political culture.

Part of the effort involved hosting a major national conference on the topic of political polarization in the church. At the first meeting, the client had shared an agenda that included lessons on how to dialogue and then had participants scheduled to dialogue in small groups on various issues during the day, culminating in a "Where do we go from here?" discussion that is a common feature of many multi-day conferences for advocacy groups.

If you're sitting there thinking, "Wow! Why did they hire Bob? They didn't really need him! What a good plan," then you don't know Bob.

He asked the conference planning committee his go-to question: "Well, what is your purpose for this event?"

Silence.

Then, different answers from committee members that were all commendable but quite different from each other. A few wanted to convene other people who had been trying to address issues of polarization to discuss strategies for how to work together. Others wanted to gather church leaders to discuss polarization and whether it should be a major focus of the church's leadership. The rest of the committee wanted to bring together folks concerned about "toxic polarization," but didn't know how to start addressing it. The risk of not clarifying the purpose upfront is that each of these goals suggests different event formats, guests, and speakers. With unlimited time and resources, all of these objectives could be addressed. However, more realistically, the committee would need to align on a single purpose to guide other design and format questions.

The work of process always starts with understanding purpose. And that work can be hard because there are many worthy purposes, but the ability of a given process or meeting or set of meetings to achieve a purpose might be limited. And so, part of this preparation work might mean reconciling conflicting purposes—or creating a process over time that allows you to address different components at different times with different process rules.

## THE WORTHINESS OF LOOSE THREADS

When it comes to purpose, most of the time we want and expect something tangible and certain:

- Our purpose is to choose what restaurant we're going to.
- Our purpose is to resolve the dispute.
- Our purpose is to sign a new three-year contract.
- Our purpose is to buy or sell the car.
- Our purpose is to enjoy the family reunion.
- Our purpose is a ceasefire and to put an end to hostilities.

Within these outcomes, we may add more nuance:

*"The dispute is resolved at low cost, without resort to litigation, and relationships between the parties are preserved."*

or

*"A new contract is signed that advances the interests of all stakeholders, allows for fair wage growth, and protects health benefits."*

or

*"We pick a restaurant to have dinner that meets everyone's dietary restrictions, that everyone will enjoy, and where the cost won't be too high."*

When outcomes like these are identified, shared, and agreed to, conflict resilience seems more in reach.

Recently, during a coffee break in the sixth month of a heated labor dispute that Bob was mediating, one of the union bargainers complained to Bob, "I'm so exhausted by this process. I can't wait to get it over with."

Despite the understandable exhaustion, which Bob shared as well, the possibility and ultimately the imperative of an agreement kept the union negotiator at the table through it all. Had that goal not been articulated and understood by the parties, the negotiation would have ended months ago. The clarity of shared purpose (a signed four-year contract), challenging as it was for all, kept the parties soldiering through the tough moments.

Even in this context, however, Bob continually had to push the parties to meet in person and face-to-face rather than on Zoom, where they could avoid direct interaction and simply use him as an information conduit.

One of the challenges in our current polarized climate, however, is that more and more frequently, we can find it harder to articulate a purpose we feel is worthy enough for our exhaustion and discomfort. That's why we often eschew engaging conflict and choose avoidance, a return to our cocoon of comfort, or kicking the can down the road. But this kind of avoidance—this aversion to discomfort—is at the heart of polarization and relationship breakdown in the U.S.

- *"Why even talk with my grandfather? He's so steeped in his biased news channel that it will just make us both upset."*
- *"There is no need to meet with the opposing school board members. We will never agree to ban a single book. We'll just have to beat them at the ballot box so that none of their people are on the board at all."*
- *"I'm not sure why I should participate in the dialogue when there is nothing we're going to agree on or do differently anyway."*
- *"I don't want to talk about why I think my son's Little League coach isn't treating the boys with proper respect. If I rock the boat, he'll just punish my son and it's not worth it."*

We get why it can feel easier to walk away from engaging differences when conflict may be high and the prospect of finding common ground or shifting views or reaching agreement seems low. But as we have already covered, there are powerful and important benefits to engaging with others even when a meeting of the minds on the substantive issue is not likely. Conflict resilience at its heart is not about reaching agreement. And becoming conflict resilient yourself will not guarantee that you will reach agreement. But without it your chances of finding common ground, bridging a gap, or remaining in relationship with those with whom we do not see eye to eye are severely diminished. Therefore, when it comes to creating a conflict-resilient space, we have to let go of "problem-solving," "agreement," or "resolution" as the main or only valuable goal or purpose.

For conflict-resilient process design, we can't stress enough the worthiness of purposes that do not require a happy ending, a signed deal, or a melding of minds. Sometimes there really isn't going to be *anything* we're going to agree on when it comes to the limits of the Second Amendment, the sanctity of life from the moment of conception, or the (un)constitutionality of affirmative action. But designing the right process, an essential part of conflict resilience, invites us to consider other purposes that can dramatically change how we relate to each other, what agreements are possible, and how we will manage differences when agreement isn't possible.

Some possible purposes for a process design might be:

- To understand others' perspective and share my own
- To build my own skills of empathy and perspective-taking
- To have a deeper sense of the contours of difference, agreement, and what might be possible or not with respect to consensus-building
- To ensure that the deep differences between us don't lead to demonization and dehumanization

None of the above purposes will mean that our conversations will end in a negotiated resolution. These exchanges, even when they do not have the possibility of consensus or agreement, are worthy and necessary, especially at a time when the gulf between so many in our country and world is widening and the motivation to come together is diminishing.

When Joel must deliver a difficult diagnosis to a patient, especially a diagnosis that they are likely to resist, his purpose in meeting with the patient has to be clear so he can know how to best design certain aspects of the process for that exchange. If the purpose is to break bad news and make sure that the patient feels supported, he'll make sure that they are in a quiet room, and he welcomes them to invite family members into it too. Good process design involves considering the environment—what to do in person versus over videoconference; even how the room is set up can matter. Similarly, if the purpose is to best support the patient in improving their quality of life and recommending a specific treatment, he will start the visit by stating the purpose of the consultation and then asking open-ended questions and listening to understand what the patient believes is the issue and what their most pressing and motivating concerns are in the moment (e.g., "I don't want to be a burden on my family," "I don't want people to think that I'm unhinged," "I want to feel in full control of my life and my body"). Without taking the why into consideration, Joel would have a much harder time figuring out the who, what, where, when, and how so that he can best serve each patient.

Thus, whether the *purpose* of a particular meeting is to resolve a conflict, brainstorm ideas, explore perspectives, or plan for the future, it's critical to align on this as the first step in process design.

Furthermore, the greater clarity you have in terms of purpose, the easier it will be to identify who should be invited and what the rest of the process will look like.

## MAKING THE GUEST LIST: EVERYONE IS *NOT* WELCOME!

Identifying the purpose for a convening or series of convenings is key because it drives the question of who should be in the room for any particular meeting and for any given part of the process.

When we work with groups, we see a bunch of common errors when it comes to identifying who should be invited:

*"Let's be as inclusive as possible and invite everyone."*

or

*"We need one person from each department (or demographic or affinity group)."*

or

*"Let's keep it small and simple so we can get something done quickly and efficiently."*

You might be scratching your head thinking to yourself, "Hey, I've said or thought these things myself. What is wrong with statements like these?"

At one level, there is nothing wrong with the idea of maximal inclusion, broad representation across departments and relevant intersectionalities, or keeping things manageable to drive decision-making.

But it is organizers' attitudes like the ones above in negotiations, dialogues, or strategic planning that also lead to common complaints like these (which we suspect you've also said to yourself before):

*"I have no idea why I have been invited to this meeting."*

or

*"I'm just here as the union (or minority or senior citizen or Southside of town) rep but I'm not really sure what I'm supposed to say or do here."*

or

*"This process is driven by a few power players. Everyone else is being left out."*

If at this point you're thinking, "I'm exhausted and this is precisely the problem: figuring out who should be part of a process is just a no-win proposition, so just do what you want and prepare for the consequences!" then brace yourself, because we're going to lean into our own conflict resilience and say, "We respectfully disagree." It's not that there is a foolproof way to design a process perfectly so everyone is 100 percent content with the level of their involvement and that of all the other stakeholders. But part of what can yield both the best possible result and the best possible experience for all is being intentional about who gets invited in a process.

When it comes to identifying who might be invited, we suggest you start by answering two questions:

1.  If your specific engagement or negotiation involves multiple meetings (or, if the idea of "meetings" feels too formal for your situation, think of these as multiple gatherings), who should be a part of the overall multi-meeting (and perhaps multi-month) process?
2.  Who should be involved in each individual meeting?

If you're organizing a one-off dialogue or mediation or negotiation session, these two questions merge. For example, consider a not-for-profit organization focused on addressing the housing crisis in your neighborhood. One of its projects involves transforming a worn-out hotel close by into permanent affordable housing. To get this approved will involve literally hundreds of negotiations with city, state, and perhaps federal officials, community leaders, architects, local businesses, and civic organizations, to name just a few. Before getting started, it makes sense to conduct a *stakeholder assessment* to understand who the various parties are and what their interests are (if you're thinking that "stakeholders" doesn't apply to your situation, think again; in addressing contentious personal matters like cutting household expenses, your spouse, each of your children, and maybe even your pets are considered relevant stakeholders). This work can be time-consuming and often gets overlooked. But the stakeholder assessment work often ends up being an exercise in wise efficiency since it can identify possible holdouts, spoilers, allies, and those who might need some convincing. To achieve a successful outcome in a long-term multiparty negotiation, broad engagement of a wide body of stakeholders is essential.

But that is entirely different from who might be invited to any given meeting. On the surface, parties will often say that they want to be invited and included in any and every meeting. But if you scratch the surface and dig under their position of "Invite me and my people to *everything*," you typically learn that what they are most afraid of is that their interests won't be met as part of the process or that they will be forgotten and taken advantage of if they are not there. At times, they're worried that while they are absent, one of their perceived opponents in the conflict will take advantage of their absence. In truth, in many circumstances stakeholders would much rather not be at every meeting where their only role is to be the person hitting a buzzer when it seems as if their interest is being forgotten or their enemy is taking advantage of their absence. In fact, good process design takes account of absent stakeholders' interests even if they are not present and then finds ways of inviting folks back to active discussion when they have an important role in moving the entire negotiation forward.

This can be done in at least two ways. First, a good stakeholder assessment will assure that there are trusted "proxies" present at important meetings to ensure that a particular stakeholder's interests get voiced. Second, when the issue is that a stakeholder wants to be there because they are afraid that a nemesis will take advantage of their absence, the correct diagnosis is a lack of trust. In a situation like this, the appropriate prescription isn't being present at every single meeting and on every single Zoom, text, and call. Rather, it's taking appropriate steps to address the low trust between the parties. For instance, it might be worth convening a separate meeting between the parties to discuss ways they might build trust, verify commitments, or raise an issue when they feel that their counterpart has breached a protocol or crossed a line. Of course, this latter work requires a lot more—you guessed it—conflict resilience than just staffing up to make sure you can send a representative to every single meeting.

As we alluded to before, once you've identified the purpose of any given meeting you are much better placed to invite the most appropriate people. For example, if the goal of a meeting is to brainstorm— let's say ideas on how a management team can respond to employee complaints—you might want to think about whether it makes sense to invite senior decision-makers to the meeting. Why? Well, first, senior decision-makers or bosses may be less inclined to "brainstorm" with their team around them because they fear that team members will hear anything they say as something they can or are prepared to do. So, they will self-censor. Self-censoring is exactly what you do *not* want when it comes to brainstorming. Even worse, subordinates may be less inclined to brainstorm if they worry that their boss is present and evaluating any ideas that come out of their mouth. That's why when it comes to a brainstorming session—as opposed to a decision-making session or an evaluation session—you may want to avoid having decision-makers in the room or folks at very different levels in the organizational hierarchy.

In Barack Obama's 2020 book, *A Promised Land*, the former president discusses times when he purposefully *un*invited himself from a meeting of senior advisors for the purpose of allowing them to brainstorm without worrying that their boss—the president—would be evaluating every idea.

Similarly, in many complex processes, like evaluating whether an affordable housing project can move forward because of regulatory and environmental concerns, lawyers will need to be involved. But if we are organizing a *brainstorming* session, we might try to keep the lawyers away, not because they aren't ultimately necessary and valuable, but because a lawyer charged with the task of avoiding potential risks will likely struggle with blue-sky brainstorming. As a risk manager, they will be eager to tell you the reasons why something can't happen or isn't a good idea or creates the following five risks and the following three violations of an obscure code. Lawyers rock. But, given their intense proclivity for risk management, maybe they're not especially suited for the brainstorming phase of a complex negotiation.

The goal in inviting folks to any given meeting is to be able to succinctly share with them *why* they are being invited. You want meeting attendees to know what their exact role is, given the clear purpose of the meeting.

Some years ago, Bob was working with colleagues to help design a series of dialogues between leaders of a large institution following numerous allegations of sexual harassment and gender discrimination that had gone on for many years. The dialogue session was primarily focused on healing—an opportunity for the organization's leadership and rank-and-file members to share their experiences of living through the trauma and shame from their very different perspectives: the "C-suite" and the "ordinary dues-paying member." Achieving success would require a strong measure of conflict resilience from everyone involved.

Selecting participants for this was extremely challenging because Bob and his team needed to make clear that the purpose was *not* to have a listening session. Some in leadership had been so traumatized during this period and the dialogue was intended to provide them an opportunity to share *their* experience and *their* story as well. Some on the leadership team seemed incapable or unwilling to share their own experience. And these individuals needed to be excluded to ensure that the purpose was met.

Similarly, there were some in the rank-and-file membership who were still hurting so badly that they simply were not in a place to be in mutual conversation. They *needed* a listening session. In Chapter 8, we discuss the limits of conflict resilience, how to know when discomfort (a requirement for conflict resilience) is touching on retriggering real trauma (something to be avoided). But for now, the challenge worth highlighting in this situation is that designing a process that enhances conflict resilience meant finding the right people for the purpose of the program. Failure to do this would mean that the team's (hopefully worthy) goals would not be met.

Consider an equally complex example where process design was key to navigating a highly polarized, extremely triggering, and very public conflict through to a successful end. In 2016, Harvard Law School retired its eighty-year-old crest. The shield displayed three sheaves of wheat, a symbol derived from the family crest of Isaac Royall, Jr., the eighteenth-century slave owner who endowed the law school's first professorship. Not until late in 2021 did the nation's oldest law school adopt a new crest. When the controversy around whether the old shield should be retained or replaced first arose in 2015, the then-dean of the school appointed Professor Bruce Mann, a legal historian and spouse of Senator Elizabeth Warren, to chair a committee composed of twelve people to make a recommendation to her on the issue. The task for Mann was gargantuan. It barely needs reminding that a place like Harvard Law School is bound to be full of passionate partisans with strong views and a penchant for rhetorical flourish. What better battleground for culture wars, history, and tradition than the question of "What to do with the historic shield of Harvard Law School?" Add to this the strong emotions and identity questions that were in play for students, faculty, and alumni of the institution around race and the legacy of slavery in the United States.

For Mann, he had to design a process that was at once inclusive but also clear about time frame and the committee's charge. The mandate of the committee was not to create a referendum or online vote; it was to make a recommendation to the dean. Mann was wise enough to know, however, that no matter how "representative" the committee itself was, its work would be dead on arrival if it was simply the product of twelve thoughtful people with diverse opinions coming to a meeting of the minds. The process had to solicit and involve the views of other stakeholders in a way that truly made them feel heard. The hearing not only had to include a thorough exploration of logical arguments and facts, but also had to be able to make space for passion and lots of emotion. It had to manage expectations of what was possible. It had to make people feel seen. It had to demonstrate that viewpoints were being heard and registered. The process could *not* feel as if it was perfunctory or just a speed bump to some predetermined result. Most people can see right through fake consultative processes. Complexifying all of this was an ambitious deadline set by the dean for the committee's work.

Mann designed a process that provided multiple ways that stakeholders could engage and share their views. These included a variety of options for in-person facilitated focus groups, opportunities to email thoughts to a monitored email address, and proactive outreach to various student and alumni affinity groups. Extra efforts were made to ensure that participants always knew how their contribution was being taken into consideration and integrated into the decision-making process. The committee also created a website with frequent updates to the wider community to ensure transparency.

In the end, the committee issued a majority opinion recommending the retiring of the Harvard Law School shield, with an eloquent dissenting opinion written by Pulitzer Prize–winning author and Harvard law professor Annette Gordon-Reed, making the case to retain the Royall crest. What is remarkable is that both opinions acknowledge that what might have seemed to be a single-issue conflict—keep the shield or get rid of it—was in reality a multi-issue conflict involving history, legacy, institutional memory, tradition, and an opportunity to learn and grow. In the lexicon of negotiation and conflict, the issue of the Harvard shield was not a win/lose, one-issue distributive negotiation but in fact an integrative negotiation with opportunities for all viewpoints to have many of their interests ultimately met. What could have descended into a long-term and pitched battle—"Do we keep the mascot/shield/emblem or not?"—that might have lingered for many years resolved in a relatively satisfactory way for most reasonable stakeholders. We'd say at least some of this relates specifically to the wisdom of the process design.

## BEST PRACTICES IN THE ROOM WHERE IT HAPPENS

In any given negotiation, whether to secure a pay raise from your boss, agree on a redevelopment plan for a community, or stay in healthy and respectful dialogue across a partisan divide, we may not know how the sausage gets made. But it turns out that once you are in the room, there are some best practices around process that can help increase the likelihood that the sausage that gets made is high-quality, ethical, and satisfying for all the stakeholders.

Again, for any meeting, gathering, or encounter, we start with being clear about its purpose. This is because the purpose will drive the process rules and agenda. Here we now broadly distinguish between the purpose of a *dialogue* across lines of difference and a *meeting*, such as a negotiation or an attempt at managing a dispute where the hope is to reach a deal or other specific outcome.

In both cases, it's critical to have an agenda. This may seem obvious, but most of us have far too much experience showing up for meetings where no agenda is announced, where a few random questions may be raised, and where decisions are either made in the last two minutes or a decision is made to "continue over email" or "schedule another meeting." There is nothing wrong with continuing over email or scheduling another meeting if that is part of the process. But in many cases, resorting to email exchange or "another meeting" is the result of a poorly prepared process, not a genuine need for more conversation or discussion. Here are six high-yield best practices for process design we recommend:

1.   Create a low-risk space
2.   Speak from your own perspective
3.   Step up, step back
4.   Listen generously
5.   Be raggedy
6.   What happens in the room stays in the room

### Best Practice #1: Create a low-risk space

For a dialogue, it is essential to establish some clear shared norms or ground rules for the interaction. A common one is to create a "safe space" for people to share their viewpoint and ideas. On paper, this sounds wonderful. In reality, we urge against using the word "safe space." Why? Because if you are bringing two people in a room where real feelings, different viewpoints, and a lifetime of experience are in play, it's simply impossible to guarantee "safety." Engaging conflict in a genuine way *always* bears some risk. That's why building *resilience* is such an essential skill.

Establishing some shared norms for a conversation on a hotly-contested issue is essential to create conditions that maximize the chances that people can assert differences with each other with honesty, integrity, and openness *and* that people can listen deeply, with generosity and grace. This means trying to create a *low-risk space* where folks—whether two friends or a focus group of ten—feel as able as possible to be authentic with each other about their views and experiences and where they are most empowered to listen with the kind of grace and grit described in Chapter 5. Much of our book is about developing the internal capacity to sit with conflict by understanding one's conflict-recognition and conflict-holding capacity and by developing the skills for deep listening and effective assertion. But once you're in the room, whether it's a one-on-one conversation or a group dialogue, establishing some shared guidelines in advance of discussing the topic can make it easier for you and the other(s) in the conversation to be conflict resilient.

## Best Practice #2: Speak from your own perspective

After establishing an aspiration to create a space for low-risk speaking and listening, consider ground rules that encourage people to speak on behalf of themselves and not on behalf of a group or an identity. This can be challenging and might feel limiting. So, let's dive a little deeper into it.

The reality is that our identities—whether as a senior, a factory worker, an imam, a person of color, a woman, or a first-generation college student—inform our viewpoints powerfully. And so they are relevant to conversations around some of the most polarizing issues of our time.

When we suggest a ground rule of "speaking for yourself" we do not mean there should be some kind of gag order that disallows someone from saying, "From my experience as someone in the evangelical community . . ." At the same time, we distinguish this from someone who might use a particular identity to speak on behalf of everyone in a particular community. While it may seem like wordsmithing, there is a meaningful difference between when someone says, "As a conservative person raised in a very liberal part of the country, I have been struck by . . ." and "Conservative people like me, raised in a liberal part of the country, are struck by . . ." The first example is providing some of the background and basis for one's personal point of view. The second example is a less helpful attempt to claim the mantle of one's identity to speak on behalf of that identity.

It's worth noting here that the opposite challenge in hard conversations across lines of difference needs to be avoided if we want to create a truly low-risk space for genuine dialogue. What do we mean? For every time Bob has been asked, "Can I ask you about your experience as a gay man . . ." (completely fine!), he's also been asked, "Bob, what do gay people in the community think about this issue?" (somewhat unhelpful and bordering on inappropriate). Unless someone is truly an objective expert on the matter, asking them to speak on behalf of one of their identities is as fraught and unhelpful as claiming the mantle of an identity yourself when in dialogue across a line of difference.

### Best Practice #3: Step up, step back

For most of us, the way we might participate or "show up" in a group differs from the way we participate or show up in a one-on-one interaction. Setting "step up, step back" as an explicit norm or ground rule invites those participating in a group dialogue to be mindful of their own default responses in a group. For those who tend to be on the quieter side, "step up" is a request and reminder that their active participation matters and that their silence is not neutral; it's a choice to say nothing and not be heard. "Step up" reminds those who tend to be quieter that their active participation is welcome and encouraged. But "step back" is a reminder to those whose hand tends to go up the second a question is asked that their active participation—even when it has the best of intentions—is not always the most constructive way to participate. "Step back" is a reminder to make space for others; it's also a reminder that thoughtful consideration of a question before offering a response can make for more valuable and authentic participation. Indeed, for those who tend to be most active in a group, one of their challenges may well be sitting quietly in discomfort. Part of being conflict resilient often calls on us to sit in the silence and not automatically talk to ease the awkwardness.

### Best Practice #4: Listen generously

For most difficult conversations where there is tension, emotion, and strong partisan perceptions, an expectation and aspiration of deep listening must be articulated. As Chapter 5 reminds us, deep listening is not sitting there passively or nodding one's head. It's much tougher. It involves asking all involved to cultivate curiosity in the moment when we might be most inclined to want to say, "Yes, but . . ."

### Best Practice #5: Be raggedy

The corollary to the "listen generously" ground rule is the "be raggedy" ground rule. It's a corollary because "be raggedy" really relates to how we can assert our views and experience across lines of difference. At times when we are in conflict and especially when we're not entirely sure how to be articulate and effective, we might be prone to simply be silent. This is especially the case if we worry that we will be judged, canceled, ostracized, misunderstood, or punished if we phrase something in a way that lands badly on others in the conversation. The invitation to "be raggedy" allows participants to ask for an extra measure of grace from others when they are trying to express a viewpoint. It signals, "I'm not sure I'm saying this the right way. I'm trying hard. If this lands badly, please let me know, but please be willing to receive what I'm saying as well-intentioned even if not well formed or articulated."

### Best Practice #6: What happens in the room stays in the room

To create conditions where people feel more comfortable sharing their perspective, establishing a norm of confidentiality can be useful. It's important here to be clear about the contours of what confidentiality might mean. In some instances, a norm of absolute confidentiality may be appropriate: we will never share anything about this exchange outside the four walls of this space. More typically, the shared norm is somewhat modified: folks agree that they can take what they learned in general from a dialogue but that they are not permitted to share what a particular person may have said or even a conclusion about that person outside the space. For example, imagine a dialogue around abortion. A ground rule that protected an individual's confidentiality but allowed someone to share learnings from the experience outside the dialogue would permit someone to say, "One of the things I learned is that some people's commitment to pro-life issues influences their views on other controversial issues such as the death penalty, gun safety, and euthanasia." What would not be permitted would be to say, "Torril's pro-life position has influenced her views on the death penalty, gun safety, and euthanasia."

As you can probably guess, a multi-person dialogue on a controversial and polarizing issue is going to likely need a more formal approach to shared norms like the ones above; in contrast, a difficult conversation that you might set up with your cousin about the way they talk about your older sibling who has Down syndrome would likely need a more informal articulation of setting norms for the conversation. In both cases, setting up some shared norms establishes a process that will help. But in the latter case, it might feel awkward and perhaps like overkill to completely formalize this part of the process.

## BEST PRACTICES FOR MAKING A DEAL

The in-the-room process expectations when negotiating a deal or a resolution to a dispute are markedly different than those we might recommend for a conversation or dialogue. When you are driving toward an agreement—whether to sign a contract, how to agree upon employment terms, how to resolve a dispute with your colleague about the best strategy to take in the legal brief, or how to respond to the negative publicity your company is receiving because of a public statement made by your CEO—getting a tangible outcome is part of the goal. Establishing a process or agenda is equally important for negotiations such as these. And all too often, process is ignored or glossed over. So, to set yourself up for success in designing a conflict-resilient deal-making process, here are five building blocks to incorporate into your process design:

1.  Identify the issues for discussion or negotiation
2.  Identify the parties' interests
3.  Generate possible options for agreement
4.  Consider alternatives and criteria
5.  Build in agreement and implementation steps

### Building Block #1: Identify the issues for discussion or negotiation

In addition to establishing the purpose of a meeting or negotiation, it's essential for parties to explicitly identify the specific issues that are to be resolved or negotiated. It's easy to assume that everyone agrees on this from the get-go. But our experience suggests that, more often than not, parties arrive at the negotiation table with different expectations about what the issues are and which are to be discussed when. Even if the parties agree entirely on the issues, naming and identifying them is useful as it establishes common ground and helps everyone to stay on track.

### Building Block #2: Identify the parties' interests

Once the issues have been clearly articulated, the process should provide an opportunity for all the parties to identify and share their interests with respect to each individual issue. This, too, supports the conflict resilience of everyone at the table by setting shared norms that are mutually beneficial, increasing the motivation to really sit with and be with the conflict-related discomfort of the negotiation. In a relatively simple negotiation, this might occur over a matter of ten or twenty minutes; in a complex and long-term negotiation, interest-sharing could take place over many multiple-hour meetings. If interest-sharing is to be genuine and real, the process needs to be agreed upon and explained before this stage. Why? Because most sophisticated negotiators will be reluctant to share their interests in a process where they aren't confident that the other parties are going to do the same, especially without enough information about how those interests will be integrated into the larger negotiation process.

Good process design and adherence to it helps reduce the likelihood that you will be exploited by unilateral disclosure of your interests, thus enhancing psychological safety for all. The challenge of information disclosure is known as the *negotiator's dilemma*. This is the tension between identifying the parties' true interests to expand the size of the negotiation pie to its maximum and claiming value for oneself, a goal often accomplished by hiding your true interests and exploiting the other person's to gain a competitive advantage.

Consider a simple example from a labor/management negotiation context. If the most important issue for a union is maintaining current levels of health care coverage, from a pure negotiation analytical perspective, where the parties are seeking to maximize joint gain, we would want this key piece of information to be revealed across the negotiation table so that the parties can arrive at an outcome that preserves that interest and allows the union to make concessions in other areas. The "risk," however, is that as soon as management knows that this is the most important issue, they can hold out and extract huge concessions around work hours, wages, and vacation time in exchange for holding the line on health care. Because of this risk and the fear of exploitation, the union will simply say, "Everything is important, and we can't give ground anywhere."

Similarly, it may be the case that management cares most about limiting wage increases in Years 2 and 3 of a three-year contract and is willing to give more in Year 1 to do that. The management interest is around managing risk of tough economic times in the future but knows it has adequate cash on hand in Year 1. Worried about being exploited by the union, management just says, "We need to hold wages down in all three years."

If both the union and management take the approach that "everything is equally important," the entire negotiation is reduced to a haggle.

It would be most conducive for the parties to share their true preferences. That is how negotiators can reach the most value-creating and optimal negotiation outcomes. But in a contentious negotiation between historic adversaries, the fear of exploitation is high, creating a significant barrier for the kind of information exchange that would produce a mutually advantageous result.

This is where careful process design can save the day. Securing an agreement from all sides to share their interests after the issues have been identified and then remaining true to the process agreement is a way that reduces the likelihood that parties will game the negotiation to their own advantage.

Without the explicit process agreement, unilateral sharing of one's interests can feel—and in fact is—riskier!

During this interest-exchange part of a negotiation process, it can be helpful to track interests using shared visuals, such as a shared Google doc or a whiteboard or flip charts. Using shared visuals for capturing and understanding interests helps to encourage transparency and openness and is useful when it is time to assess the relative strength of the ideas that might emerge.

It's also critical at this stage that parties distinguish questions that help everyone get a clearer understanding of interests from questions that criticize or evaluate interests. Here we remind you of the difference between "hot" or "triggering" inquiry that we discussed in Chapter 5, on deep listening.

During the part of a negotiation where parties are sharing and learning about each other's interests, it can be very helpful to ask questions about why someone cares about a particular item they've identified as an interest. Indeed, it can often be the case that what they are articulating as an "interest" really is just a position that represents a bunch of underlying interests.

Saying "I want to retain Dad's watch as we divide his belongings" might mean that the interest is in the watch. But it might also mean "I want something to remember Dad by that was really important to him and that I can see and feel every day." Questions that invite parties to think past positions to their interests—encompassing those that are substantive, emotional, and relational—are extremely valuable at this stage in the process.

Questions that challenge or dispute one's interests tend to be counter-productive in a negotiation. For example, responding by saying, "That watch isn't worth very much," or "You can't possibly want the watch," or "I don't see how the watch can be that important here," tends not to be productive in this part of a negotiation process.

**Building Block #3: Generate possible options for agreement**
In terms of how to best order the sequence of topics in your conflict-resilient process, only after interests have been articulated clearly does it make sense to move to the next stage in a negotiation. Once all the interests have been mapped and understood, a wise negotiation process creates an opportunity for parties to brainstorm possible outcomes that can meet the parties' interests.

During this phase of a negotiation, it's important to be even clearer about the ground rules. For many of us who spend hours and hours of our work lives in meetings, the mere mention of the word *brainstorm* is apt to trigger an internal eye roll and a loud voice that says, "Ugh. Another hour of my life gone down the drain!"

In our experience the problem with brainstorming is not the premise *(or promise)* of brainstorming, but the failure to execute it well or at the right time. To prevent this, when designing a process to yield a negoti-ated outcome, it's important to be clear about the *when* and the *how* of the brainstorming stage.

First, starting off a negotiation or dialogue with brainstorming should be avoided. Brainstorming detached from an understanding of parties' interests is random, frustrating, and a sure way to wear down everyone's resilience to the distress of conflict.

Once interests are clearly identified, brainstorming can be generative, disciplined, and worth the effort. When beginning a brainstorming-for-possibilities phase, it's important to be clear that all ideas are welcome ideas. This means not evaluating ideas—either with positive affirmations (i.e., "Great idea, Rehema!") or negative ones (i.e., "I'm not sure something like that would really work in this context, Rehema"). When ideas get evaluated, folks start to self-censor. They wonder, "How will this be received?" or "Will this make me look smart, constructive, or creative?" The whole idea of brainstorming is to mute the internal self-evaluation so you can generate some truly creative and innovative options that weren't apparent before. One critical way to allow these options to emerge is to eliminate all forms of evaluation during brainstorming in a group.

In addition, it should be made clear that just because someone suggests an idea for an option, that does not in any way mean it is something they would support, like, or are willing to agree to. One way to demonstrate seriousness about this rule is to begin a brainstorming session by throwing out at least one idea that would land you an outcome that is wildly not in your favor and one that would be wildly in your favor. Throwing out extreme outcomes on all sides demonstrates a commitment for this phase of the negotiation to truly be a nonevaluative and out-of-the-box idea-generation session.

During brainstorming, parties should work to separate ideas from those who suggest them to avoid suffering the consequences of *reactive devaluation*. *Reactive devaluation* is a psychological bias whereby humans tend to automatically discount the value of ideas that come from another party. Our brains have a natural, instantaneous reflex to evaluate information in the world as soon as it is perceived to quickly decide whether and how to act—you can imagine how beneficial this would be for survival out on the prehistoric savanna. Similar to issues of implicit bias, reactive devaluation is a relatively low-energy and minimal-thinking shortcut for your brain to dismiss the ideas of others, especially if you view your counterpart in negative terms, as possibly posing a threat to your values and interests (e.g., your identity, your place in a hierarchy, your well-being). That's why the more you can consciously detach a brainstormed idea from belonging to a particular person, side, or viewpoint, the more successful you will be at assessing it on its merits. So, rather than collecting Josue's idea or Mary's idea, it's helpful just to collect ideas. This is definitely more challenging than it sounds. It takes real practice and commitment! Luckily, technology can often be helpful here. For example, having participants type ideas into a document that does not connect the idea to an individual can effectively eliminate the problem of reactive devaluation.

### Building Block #4: Consider alternatives and criteria

After parties have brainstormed various options that meet the parties' interests, ultimately, the parties will either come to some kind of agreement on the possibilities or walk to their BATNA, which stands for Best Alternative to a Negotiated Agreement. *BATNA* is a term coined by Roger Fisher and William Ury in *Getting to Yes*. It is defined as the best course of action one might take if they do not reach agreement with a counterpart. Inherent in the concept of BATNA is that the course of action one would take is one that does not require an agreement with the counterpart in any way.

We explore how to think about your BATNA in the context of conflict resilience in detail in Chapter 8. For now, let's consider a simple example. Zach needs a reliable way to get to work in downtown Salt Lake City. His neighbor drives into the city each morning, so Zach considers asking for a ride. Before negotiating, though, Zach should evaluate what alternatives he has if he can't reach an agreement. These might include:

- Taking public transportation
- Buying his own car
- Asking someone else for a ride
- Taking a bike
- Hitchhiking
- Working from home

Zach then needs to determine which of these options is his best alternative if he and his neighbor don't reach a deal. That alternative becomes his BATNA. By identifying his BATNA ahead of time, Zach can avoid agreeing to anything that would be worse than it— the best away-from-the-table way to meet his interests.

Even better, negotiators are advised to improve their BATNA before starting negotiations. For example, if Zach's current BATNA is taking the bus, he might first ask a colleague who passes his house for a ride. Although the colleague's old Chevy is less appealing than his neighbor's new car, it's still better than the bus. Securing this option improves Zach's BATNA from what it otherwise would have been, putting him in a stronger negotiating position.

When it comes time for parties to choose among options, they often engage in a protracted battle of wills where sides dig in and try to trade tiny concessions in exchange for large ones, amounting to a predictable puerile game of haggling and horse-trading. Whatever you may have read or been told, this is by no means a shrewd way to approach a negotiation or conflict. Haggling and bargaining typically puts an unnecessary strain on relationships, diminishes trust, and breeds acrimony. Moreover, this approach can result in arbitrary outcomes, rewarding those who are more willing to dig in, bluff, puff, use insults, and hold out.

To avoid exploitation, to be more prepared when it comes time to choose among possible brainstormed options, and to make tough distributive questions, parties should instead look to widely recognized *criteria* to help decide the best option from the many options that were brainstormed. The idea here is to work collaboratively to identify some principle for making a choice that stands independently of the parties themselves and independent of their relative power and leverage in the negotiation or dispute.

In some cases, an objective criterion might be a market price, a standard of care, or an industry standard—some sort of benchmark that is external to the parties and could be seen as having a degree of legitimacy. For example, in negotiating a child custody clause, parties might look to guidelines established by the law or local practice. Grounding your result in such third-party criteria first acts as a shield against exploitation.

Imagine a situation where one side starts with a very extreme offer or demand. In a purely distributive or haggling approach to bargaining, the other side would respond with an outrageous offer in the opposite direction. What tends to follow is a classic exchange of back-and-forth offers where each side is making concessions. The goal of such an approach is to make fewer and smaller concessions than your counterpart so that you claim a larger piece of the negotiation pie.

The problems with this approach are manifold. First, you become susceptible to arbitrary outcomes. If your counterpart makes an extreme initial offer and you simply counter that offer, you've already allowed their demand to function as a sort of anchor in the negotiation whether or not it is grounded in anything legitimate. If, on the other hand, you ask what criteria or norms support the offer, you can suss out whether the offer is grounded in anything more than an attempt to take advantage of you. For example, if they say, "That's what we think is fair," or "That's what's in our budget," you should immediately reject such thinking by responding, "We'd be delighted to entertain any offer that is based on some kind of defensible standard but we are not in a position to respond or counter an offer that isn't connected to some legitimate market standard."

The second problem of playing an offer-counteroffer bargaining game is that it undermines the ability to engage in productive mutual-gains negotiation. It's very hard to sustain an interest-based, conflict-resilient approach to negotiation that seeks to create value while at the same time looking to use your leverage to "get the best" of the other side. However, if all sides are committed to using some kind of objective and defensible criteria when it comes time to evaluate and assess outcomes, it builds trust for the parties to share (1) their true interests and (2) the relative preference of those interests. This is what drives the most value-creating outcome.

When it comes to preparation, spending time researching and preparing criteria and standards of legitimacy can help serve as a *shield* from exploitation and a *sword* toward persuasion. Few parties in a negotiation want to be unfair and even fewer want to be seen as unfair. If, by reference to legitimate criteria, you can make a strong case for your preferred outcome based on a norm or standard that is external to your own perception of fairness, it often has persuasive power with the other side.

Consider the example of Danilo. Recently promoted to the rank of associate professor of surgery at the state School of Medicine, Danilo arranged a meeting with his dean to discuss the terms of his new contract. Among the issues to be negotiated was new office space. Danilo had spent the last five years in a very small office because of space constraints at the school. When Danilo mentioned his interest in acquiring a bigger office, the dean said, "I wish I could do that, but there is just no space available." Aware that every one of his colleagues had received a larger office upon promotion, Danilo felt more confident in asserting, "I appreciate you are working with constraints that are out of your control. At the same time, it's important to me that I receive the same set of benefits that all promoted faculty receive. If you feel I'm pushing beyond what is appropriate, let me know. And if it is simply a matter of space right now, I'd like to work with you on an assurance that I'd be given the next full-size office that becomes available." Without the benefit of being able to reference the external standard, Danilo would likely have either caved or pushed back in a way that felt entitled and even selfish, a self-image that did not comport with Danilo's own vision of himself as a team player.

Of course, in most negotiations there might be more than a single "norm" or "standard" to guide a question of distribution.

In cases like this, what might be done?

A common error is that parties start to get positional about what are the right benchmarks or criteria.

Some years ago, Bob was invited to mediate a labor dispute. The most contentious issue was related to wage increases over a five-year contract. On the good-news front, both sides were committed to identifying norms and criteria to guide the resolution of the wage-increase program. On the bad-news front, by the time Bob arrived on the scene, each side was already dug in on whose criteria was more accurate or fair. Was the "right" answer inflation data from the Bureau of Labor Statistics? Or instead, should the parties look at local wage increases for similarly situated unions in the Midwest over the past year? Or maybe neither of these was the best approach and the parties should instead defer to the opinion of a leading and well-respected authority at the local university? But if that were the best way forward, how to agree upon who was the most appropriate, well-respected, and leading economist?

The goal in identifying criteria isn't to move the battle from arguments over positions to another argument over criteria. But all too often, this is what can happen. A perfectly elegant interest-based negotiation gets stuck as parties become positional over which norm, criteria, or benchmark to use. A well-designed process encourages parties to find a criterion that everyone can agree upon, even if it would have little persuasive traction outside the parties at the negotiation table.

At times it's simply not possible for parties to agree upon or identify such criteria. But when that happens, often the parties can at least identify some kind of normative approach for closing a gap. What is the difference between an objective criterion or legitimate standard and a "normative approach"?

A criterion or legitimate standard is specific to the issue being negotiated. For example, looking at recent salaries of rookie professional baseball players is a relevant criterion for the New York Yankees to negotiate the acquisition of new talent.

A normative approach or standard is a more generic way of choosing that is not specific to a particular context but that parties may be prepared to defer to because it is commonly used by parties to make allocational choices of who should get what.

Consider a few examples:

- *First come, first served:* When Taylor Swift goes on tour, tickets are sold on a first-come, first-served basis. As stressful and unpleasant as it may feel to be hitting "refresh" on your Ticketmaster button to get those tickets, most people simply accept that this is the way you get Taylor Swift concert tickets unless you want to go on the secondary market and pay thousands of dollars.
- *Seniority:* Each year the U.S. Supreme Court sits for an annual photo. Where the justices sit is predetermined based on seniority. The chief justice sits in the front middle and then the most senior justice sits to his left, the second most to his right. The most junior justices stand in the back, with the most junior on the back left. Despite the increasing contentiousness of the current Supreme Court, as far as we know, there are no reports of Justice Barrett elbowing out Justice Sotomayor for a better seat for the annual photo. Seniority works as a commonly understood normative standard for resolving an important "distributional" question: where you sit/stand for the annual portrait of the Supreme Court.
- *Need:* Similarly, in some contexts, need ends up being an acceptable norm for dividing a resource in limited supply. You're sitting on the subway and an elderly person steps into your car from the subway platform, or perhaps a parent with a baby on his arm. Assuming you are able-bodied, the common convention is that you get up and offer your seat to that person because their need for the scarce resource of a subway seat is higher. Indeed, a decision to buck the normative standard and continue to sit in a seat

when an older person boards is at best seen as rude and selfish and, at worst, likely against the rules of riding as posted on signs in the subway car.

The point here is that when it's hard for parties to agree on a criterion to choose among the brainstormed options, sometimes they can identify a normative approach that helps them decide and that doesn't involve using leverage, bullying, or threatening the relationship— "It's my way or the highway!"

At times, parties can't even agree on a normative standard or approach.

Even then, a well-designed process can create space for driving decision-making that doesn't result in the exercise of leverage and power.

For example, at times parties can design their own way of making a distributional choice that works for them. Or they can agree to bring in a third party—perhaps a mediator, a trusted advisor, or expert— to help them work things through.

All these approaches are better than resorting to leverage and power.

The first time Bob had the chance to teach a full-fledged negotiation and conflict resolution course, he was working with a colleague who, like him, was a rookie instructor. In one of their planning sessions, Bob and his colleague had a disagreement about how to teach a particular unit. Unlike trying to agree to a wage level, a price point, or even a fair distribution of water resources between two communities using a shared reservoir, it turns out that there are no objective criteria—no *Kelley Blue Book*—for how to teach a bespoke unit in a semester-long law school negotiation class.

Though it was tough to make a credible reference to a normative approach, Bob could have argued that he was the senior teacher since he had one additional semester of experience serving as a teaching fellow before landing the gig as a co–course leader. But such an argument would not have landed well with his colleague, would have hurt their friendship and budding collaboration, and would have been a bit of a stretch in any event given his relative lack of experience in general.

Just at the moment things felt really stuck, Bob's colleague had a brilliant idea that drew upon the kind of best practice they would teach in their course together. Both Bob and his colleague had taken negotiation under the tutelage of the same professor at Harvard Law School. And both Bob and his colleague respected and valued the professor as an outstanding and skillful teacher. What about presenting the two approaches to the professor in a neutral way, without reference to who preferred which approach, and just ask her what she would do? This creative idea had huge appeal for both Bob and his colleague as a way to resolve the question. After all, part of the reason why they were so stuck was that each of them thought they were right and that surely their teacher and mentor would rule in their favor! It allowed them to find a workable solution without either of them backing down and losing face. Of course, Bob remembers the story well because, even though the idea for how to resolve the conflict was his colleague's, their professor picked his approach as the way to go!

The point here is that any good process that needs to drive a decision and reach an outcome should be clear about the way decisions and options will be selected as part of the process design. It should seek to use criteria and legitimate standards first, followed by a deference to commonly agreed-upon norms, and, when all else fails, a willingness to develop a process for resolving the question without resorting to mere leverage or escalation.

### Building Block #5: Build in agreement and implementation steps

This best practice works for more than just a conflict situation with a goal of making a deal. Whether you're designing a process to allow for a tough dialogue along lines of difference or a process for helping negotiate a deal or resolve a conflict, it's important to build in time to address what comes after the meeting, conversation, or negotiation is over.

This sounds simple and obvious but all too often, it's forgotten.

In the case of dialogue, sometimes the meat of the conversation is so rich and valuable that it's easy to push forward to the end of the allocated time and say, "Oh well, we're out of time but we'll follow up for next steps!" In the case of a negotiation, it's equally easy to say, "Yes! We finally worked it out! Let's go out and celebrate!"

We want to encourage you to have the discipline to build in a "Next Steps" or "Follow-up" phase into your process. Factoring this critical part into the process you're designing will also facilitate your ability to remain conflict resilient in all the moments leading up to and through this part of the process.

What might this look like?

In processes that are not designed to drive toward a specific substantive outcome, there might be a designated time to ask parties if there is interest or desire to continue a conversation—on either the same topic or a related one. Depending on how the conversation went, it might be a proposal for taking some joint action together. Maybe neither of these is in the cards. Even then, it might mean inviting participants to offer some feedback about the experience or a learning or a takeaway. It's important to remember that the purpose is not to tie up a hard conversation in a saccharine bow of good feeling or false consensus. If good feeling exists, wonderful; if not, simply naming the experience and allowing participants to reflect on and hold the tension is part of what it means to have designed a conflict-resilient process. Encouraging parties to reflect on the discomfort and to encode the reality that they survived the experience and may have gained insights, empathy, or knowledge of self or other from the experience is highly valuable.

The kinds of questions that can offer closure after a tough dialogue, full of differences and tension and without a next step as a group, might be:

- "What is one thing you learned today that surprised you?"
- "What is one question you still have about this issue or the other party (parties)?"
- "What have you learned today that will shift the way you engage with others (or yourself) on this issue?"

Depending on the nature and sensitivity of the closure question you provide, a facilitator may ask everyone to share their answer, may provide an opportunity for those who wish to share to do so, or may simply invite people to consider the answer to the question and write it down (or even put it into a note on their phone) and take it with them. The point is that some kind of closure or invitation to further engagement, reflection, and learning is key.

In the case of "next steps" coming from a process that was driving a negotiated resolution or deal, the "next steps" will be different. If there is a process in place to formalize an agreement—perhaps drafting and signing a deal—it's important that all the parties know who is responsible for the next task, when it will be done, and what comes next. In most contexts (even as commonplace as negotiating who will host the family reunion next year or figuring out phone etiquette at the dinner table), it's important that a process be in place to monitor and ensure implementation and to allow for ongoing feedback and revision of an agreement as needed. Imagine a negotiation between several gun-safety NGOs working together to have a coordinated legislative and public relations strategy to advance gun regulation legislation at the national level. Agreeing on how the interorganizational consortium will work is only the beginning of an ongoing series of negotiations that will occur over weeks, months, or even years.

Good process design acknowledges this and builds in set times when the parties will reconvene to assess how the collaboration is going, what is working, what isn't, and what might need to be changed, amplified, or eliminated.

By designing these next steps into the process up front, parties avoid the awkwardness of needing to "call a meeting" if things aren't going well in some phase of implementation. It also acknowledges that when it comes to working through differences or negotiating deals, structure *and* flexibility go hand in hand. That the original approach might not be working as planned is not a sign of failure, just a recognition of the complexity of the issues that have been worked out. Because the process has built-in feedback and review, the fact that some things aren't going as planned becomes normalized and there is opportunity built into the process for further discussion, negotiations, or modifications if needed.

Indeed, this is what makes a process conflict resilient: that parties could reach a conclusion and still feel that relationships and trust are sufficiently intact that they can bring up ongoing differences, disputes, and speed bumps, without feeling that the entire agreement is in jeopardy. This ongoing experience of being in conflict, addressing it in a way that is mutually valuable to everyone involved, and surviving the process again and again truly builds those conflict resilience muscles to not only become stronger, but also gain flexibility, stamina, and coordination with all the other muscle groups of conflict resilience.

## BUT REALLY . . .

If you've made it this far, you might be thinking, "Thanks, but I rarely find myself leading multiparty dialogues or participating in major negotiations! This stuff just doesn't apply to the conversation I want to have with my mom about the way she talks about my brother ever since he refused to go to synagogue during the high holidays last year and declared he is 'leaning into' Buddhism."

Or maybe you're thinking, "I like what you have to say here, but how does this work in the moment when you're powering through your day and suddenly your boss casually tells your colleague not to act so 'retarded' in the middle of your weekly meeting?"

Or maybe you're more skeptical, thinking, "I really can't imagine introducing some of these norms into the monthly PTA meeting. Plus, we already have a set of formal meeting rules in place. How can I ever change that?"

These are great questions, and we admit that this chapter has approached process design from a more formal and planful stance. And we get that you're unlikely to interrupt your boss mid-meeting to impose a bunch of process rules around a difficult conversation about how you think he should be more careful with the language he uses. We also agree that whether it's a PTA meeting, a conversation with your best friend about your radically different views on election integrity, or a family meeting around summer vacation planning, context and past practice matter and will influence how you might deploy the advice in this chapter.

At the same time, the tips around process in this chapter do have application in the day-to-day conversations we have where we need to be conflict resilient and where we want to create the conditions to maximize the chances for others to engage conflict constructively. First, we want to draw a distinction between how you might respond in the moment to a comment that feels triggering, upsetting, or downright offensive and how you might engage the larger issues embedded in the difference constructively. In the moment when we feel triggered by the boss's comment, we may be apt to fight, flee, freeze, fawn, or fester. Advice we provide in other parts of this book relating to mindful awareness, to pausing, to becoming aware of the limbic irritability in our brains—all are critical in the moment your boss uses the R-word or tells you your idea would "never work," in front of your entire team.

But when you return to raise the issue with your boss or have your conversation with your mom about her treatment of your newly minted Buddhist brother, deploying some of the process advice here can help make the difference between success and failure, between having an authentic, fruitful, and learning conversation and having an escalatory and tense contest of wills. While not every piece of process advice is useful for that convo with Mom or your boss, some of it really is. For example, being clear about the purpose of the conversation and setting up some ground rules and shared norms can make it easier for both of you to stay resilient and present in the face of your differences, especially when emotions are running high. Or, in the PTA meeting, shifting from traditional meeting rules to an approach that identifies interests and creates space for brainstorming can allow for more generative thinking and more creative ideas that would never come up through a more stilted and formal set of process norms.

When U.S. Supreme Court justice Elena Kagan was named the dean of Harvard Law School in the early 2000s, the first-year curriculum at most U.S. law schools, including Harvard, had been largely stagnant for nearly a century. Kagan had it in her mind to make a profound reform to legal education, especially around the first-year curriculum. But to succeed, she would need to persuade a fractious faculty of strong-willed individuals replete with hunkered-down factions. Ultimately, she was able to succeed in effecting the most extensive changes in the school's curriculum in decades. She accomplished this in a landslide vote of a faculty that was traditionally deadlocked and frequently at each other's throats.

Bob was a junior faculty member at Harvard Law School at the time and he would argue that the single most important factor in the success of Kagan's initiative was not the brilliance or even soundness of the reforms themselves. Instead, the success was due to her careful implementation of a process that involved key stakeholders over a multi-month period, sought to understand interests, was open to creative ideas, and ultimately created a glide path to a largely supportive vote of the faculty within a reasonable set time frame. The process even built in opportunities for review and feedback on changes. This paved the way for modifications and revisions in the ensuing years, from a mandatory "Problem-Solving Workshop" for first-year law students in the winter semester to a more flexible set of problem-solving courses. The latter gave students more autonomy in choosing a course tailored to their own curricular and professional interests and, ultimately, to requiring a negotiation or leadership class for all students graduating from Harvard Law School.

Building a conflict-resilient process doesn't guarantee consensus, a deal, or a melding of viewpoints. And having a thoughtful process in place doesn't make differences between individuals melt away—nor should it. Differences and healthy conflict are the lifeblood of dynamism and creativity. At times, a process that encourages and invites the expression of differences can surface conflicts and mismatches that are even deeper than we imagined. The beauty of a conflict-resilient process, above all, is that it helps you identify what's really at stake, which may often not be what the conflict first presents itself as being about. Once surfaced, conflict resilience helps us live in and with the tension, with real integrity rather than the haze and instability that come from swirls of polarization, sublimation, self-hate, or demonization of the other. Compared to the results from quick-and-dirty methods like haggling or horse-trading, this is what ultimately leads to the creation of much greater value—substantive as well as emotional and relational—for everyone involved. It's also part of what helps us come together in a conflicted world.

An awakening of the internal conflicts we hold, an increase in skills of handling conflict—of deep listening and effective assertion—and a process built to create low-risk space for exchange and exploration are all essential in helping individuals, organizations, parties, and even nation-states make enlightened choices about whether and how to move forward. That's what we take on in our next chapter.

# Chapter 8

# DECIDING THE FUTURE—TOGETHER OR APART

## Guidelines for Determining Whether and How to Move Forward

Joel—ever the scientist and problem-solver—is meticulous when it comes to his work, but he is infinitely more obsessive when it comes to getting his romantic relationships "right." His first long-term romance, in his early twenties, lasted five years, on and off, and was plagued by recurrent struggles around weak boundaries for both parties. Joel's own default tendency to avoid engaging conflict at all costs didn't help. It was only until he was completely miserable with his partner that he finally decided to end the relationship. This itself was agonizing, akin to a physical wound.

Years later, Joel married, vowing to take the lessons from his past relationship into the next. But that relationship was marked with the same patterns, and it ended in a similar, agonizing way, except with *a lot* more paperwork.

Joel's pattern in romantic relationships is not uncommon and often extends into professional relationships as well: How many of us, painfully aware of the high conflict in which we find ourselves, nonetheless choose to remain in the situation without engaging directly until it reaches a boiling point?

Then there are some who seem to have an almost pathologic compulsion to magnify and exacerbate conflict, usually to the detriment of themselves and their relationships.

Still others, as we have discussed repeatedly, walk away from a relationship without ever engaging at all.

Consider some examples:

- The talks about the possible joint venture between your start-up and a market competitor have been moving at a snail's pace for months. While you've reached an accord on many parts of the joint project, progress on key sticking points regarding staff retention and decision-making has stalled. Your investors have had it. They say it's time to make some key concessions or they will walk away from the deal. At this point, is it reasonable for you to concede?

- There is so much you love about accepting a job offer that will bring you and your family back to Chicago from Nashville. You'd be close to your extended family, become affiliated with a leading research institution, and be surrounded by brilliant colleagues. At the same time, the cost of living in Chicago is higher, the pay is lower, and your spouse is less than thrilled about Chicago winters. How do you navigate whether to accept the new job or stay where you are at?

- You've been negotiating a settlement with the French company over patent litigation for months. Your counterparties have indicated that their "last and final offer" is "take it or leave it." You realize this is not a bluff. Should you take the deal or proceed with the protracted litigation?

- A client often comments on how "fit" and "well-dressed" you are at the end of a professional meeting but rarely says anything about the quality of your representation or the hard work you do on your client's behalf. You don't sense the comments are coming from a bad place, and you believe the client clearly thinks you're at the top of your field. But that doesn't make the client's comments any less upsetting or inappropriate. You want to say something, but you also don't want to hurt your client's feelings or the relationship. Should you speak up or just let it go?

- Before a holiday dinner, your Jewish family prayed for the "innocent Palestinians who are losing their lives to violence in Gaza."

During the prayer, your sixty-three-year-old aunt, seated next to you, audibly grumbled, "I hope the Israelis kill them all." No one said a word afterward. But the comment has been sitting with you for months. Should you raise it with your aunt or keep the peace by remaining silent?

## WRESTLING WITH UNCERTAINTIES

Imagine standing at a crossroads in a forest, each path leading to a different destiny. This is the tantalizing premise at the heart of many stories in film and literature, where the concept of alternate universes captivates our imagination. Take *Sliding Doors*, for example, where Gwyneth Paltrow's character missing her train propels her into a parallel life that contrasts starkly with her existing one. This film, much like the transformative journey in *& Juliet*, a musical reimagining of Shakespeare's tragic heroine's fate had she not (spoiler alert) stabbed herself with Romeo's dagger at the end, delves into an expanding emotional whirlpool of what-ifs. Similarly, the *Back to the Future* trilogy, *The Family Man*, and the timeless *It's a Wonderful Life* not only showcase alternate realities for their characters, but also ponder the profound impacts of our choices and how our place in our relationships influences the lives of others.

In real life, we don't have the luxury of omniscience or time travel to see all the alternate outcomes that result from our different choices. Whether to say yes to an offer, accept the settlement, stay in a particular relationship, engage a hard issue with a colleague, friend, or family member, or walk away from it all—we can never know for certain the full consequence of one decision or another.

As we've demonstrated throughout this book, a lack of conflict resilience leads to lost opportunities. Too many of us are choosing to *not* engage in the hard-yet-important stuff. We can be too quick to walk away, fold, avoid, or escalate out of anger and frustration. The costs of this tendency, as we demonstrate, play out in increasing silos, frightening political polarization, damaged or ruined friendships, and balkanized family relationships that result in misunderstanding, alienation, and a reduced ability to engage the hardest issues of the day.

But let us be clear. Despite the urgency of our message, we do *not* believe that any of us should choose to engage differences and conflict in every instance, with everyone we disagree with, and at all times. As we deliver keynote talks and teach workshops on conflict resilience, we are careful to articulate the limits of our argument and to ensure that our message not be misunderstood as "To be conflict resilient means to engage all differences and conflicts with everyone in a constructive and skillful way one hundred percent of the time." Nothing could be further from our message on this. Sitting with the discomfort and unpleasantness of conflict as a way to grow and learn is different from subjecting yourself to real trauma and abuse. All too often these two concepts can get confused or conflated. Even worse, they can be co-opted. On the one hand, those who find engaging in conflict uncomfortable or difficult can wave a flag of "harm" or "trauma" as a defensive shield to avoid the hard work that is so central to conflict resilience. At the same time, trauma and abuse are real. Dismissing them with name-calling, "She's such a snowflake," or one-line aphorisms, "If you can't stand the heat, get out of the kitchen," is unfair, misguided, and sometimes even cruel.

In this chapter, we offer guidance on how you can assess when to stay and when to go. More specifically, we unpack what it means to be conflict resilient in several contexts.

## ENTER BATNA!

Deciding whether to stay in a negotiation, close a deal, or just walk away can be confounding. In the course of a challenging or high-stakes negotiation, a range of emotions, psychological biases, and general or acute anxieties can easily overwhelm you.

- It's the house of your dreams, but you've already exceeded your budget! Should you say no and keep looking or suck it up and say yes, knowing it might mean additional financial stress and possibly delaying retirement by several years just to meet the mortgage payments?
- You're ready for a change, and you love the colleagues you've met, but the job title and salary feel like a demotion. You've pushed as hard as you can, but your new boss has said that she's done all she can do. You just need to decide.
- The offer from the negligent contractor still feels like a rip-off, but you're not sure you can take the risk of losing in court. Plus, this unexpected dispute over the bathroom renovation has already kept you up for too many nights. Maybe it's just time to take their lowball offer and move on. Both options feel bad to you.

Dilemmas like these are challenging to assess. And advice from family and friends is often contradictory, which makes it hard for you to feel like you're making the most informed and correct decision. As a result, decision paralysis can take over. Despite these realities, there is advance work we can do to guide decision-making in situations like these.

Earlier we introduced the concept of BATNA (Best Alternative to a Negotiated Agreement) in discussing process design. Here we will explore it in greater detail because it can provide rapid clarity in even the most chaotic dilemmas. Whether we say yes to anything is ideally decided in relation to what we could or would do if we said no and walked away from the interaction. To help sort through these questions, before you enter *any* negotiation or conflict management process where part of the goal is to potentially reach an agreement with the other side, it's critical to understand what alternatives might be available to you if you do *not* reach an agreement.

For Meryl, a financial manager and mother of two, life was akin to piloting a supersonic jet—fast, exhilarating, but requiring constant vigilance. Her latest challenge was a critical midcareer maneuver: negotiating for a well-deserved promotion and raise with her boss Alejandro. This wasn't just a professional hurdle; it was about steering her life toward a destination that valued her worth, a validation of her hard work, and a recognition she earnestly sought amid the daily chaos of meetings and motherhood.

As she prepared for this anxiety-inducing meeting with Alejandro, Meryl had followed the counsel we laid out throughout this book: She acknowledged her discomfort about negotiations with inherent power differences and devised strategies to manage feelings around her identity and the internal narratives that might come up as a result of the negotiation. She did her chair work, rehearsing the exchange with a trusted colleague, and had identified her substantive, emotional, and relational interests, while also considering what they might be for Alejandro and other relevant players external to this negotiation, but who might be able to influence the result. She was ready to deeply listen and assert effectively—and she had even deliberately proposed a process for the exchange.

But she didn't know what to do if Alejandro rejected her request outright. Or what if he offered her something better than the status quo, but less than what she deemed as fair or appropriate?

If her boss did not give her the raise and promotion she felt she deserved, some of Meryl's "alternatives" would include:

- Staying in her job and doing nothing
- Quitting
- Accepting an offer at a competing firm
- Staying in her job for now while updating her resume/CV and reaching out to a recruiter
- Suing her boss for gender discrimination
- Starting a social media campaign calling out the deficiencies and bad behavior of her employer
- Going back to school for another degree

As you read this, you may think, "Well, OK. But some of these alternatives would be strategically poor or even a losing proposition for her." We agree with this, of course. Suing her boss for discrimination, for instance, would likely cost Meryl thousands of dollars and, short of compelling evidence supporting gender discrimination, result in a loss in court and a hit to her reputation if she had no evidence.

As you prepare for any negotiation, we encourage you to make the longest possible list of alternatives—things you can do that do not require an agreement with the other side. Adding ones that seem unlikely or even not attractive to you helps get the creativity juices flowing. Once Meryl has generated this list, she needs to consider which one of these alternatives she would actually choose if she did not reach an agreement with Alejandro because that "thing" is the best of her alternatives—what we call her BATNA.

Meryl should only say "yes" to Alejandro if what is being offered is better than her BATNA. Anything less than what she would achieve by accepting Alejandro's offer should yield a "no" from her.

Analytically, this seems straightforward and easy enough. But in practice it can get messy.

This is where her earlier prep work matters. The way you assess your BATNA is based on how well you understand what your interests are—substantive, emotional, relational—and how to prioritize them. For example, if Meryl has young children, works close to her children's daycare, and doesn't want to relocate, she may think that simply staying where she is, without a promotion or raise, is her BATNA. On the other hand, if one of her most important interests is being paid fairly, getting public recognition for her work, and feeling appreciated, she may assess that looking for a new opportunity is her BATNA. Of course, it's likely that Meryl may want fair pay, recognition, and appreciation while also wanting to keep stability in terms of location and convenience for daycare. In determining what her BATNA is, Meryl will need to weigh the relative importance of these interests against each other to determine what she will do in the absence of an agreement. That is, your BATNA is always decided in relation to the *full set of interests you bring to the table*. It also explains why preparation is so important. If you've failed to think through your interests thoroughly in advance, it becomes hard to assess whether accepting a specific offer or resolution is the best or right decision.

All too often, parties mis-assess their BATNA because they are over-focused on one or two highly salient interests—like salary or prestige. This is called *vividness bias*—the tendency to over-weight the more immediate and prestigious attributes of a decision, such as salary or an employer's status, and under-weight less impressive issues like location or rapport with colleagues. This is why it's critical to conduct a careful assessment of not only your interests but also the relative weight of those interests *before* you determine your BATNA.

Once you assess your BATNA based on a frank and honest assessment of your full range of interests, you are more empowered to decide whether to say yes or walk away from the negotiation.

Let's imagine that, for the purposes of our example, Meryl has assessed that her BATNA is to simply stay in her current job if Alejandro denies her requests for a promotion and salary increase. In our consulting work with clients, sometimes we hear folks in a situation like this say something like "I have no BATNA here because I can't afford to quit or change my job." We get where this is coming from. But it is not quite accurate. Meryl *does* have a BATNA. It's staying where she is at, without a new agreement, and doing nothing. Her BATNA just happens to be "do nothing" and stick with the status quo. "Do nothing" is still a BATNA if you can do it without an agreement with your negotiation counterpart. Your BATNA need not be "good" or "strong" for it to exist.

Working through and identifying your BATNA can help you think about how you might improve it before you begin a negotiation. What might this look like for Meryl? Well, first, she might update her resume/CV and interview to obtain a tentative competing offer from another firm before she begins her negotiation with Alejandro. But even the decision to interview elsewhere should be assessed in relation to Meryl's interests. For example, is this worth the time and effort it would take? Or is there a risk that interviewing elsewhere will leak back to Alejandro and hurt her standing and reputation in her current job? Answers to these questions will help guide her decision-making in whether and how best to improve her BATNA before speaking with Alejandro.

In a mutual-gains negotiation, we don't want to focus our energy and time solely on figuring out "whose BATNA is better." Instead, we want to focus our energy and time on the parties' underlying interests. This is how you will increase the chances that the negotiation will result in creating value for all sides—value that may not have existed beforehand.

But even when people do prepare and know their BATNA ahead of entering a negotiation, they still often reach deals that are worse than their BATNA because they fall victim to a psychological dynamic called the "sunk costs" or "escalation of commitment" problem. Bob has seen this happen dozens of times. Some years ago, he offered strategic negotiation consulting to government officials working on a complex multiparty negotiation over the redevelopment plan for an abandoned industrial park that involved hundreds of stakeholders. Painstaking efforts were made to drive a value-creating process and address some of the thorniest issues that had been ignored by local officials for decades. As the date for a major decision-making deadline approached, however, some negotiators started to soften on key issues. Bob would press these officials, reminding them that, by any measure of how they assessed their interests, their BATNA was extremely strong. Walking away—even considering the intangible optics of no-deal at a major progress deadline—was better than the current deal on the table. Still, the officials said they wanted an agreement. It was clear to Bob that escalation of commitment bias was in play. These negotiators had spent eighteen months in intense and often exhausting negotiations. The thought of walking away was too painful. It would be a blow to their identity and, in their mind, to their efforts, and it would result in what seemed to be a failure of the entire process. Bob sympathized. Deeply. He had been there, advising this team from the start. But the beauty of understanding and preparing your BATNA is that it becomes the benchmark for deciding whether to agree or walk away. Success is *not* an agreement at any cost. It's only success if the deal on the table is better than your BATNA.

The same could be said in reverse. We have worked with clients who, because of their failure to manage their emotions or their identity, have walked away from a deal that, overall, while perhaps not their desired result, was still meaningfully better than their BATNA. Consider a situation where an inventor discovers that one of his patents has been infringed upon. His counsel reaches out to the infringer. As time wears on, it's clear that the alleged infringer is prepared to make a substantial payment to the inventor for a license. From the infringer's perspective, the proposed payment amount is based on their assessment of the likelihood of losing at trial. But the inventor, suffering from overconfidence bias, refuses to calculate any discount in his settlement price for the chance, however small, that he could lose at trial. Moreover, he fails to consider the cost of litigation—in terms of time, money, and sleepless nights—that could reduce the value of any court victory. His legal counsel, advisors, and others urge him to accept the generous, if not entirely satisfying, settlement offer. But the inventor walks away to an uncertain, costly, and time-consuming BATNA of litigation.

In both cases, BATNA assessment, done carefully and with a full consideration of the wide range of interests that you may bring to the table, can help you decide when to agree and when to walk away.

## TO ENGAGE OR TO AVOID, THAT IS THE QUESTION

BATNA is a helpful concept for an exchange that has the markings of a traditional negotiation. Whether to accept a job offer, sell your home, hire the nanny, or settle a business dispute—all fall into this traditional idea of a negotiation.

But how do you decide whether to engage in many of the toughest conversations that we discuss in this book—the ones that cut to the core of your identity, belief, and meaning—the kinds of conversations that are ripping our country, community, and families apart?

Consider some common examples:

- A conversation about marriage equality will hit differently with profoundly unequal real-world consequences for an LGBTQ+ person than it does for a straight one.
- A conversation about whether your undocumented cousin should be sent back to Guatemala, where he's at risk of being murdered for his political beliefs, is fundamentally different for you than it is for your best friend whose family arrived from Ireland in the early part of the twentieth century.
- A debate about whether to approve the proposed public school budget has experientially different implications for you with three elementary-school-age children than it does for the wealthy couple who decided to forgo children and who would prefer lower property taxes.

We are deeply aware of the pain and hurt that some individuals and groups endure in a world where others make arguments and hold on to beliefs that are or may be experienced by others as racist, sexist, ableist, ageist, homophobic, xenophobic, anti-Christian, anti-Semitic, Islamophobic, or in some way unfairly prejudiced or intolerant. We wish we lived in a world where the dignity, freedom, and rights of all were seen and universally respected and honored. But unfortunately, that is not the world in which we live. Moreover, at times there are genuinely challenging issues where the rights of one group might rub against, impinge upon, or be in tension with the rights of another group. The decision by a Christian university to fire a theology professor who marries someone of the same gender necessarily pits competing constitutional rights against each other—the free exercise of religion versus the right to marriage as a substantive-due-process right of the Fourteenth Amendment.

As you assess whether to engage some of these especially hard conversations, let us be clear: we want to invite you to increase your tolerance for discomfort around conflict and your capacity to handle that discomfort rather than run from or avoid it. That is the necessary work of conflict resilience. But there are limits to this: there is a distinction between discomfort, displeasure, and frustration, and genuine trauma. *We don't want you to put yourself in the face of danger from any form of harm, abuse, or trauma.* And we acknowledge that there's often a marked power imbalance in play in very hard conversations that can't be equalized fully before the hard dialogue begins. In the case of an LGBTQ+ person, the stakes over whether they can be fired because of who they love will land differently for them than it might for a straight person who, while they may have strong views on the topic, do not have their livelihood at risk by whether their view ultimately prevails in the public square.

*Conflict resilience means being able and strong enough to sit with and through the discomfort of disagreement to strengthen connection and discover valuable insights—insights about ourselves and others and how we can better relate to each other as family, colleagues, or fellow citizens.* Part of our overall premise here is that we find ourselves in a political and historical moment where it can simply be too convenient to avoid the dialogue or conflict and rationalize your avoidance on some external factor: "Talking to them legitimates their viewpoint." Or "What's the point? They are beyond persuasion, and I'll only leave upset." Or, "Because their view is entirely based on misinformation, acknowledging it further legitimizes ideas that are neither reasonable nor acceptable, and I refuse to contribute to that." In many cases, we have neither the mindset to be open to conflict-related discomfort nor the skills to handle it. Much like a form of socio-emotional intelligence, mindset cannot be emphasized enough. But neither can the behavioral skill set (what you actually say and how you say it) be minimized, because it allows us to translate that mindset into action. This includes assessing when, in a given context or moment, you can choose to apply the skills or walk away.

So, how do we go about deciding whether to stay or go in these scenarios, assuming choice is in our control? We propose considering each scenario across three sets of context-oriented questions:

1. Situation
2. Dynamics
3. History

## 1. Situation

This may be the easiest one to take on. This context is relevant in the moment when you have three minutes left in a meeting, there are twelve people present in the room, and someone unexpectedly says, "All of you types should go back to your home country" or "I can't believe how many brainwashed sheep there are like you. I wish you could just do the hard work of understanding the truth or be put out of your misery." Neither of these triggering moments is ideal for a conflict-resilient dialogue in the moment. Situational factors are not only about timing and setting; they are also about the circumstances and conditions of the environment. Circumstances here refers to givens of the situation, factors that are not easy or are unlikely to change in the moment, like the country you live in, your health, your financial security. Whereas conditions refers to variable modifiable factors that are easy or likely to change in the moment—the noise level of the room, the uncomfortable chairs you're sitting in, feelings of hunger, fatigue, or lightheadedness because you've had a glass of wine on an empty stomach. Put another way: circumstances are to a region's climate just as conditions are to the weather happening right now. Here are a few questions you can ask yourself to clarify the suitability of this context for you if it isn't readily apparent:

- *Time and Setting:* Is there sufficient time and an appropriate setting to address this conflict effectively? For instance, with only a few minutes left in a meeting and multiple participants involved, is it realistic to expect to start a productive discussion?

- *Circumstantial Constraints:* What are the immutable factors in this situation that might impact the process of navigating conflict? Consider aspects like the cultural or legal context, the physical environment, or resource limitations that are unlikely to change in the immediate moment.

- *Current Conditions:* Are there temporary factors influencing the situation that could affect the outcome of the discussion? This includes variables like the current mood of the participants, environmental discomforts (noise level, seating arrangements), physical states (hunger, fatigue), or even recent consumption of substances like alcohol or medication that could influence how you or the others in the conversation engage in the conversation.

- *Immediate Relevance:* How directly relevant is the topic of conflict to the current situation or agenda? If the disagreement is tangential or unrelated to the immediate goals of the gathering, for instance, it might be more productive to address it in a later encounter directly dedicated to working through the disagreement and nothing else.

- *Safety and Respect:* Will engaging in this dialogue maintain a low-risk and respectful environment for all involved? If the conflict involves harmful or disrespectful remarks or derogatory comments about one's background, it's crucial to consider whether engaging the conflict on the spot will uphold or undermine a respectful, direct, authentic, and low-risk space for dialogue.

These questions are designed to help you assess whether the current situation is conducive to constructive conflict-resilient engagement or if it might be better to address the disagreement in a different setting or at a later time.

We acknowledge that there also exist situations when walking away from the scenario without saying anything at all may be a challenge, even after you recognize that now is not the time or place to stay and engage a difficult conversation with conflict resilience. In situations like this, your purpose may be less in the direction of an actual conversation and more about either noting disagreement, offering support to someone else who may need to hear it in the moment, or upholding an important value. Before making a comment, carefully consider your purposes. If it is simply coming from a place of anger or frustration, consider naming those emotions to yourself and asking whether speaking may produce more negative and unhelpful externalities and whether there may be other ways to quell or manage your inner anger or sense of hurt. However, if you decide you must say something in the moment, here are some potential non-escalatory responses you can consider using or adapting to help you walk away for the moment while asserting your interests and not endorsing the other party's view:

- I'm not able to join or say yes on this, and you seem to really want me to. I wonder if we can find a different time to talk this through some more when we both feel ready to engage?
- I recognize and acknowledge your view on this matter, yet I hold a different view. If this is something you would be open to talking through when we have more time to do so, I'd be open to that.
- This might be a really good topic for a longer conversation, and I confess I'm not prepared right now to do so. For now, let me simply register my disagreement and curiosity to discuss more, if there is openness to this, and we can go from there.

## 2. Dynamics

These questions are not just about your relationship with the other person. They are also about how you and they are situated in the context of, say, a community, organization, or even family. This type of context relates primarily to implicit and explicit social dynamics. Let's say you and I work at the Department of Widgets or are in the same family. We don't have much of a relationship except that we work in the same place or share relatives. If it weren't for the fact that we share a workplace or a family, there wouldn't be much of a relationship at all. Still, we bump into each other enough that it might be valuable—or even necessary—to talk through our issues. By doing so, we could learn from each other and find ways to manage our differences more effectively, especially since we're likely to be in each other's presence regularly due to our shared context. Although there might be some possibility of alignment or problem-solving from the conversation, neither the possibility of alignment nor problem-solving should be a precondition to the conversation. This context of dynamics also includes the structures or systems in place where one party may be more likely to have greater influence or authority to impact a relevant situation.

One of the most common related frustrations in conflict is when we have an actual or perceived imbalance of power, especially if we are or feel disadvantaged by those dynamics. It's important to note that, although it may not always seem this way, these dynamics have the potential to change based on factors that at times (even if only rarely) may be in our control and other times may be completely out of our control. Some questions to consider that may clarify how the dynamics at play can influence whether it makes sense for you to engage or walk away in the moment:

- *Shared Context:* How does our shared context (like working in the same office or being part of the same family) influence the need or opportunity to address this conflict? Consider whether shared environment, resources, or supports make it helpful to find a way forward despite differences or provide an opportunity for mutual growth and learning even if persuasion is not a possibility.

- *Relationship Beyond Context:* Aside from our shared context, do we have any significant relationship or interaction? For example: Is it a parent-child relationship? Are you married, in a domestic partnership, or in a coparenting agreement? Are you housemates in a twelve-month lease, teammates for the next hour, or complete strangers carpooling in a five-minute rideshare? What do you know about the relationship on their side and how much do you know about who they are? Assess if the conflict is worth addressing with a good-faith effort given the nature and depth of your relationship outside the shared context.

  As you do this, we invite you to pause and also consider: What relationship might I hope or prefer to have if this and related differences were not standing in the way? Too often, our strong, salient feelings about a sensitive and important disagreement blind us to what we might gain from getting to know someone better. As a result, we quickly dismiss the possibility, telling ourselves, "This just isn't worth it," without giving it any further thought. Given the discomfort involved in the direct conflict, we appreciate the tendency to write the relationship off. We also invite you to consider the great cost of quickly dismissing what's possible and what might be missed by avoiding a hard conversation or coming together even in the discomfort of your disagreement.

  Take even twenty seconds to pause and consider: If the hard issues of disagreement didn't stand in the way, what kind of relationship would I prefer to have with this individual?

- *Influence Dynamics:* Is there an imbalance that may affect the ability to influence others or the course of events between us within our shared context (e.g., due to legal authority, hierarchy, seniority, social network, systemic inequities, political will, etc.)? How does this affect the conflict? Assess whether the dynamics make it more challenging to address the issue in a low-risk way and how you might be able to address these concerns adequately before or during the conversation.

- The notion that the conversation should only happen if there are no power or authority differentials is not one we can endorse. Indeed, part of what makes so many conflicts so challenging is the inherent power dynamics in play. If we were to wait for power between parties to equalize before a hard conversation could happen or before a conflict could be engaged, the wait might (literally) last a lifetime. Whenever there is a serious risk that someone has more power in a dynamic, assessing these issues can often create some safeguards to facilitate the engagement of the conflict. These can include some of the process features we discuss earlier in Chapter 7, including shared ground rules, the use of a facilitator, and an agreed-upon agenda.

- *Potential for Change of Dynamics:* How motivated or open is the other party to a genuine dialogue? Note how we frame this not as potential for change of *opinion*, but rather of *dynamics*. We usually avoid conflict because we think there is no way of persuading our counterpart. But this misses an essential value of conflict: the chance to learn from them, and perhaps even be changed or persuaded about something ourselves. So, the question is not so much whether you can persuade them, but whether you can change a destructive or toxic dynamic into a more authentic, even if somewhat uncomfortable, conversation. As you consider this, ask yourself whether there might be factors within your control that could alter the dynamics positively or negatively.

We distinguish assessing the likelihood of having a persuasive outcome, which we think should not be a factor, from whether the counterpart is genuinely open to a dialogue that they can come to in good faith. Engaging in a difficult dialogue requires real vulnerability. There must be some degree of mutuality and preparedness for this on all sides, acknowledging that individual capacities to engage at this level may vary. If one side is keen for a dialogue and the other simply wants to use the time to drive and defend their own point of view or, even worse, extract important substantive concessions and impose emotional "work" on you at your expense, the dynamics may counsel against a conversation.

- *Frustration from Imbalance:* How does any perceived or actual imbalance of influence contribute to the frustration in this conflict, and is it possible to address this imbalance? Think about whether the dynamics are causing additional stress or frustration in the conflict, and if there's a way to mitigate this impact to facilitate a more balanced dialogue. Or, when the interaction is part of an attempt to negotiate an outcome or resolve a dispute, to facilitate creative problem-solving between the parties. For example, the use of a facilitator or a pre-agreement to ground rules that empower or enable the voices of those who may have less structural power in a situation can often address some of the frustrations around power inequities leaking into the conversational space. Sometimes, though, just admitting the frustration to yourself and deciding that, for the time being, you will put that aside to do the hard work of being conflict resilient in the conversation is enough.

Consider a dialogue in a corporate workplace in the months following COVID about workplace policies that would govern expectations around hybrid work going forward. Tensions were high between management, longtime employees, and employees who had been hired since the pandemic had started. On various occasions, management had set up listening sessions for their employees. But these had done little to ease divisions and resentment. The power dynamics within the organization were palpable. And there was resistance from many frontline workers to yet another "conversation."

The introduction of Bob as a facilitator helped. But of equal importance was an agreed-upon ground rule: this would not be a "listening session." Instead it would be a genuine dialogue in which management would be invited and expected to become vulnerable about their own doubts, struggles, and insecurities in navigating the organization both through and since COVID. The rules required people to speak about their personal struggle and experience—and *not* about the substantive issues, what the company policy was, why it was unfair, outdated, appropriate, nonsensical, or balanced. While some expressed doubt about whether this would help solve the substantive questions, enough members of management and frontline staff agreed to participate.

The conversation ended up being transformative. For the first time in a very long time, individuals saw folks on the other side as "humans" and not as enemies with huge power differentials. The positive experience led to others wanting to participate. None of these conversations did much to shift substantive views on the "best" or "right" or even "acceptable" answer on post-COVID work rules. But it did enable a less stressful and more joint-problem-solving approach to these conversations. Why? It helped humanize viewpoints and stories. And it built trust.

Admittedly, not every dialogue went well. And there were moments when parties resorted to their power positions. But a shift in ground rules and a considered focus on what the dialogues would be about fundamentally shifted workplace culture, the stories each group told about the other, and the willingness to work with each other from a collaborative rather than a divisive zero-sum stance.

Answering these questions can help you better understand the dynamics at play in a conflict and whether engaging in the disagreement in the moment is likely to be productive.

### 3. History (dealing with trauma, mental health, and other complexifying factors)

First, if you believe or are unsure whether the dynamics of your specific scenario are abusive in any way or put you at risk for or relate to any kind of violence, harassment, or assault, we address some of these questions later in this chapter. Similarly, if you are uncertain about how to approach a situation where the dynamics are influenced by mental health issues—personality disorders or tendencies like borderline personality disorder or narcissistic traits or psychiatric disorders like major depression, substance use disorders, or delusional disorders—we will address this especially sensitive and complex matter below.

That said, we haven't forgotten about the third set of context-oriented questions; we wanted to appropriately introduce it given how complex it can be. This third context may be the most challenging to address, because it is about events that have already happened. For example, if you are a survivor of trauma or have been unjustly accused of causing trauma of whatever type, this is likely a scenario where you don't need to charge into a challenging conflict-resilient dialogue. That is, staying or going may be decided based on how much distress or harm you are likely to experience in engaging the current conflict because of something that happened in your life related to the context.

Furthermore, you may be a person or belong to a group that has been historically subordinated or targeted by the other party or the group they belong to. Engaging in dialogue has the potential to create a scenario that is unjust, unfair, harmful, or traumatizing. In this latter case, the fact that you find yourself in a historically subordinated or targeted group does not mean you should not engage the conflict. But it certainly would be a consideration in your decision-making. One way of thinking about conflict resilience is a capacity each of us should have and be able to draw upon. But, like emotional intelligence, it's not the case that even the best leader can be expected to display these qualities in every context and at every moment.

Below are some questions to consider as you evaluate whether a particular conflict or dialogue is one that you should participate in directly:

- *Personal Trauma and Past Experiences:* Have past traumatic experiences or injustices you've faced made you particularly vulnerable in this conflict? Reflect on whether the conflict might reopen old wounds or cause undue distress due to your personal history. For example, if you have been the victim of a sexual assault, or perhaps unjustly accused of harassment in the workplace, it may be harder for you to engage a dialogue on these issues. Being conflict resilient does not mean soldiering on. It also means using the wisdom to say, "Participating here may re-traumatize me or cause me further, deeper pain and harm."

- *Historical Relationship with the Other Party:* What has been your past experience or historical relationship with the other party? In this case, we are asking more than whether you have a history of exhausting, painful, or bad interactions with the other person or set of persons. If bad history in general or around this issue were a disqualifier, it would eliminate a wide swath of dialogues that need to happen. And it would take away the possibility that conflict resilience provides for improved under-standing, forgiveness, and even restoration of the relationship.

  Instead, we invite you to consider the extent to which you believe that the other person—however challenging their behaviors—might be coming from a place of good faith. If in-vited into a more purposeful dialogue, the question in our mind is not "Could they do this well?" but rather "Could they at least enter this with an intention—to the best of whatever their ability may be—to join with me?"

  That question is fraught and hard to know ex ante. It's one of the reasons why being conflict resilient requires so much courage. To assess this, we invite you to broaden the lens beyond just the set of a few past bad interactions to the widest possible angle of your experience and history with them.

- *Hope for Improved Understanding, Connection, or Possible Resolution:* Despite a difficult history, is there a genuine possi-bility or hope for increased mutual understanding, growth, re-demption, repair, or positive change that could motivate you to engage in this dialogue? In the past, how often has either party been open and willing to reflect critically on their own beliefs or assumptions? If this is something that continues to be on your mind, there is likely something there that makes you hold out a hope—however slim—for some kind of improved understanding, connection, or resolution. Balance the challenges of the past with the potential for a constructive and healing future outcome.

We're suggesting these questions to help you consider the impact of historical contexts as you assess whether you should engage a particular conflict or hard conversation. They're designed to encourage a thoughtful assessment of past experiences and their potential influence on present conflicts, as well as the prospects for future resolution and healing.

But here it's important for us to again underscore our purposes. People struggle to stay in any kind of conflict, often because they have limited patience and skills for conflict and, importantly, limited resilience for conflict. And that ends up destroying all sorts of value. That's our main premise.

At this point, we hope you know that we are inviting you to stretch your mindset and skill set around conflict, not enter headlong into every single area of conflict in your life regardless of the circumstances or person on the other side. We are making the case that doing so offers benefits for you, your family, your career, and your well-being. We're also urging that both the individual and collective failure to do this work imposes high costs and will have dire consequences for ourselves, our families, and our nation.

Precisely because our call is not one that applies "always" and "at all times," we are focused here on helping you think about how to decide if you should engage and stay, or walk away. What we're recommending here is to ask yourself with real integrity, "Does this situation call for the stretch of skill with a conflict-resilient approach? Or does prudence, a healthy self-regard, and an acknowledgment that not every conflict situation should be engaged directly, counsel me to step away from this situation—at least for the time being?"

We've been providing guidance, broadly, at two levels. One is around the substantive negotiation tools and the second is around "staying with and in the difference" tools. For the latter, the hope is that it will help you, for your physical, mental, material, and social well-being, to more mindfully gauge when to stay or go.

We want to avoid sweeping categories here. It would be too convenient to say, "Well, if you are a Jewish person, you are exempt from a conversation with someone who thinks that Israel is a neocolonial project and should be destroyed." That might be true for you, given your own history, context, and experience of past trauma and harm. But we also think it's helpful for some Jewish people who believe in the right and necessity of Israel to exist to engage a serious and hard dialogue with people on the other side of the issue. The point here is that we want to encourage you to develop your conflict resilience skills—to be truly brave, but also to be thoughtful and wise about your well-being. That is very different from simply putting some conflicts or topics beyond conversation or saying that you automatically get a "pass" if you are personally implicated and "no pass" if you are not. It's a highly individualized consideration.

## IS THIS TRAUMA OR DISCOMFORT?

If you're unsure whether what you might be experiencing in the face of conflict is expected transient discomfort or longer-lasting trauma, you're not alone. It can help to have some definitions for these terms as well as some tools to assess this for yourself. First, we need to complicate things slightly by pointing out that somewhere in between the extremes of discomfort and trauma is something else—what is widely called "adverse life experiences."

Let's start by getting the definition of discomfort out of the way. Discomfort is about feeling moderate reduction in the amount of physical or mental calm that you would usually feel. This might be described as a mild-to-moderate feeling of unease. This feeling is usually temporary and goes away soon after whatever is causing the discomfort stops or is no longer present.

Next, understanding the distinction between a trauma and an adverse life experience is essential. Daniela Montalto, PhD, clinical associate professor in the Department of Psychiatry at NYU Langone Health and clinical director of the Neuropsychology and Learning Service, notes an interesting shift in language usage over the past decades. "Over the last 30 years, with the rise of medically focused media, clinical language has become more accessible," Dr. Montalto explains. People now commonly describe feeling down as "depression" or label frightening or challenging events as "traumatic." Dr. Montalto points out that approximately 75 percent of individuals report that they were exposed to a trauma.

Trauma can be defined as experiencing or witnessing an incident that was life-threatening or took away someone's bodily autonomy, resulting in intense fear or helplessness. In contrast, adverse life experiences are unpleasant situations that are not life-threatening and not all that sudden and unexpected. Dr. Montalto compares most adverse life experiences to a mosquito bite: bothersome and distracting in the moment but it will eventually fade away. Conversely, a bee sting could represent a more intense adverse life experience—it hijacks all our attention when it happens, is very painful, usually requires removal of a stinger, and needs more time to overcome, though it too eventually becomes a distant memory. But an allergic reaction to a bee sting could suddenly be traumatic, particularly if it's severe and epinephrine isn't readily available, as Dr. Montalto notes.

Consider a real-life example. As we wrote this chapter, our book agent reached out to settle on a final date by which we would submit it to our publisher for review. We were already late on the manuscript, due to a number of complicating personal and professional commitments that knocked us off schedule and—let's face it—the tendency to delay writing in favor of any other activity that can give a steady stream of dopamine and serotonin. Even worse, on the day that our agent reached out to us, Bob was asked to join a high-level negotiation team in Abu Dhabi for a round of critical talks. The unexpected trip would take him away for ten days, forcing us to either give our literary agent, Roger, a date much later than he wanted to hear or to placate him with an earlier date on which we both knew we couldn't deliver. We decided to ask him for a conversation instead. In the lead-up to the conversation, Bob slept poorly and felt a fair bit of anxiety and dread. On the one hand, you might be thinking, "What's the big deal? You were just asked to participate in extremely consequential set of international negotiations that could only add more credibility to this book. What are you fretting about for a short and reasonable extension on the deadline?"

But for Bob, the entire conversation felt deeply uncomfortable because it hit one of Bob's biggest identity triggers—disappointing people. Luckily, given Joel's experience as a neurologist who is regularly forced to deliver bad news to patients about their serious medical diagnoses, the conversation with Roger was a bit unpleasant but not particularly earth-shattering either. What's important to stress is that for neither Bob nor Joel would this conversation rise to the level of trauma, even though it meant a lot more discomfort for Bob than for Joel or even the average person.

Consider another example involving Shankar, who had been unjustly accused of harassment at the height of the MeToo movement. Years later, Shankar found himself at a cocktail party. A debate ensued around a highly publicized incident involving a CEO and founder who was unceremoniously removed from his position with what seemed to be very little or no process after a three-decade career. One of Shankar's friends quipped cavalierly, "You know, the CEO may well be innocent, but given the history of inappropriate behavior that went unchecked for so many years in our society, we have to be OK with some innocent people going down for the greater good and as an example to show that this kind of behavior is just unacceptable." Shankar froze. His feet and hands went cold. He felt as if he could not breathe. Shankar left the room. And then the party. Later, in a coaching session,

Shankar raised this issue with Bob, feeling shame that he had not been conflict resilient.

While we are not perfect diagnosticians, in our conversations with experts and our understanding of the literature and symptoms, what Shankar was experiencing was genuine trauma, not just mere discomfort. That a single statement in a casual conversation created palpable, extreme physical and lasting symptoms and, as Shankar later shared, "set me back months on my healing journey" suggests that exit from the conversation was the right call. Conflict resilience does not expect or demand this level of discomfort.

Some people who experience trauma will develop an acute stress disorder or post-traumatic stress disorder (PTSD). The possibility of developing PTSD is a significant concern for many who have experienced a traumatic event. An anxiety disorder, PTSD can develop after witnessing or experiencing a trauma as defined above. While initial reactions like shock, nightmares, trouble sleeping, jumpiness, increased reactivity, and reexperiencing fear of the trauma at various points through the day are common after trauma, these reactions typically diminish over time. However, in PTSD, these feelings persist and are as vivid and intense as when the traumatic event first occurred.

Interestingly, Dr. Montalto explains that the fear of PTSD has become greater than the actual prevalence of PTSD, with only 8 to 12 percent of those experiencing a trauma developing significant symptoms. A person with significant symptoms of PTSD is someone whose limbic system was suddenly programmed to repeatedly sound the alarm that a threat to life or autonomy is imminent whenever something even remotely resembles the original event.

Dr. Montalto further clarifies that not every traumatic response constitutes PTSD. The disorder is diagnosed only when symptoms substantially disrupt daily life. She highlights that 90 percent of people with post-traumatic symptoms recover completely within eight months, and this applies to 90 percent of the 10 percent who exhibit significant symptoms.

Fewer people than you may think develop PTSD. A more common phenomenon is post-traumatic growth. The term *post-traumatic growth* can be traced to Professor Richard Tedeschi of the University of North Carolina at Charlotte, who observed that following terrible trauma—including 9/11 and veterans returning from Iraq and Afghanistan—people often had a renewed appreciation for life, felt more personal strength, and were more connected to the individuals around them. Dr. Alan Schlechter, clinical associate professor of psychiatry at the NYU Grossman School of Medicine, emphasizes the role of coping through acceptance and the ability to share experiences as catalysts for growth. Related to this, you may recall the story about Pete Buttigieg from Chapter 4. Part of what gave him the courage to come out as gay was his experience returning from the trauma of serving in Afghanistan. That experience gave him a renewed appreciation for life's fragility and reinforced the importance of living authentically—even if it meant causing conflict and, in his case, risking the loss of a long-desired career.

Schlechter also notes the significance of emotional disclosure in processing new realities and its role in reducing the likelihood of developing PTSD. This emotional sharing is part of what can make a difficult conversation along a deeply held line of difference "connecting" rather than alienating—even if there is no agreement or meeting of the minds on the substance. The experience of being listened to, especially by someone who sees the world very differently, can aid in humanizing the other and building a relationship.

To explore whether you may be experiencing symptoms of PTSD, below are questions based on the PTSD Checklist for DSM-5 (PCL-5), which was developed at the U.S. Department of Veterans Affairs' National Center for PTSD and is publicly available. Of note, these questions may help you determine if you have PTSD symptoms that may benefit from professional attention by a qualified health professional and are not meant to be used to make a diagnosis of PTSD.

## PTSD CHECKLIST

1. If you feel comfortable doing so, identify the event that happened.
2. Did it involve actual or threatened death, serious injury, or sexual violence?
3. Did it happen to you directly? Did you witness it? Did you learn about it happening to a close family member or close friend? Were you repeatedly exposed to details about it as part of your job (e.g., paramedic, police, military, or another first responder)?
4. If the event involved the death of a close family member or close friend, was it due to some kind of accident or violence, or was it due to natural causes?
5. Below is a list of problems that people sometimes have in response to a very stressful experience. Keeping the event above in mind, how much were you bothered by the problems below in the past month?

   - Repeated, disturbing, and unwanted memories of the stressful experience
   - Repeated, disturbing dreams of the stressful experience
   - Suddenly feeling or acting as if the stressful experience were happening again, as if you were back there reliving it
   - Feeling upset when something reminded you of the stressful experience
   - Having strong physical reactions (heart pounding, trouble breathing, sweating) when something reminded you of the stressful experience
   - Avoiding memories, thoughts, or feelings related to the stressful experience
   - Avoiding external reminders of the stressful experience, including people, places, conversations, activities, objects, or situations
   - Trouble remembering important parts of the stressful experience

- Having strong negative beliefs about yourself, other people, or the world (for example, having thoughts such as: I am bad, there is something seriously wrong with me, no one can be trusted, the world is completely dangerous)
- Blaming yourself or someone else for the stressful experience or what happened after it
- Having strong negative feelings, including fear, horror, anger, guilt, or shame
- Loss of interest in activities that you used to enjoy
- Feeling distant or cut off from other people
- Trouble experiencing positive feelings like being unable to feel happiness or have loving feelings for people close to you
- Irritable behavior, angry outbursts, or acting aggressively
- Taking too many risks or doing things that could cause you harm
- Being "super alert" or watchful or on guard
- Feeling jumpy or easily startled
- Having difficulty concentrating
- Trouble falling or staying asleep

The greater the number of symptoms above that you've been experiencing and the greater the severity, the more likely it is that you are at risk of having PTSD. For someone who has PTSD or has a highly distressing response similar to that of someone who has experienced a recent trauma or a very intense adverse life experience, the decision not to engage in a conflict situation that will remind them of the stressful experience—or walk away altogether—is consistent with appropriate and laudable self-care, not an indication that they need to be more conflict resilient. However, it is of the utmost importance to remember that experiences of discomfort, adverse life experiences, and trauma are hard, but they are not all bad. As in the case of post-traumatic growth, even trauma can one day become a source of good.

We've already described several ways to manage feelings of distress, especially in Chapter 6, such as coping techniques like the intentional breathwork of box breathing or cyclic sighing. Interestingly, although they are becoming increasingly common, it's unclear how helpful "trigger warnings" are to manage distress for someone who has experienced trauma in the past. The intent is to give a viewer, reader, or audience member a heads-up that a topic will be discussed that may cause feelings of discomfort or some other emotional disturbance, especially for people with PTSD. In a way, trigger warnings aren't that different from other kinds of common warnings, like the $M$ accorded to a video game for mature audiences or a warning at the beginning of a streaming movie that "viewer discretion is advised." To better understand the effect of trigger warnings, Payton J. Jones, Benjamin W. Bellet, and Professor Richard J. McNally from Harvard University's Department of Psychology conducted a study that involved 451 trauma survivors randomly assigned to either receive or not receive trigger warnings before reading potentially distressing passages from literature. The aim was to determine whether these warnings helped trauma survivors, including those who self-reported a PTSD diagnosis or met the criteria for probable PTSD, especially when the content of the readings was related to their own traumatic experiences.

What was surprising is that the study found no evidence that trigger warnings were beneficial to trauma survivors; in fact, findings suggested that trigger warnings might inadvertently reinforce the idea that trauma is a central component of the survivors' identity, which could be countertherapeutic—possibly having the opposite of its intended effect by causing harm, worsening symptoms, or impeding recovery. Furthermore, in terms of replicating previous research findings, the study concluded that evidence was either unclear or strongly supported the notion that trigger warnings do not have a significantly useful effect. This suggests that trigger warnings may not always be helpful for trauma survivors and could potentially have adverse effects on their perception of their trauma.

Certainly, more research is required to have more concrete recommendations around the use of trigger warnings, but what is notable from this work is that, however well-intentioned they may be, our typical assumptions about protecting ourselves and others from harm by flagging the potential for it and leaving the door open for us to walk away (potentially losing out on a powerful and ultimately positive experience) might sometimes be misplaced and need to be reevaluated. In some respects, trigger warnings may be more a symptom of the problem this book addresses—the increasing unwillingness to sit with the discomfort of conflict and disagreement—than they are a remedy for trauma.

## ASSESSING THE RELATIONSHIP ITSELF: DO I STAY OR DO I GO?

Sometimes the question is harder than "Do I say yes to this offer or walk?" or "Do I engage this really challenging topic with this person or group?"

Sometimes, we all have to ask, "Do I stay in this relationship, or do I walk or exit?"

Whatever useful words of guidance we can offer here, whether you can "exit" or leave a relationship isn't always practically implementable. As the saying goes, "We choose our friends but not our family." A daughter might be able to do something to extricate herself from a poisonous relationship with a parent, but she will always be her parents' daughter. Similarly, a worker in his late fifties with two teenagers heading to college and more than three decades at the same company may find it harder to walk away from a job with a new, twentysomething boss who is rude, disrespectful, and ageist. In contrast, a fresh MBA graduate of Harvard Business School who abhors the climate at his private-equity firm in New York City might have no trouble leaving, knowing he'll be quickly scooped up by another employer.

With that backdrop, though, there are times when your assessment about how to engage may extend beyond the simple question of tackling a hard topic to whether you should completely minimize or end the relationship entirely.

Consider the experience of Dolly Parton. In 1966, a twenty-one-year-old Parton crossed paths with Porter Wagoner, a renowned figure in country music. Porter, a legend with his own popular TV show, was known for his flamboyant rhinestone attire and hit records. In contrast, at that time, Dolly was grappling with the challenges of establishing her career as a woman in the fiercely competitive and male-dominated country music industry.

Appearing on TV singing a song called "Dumb Blonde," Dolly caught Porter's attention, leading to an unexpected offer to join his show as the "girl singer," replacing Norma Jean Beasley. Dolly and Porter's harmonies soon captivated audiences, bringing her to the forefront of the country music scene, but not without its complexities. As Dolly's star ascended, she eclipsed Porter, and she understandably began to crave creative independence and recognition as an artist in her own right. She longed to establish herself beyond the "second" in a duet or as the mere "girl singer." This desire for autonomy led to friction with Porter, who was reluctant to loosen his grip on their partnership.

With increasing tension between her and Porter, Dolly reached a breaking point. "I just finally just thought I'm going to break myself if I don't go," she later recalled, "because all we were doing was fighting, and it just wasn't working. I couldn't think. I couldn't sleep. I couldn't eat."

In the end, Dolly made a series of hard decisions. From a pure business negotiation perspective, she assessed that her interests were better met by stepping away from an ongoing partnership with Porter. This decision drew a painful lawsuit from him. Notably, however, to this day she expresses a love, admiration, and respect for Porter, who passed away in 2007, and continued to find ways to support and honor him and the role he played in her life.

Quite apart from the impact her decision had on her own career and on the country music industry generally, her capacity to hold what might seem to be incompatible realities simultaneously demonstrates a remarkable ability to be conflict resilient by managing competing identities within herself while still being mindful about the across-the-table negotiations with Porter. From a pure business and career-interest perspective, Dolly made an assessment that her BATNA, complete with all the attendant risks and uncertainties, was better than continuing to play "second fiddle" to Porter. She also assessed the impact that such an exit might have on her personal relationship with him. Despite the loss of that relationship, however, she was also able to retain an admiration, love, and respect for Porter.

Simultaneously holding these two realities, full of tension and yet fully authentic to her feelings and interests, embodies a commendable level of conflict resilience. Indeed, years later, when Porter lost his record contract and ended up in dire financial straits, it was Dolly who bailed him out—not from a place of pity or guilt, but from a stance of genuinely holding the rightness of the decision to exit a long-term business relationship with the soundness and certainty of her feelings of connection, appreciation, and love for Porter even as the day-to-day friendship and business relationship had faded years earlier. In a very real sense, she had managed her negotiations within and her negotiations across the table masterfully.

Dolly provides an example of the complexity behind the decision to stay and the decision to leave. Sometimes we may choose to exit a particular negotiation or not engage a hard series of conversations but still stay in a relationship. At other times, exit may be the right answer. Being conflict resilient empowers you to work through even these deeply challenging and uncomfortable questions rather than take the convenient route of cancellation, exit, or ghosting. In a world of deep polarization, we need to engage these hard questions with tenacity and grit and resist the urge to flee, ghost, and avoid.

## GETTING UNSTUCK

The only thing more unthinkable than leaving was staying;
the only thing more impossible than staying was leaving.
—Elizabeth Gilbert, *Eat, Pray, Love*

In articulating the gifts of being conflict resilient, we've focused on the downsides of mindless avoidance and pointless escalatory fighting. But, as often as we see these behaviors playing out in the public square, we also see something else, equally painful: the inertia of resigned or debilitating "stuckness":

- "I love my annual visits to my cousins in Nebraska, but I can't stand the way they all treat their gay son and his boyfriend. It's just too hard to bear. I've tried to talk with them, but they have dismissed me as 'brainwashed by the woke mob.' It feels hopeless and sad."
- "We have so many fond memories together, and I really want to have my friend back. But she has changed so much, and I don't know what's left beside memories and constant awkward, avoidant interactions. These days, she doesn't even respond to my texts. I don't know what to do."
- "I helped build this company from when it was only a start-up and need to finish out my career here. But the current management is the opposite of everything we stood for in the early days and I've been told to get in line or head for the door. I'm trapped and counting the days until retirement. It's not what I imagined or wanted at all."

If any of these examples resonate for you, you are not alone. Each of these vignettes embodies a common dilemma that is related to, but different from, the question of whether to engage or avoid: it's the sense of just feeling stuck.

At some level, being conflict resilient is an invitation to sit on occasion with the discomfort of being "stuck": you've put forward your perspective with skill, listened deeply, and the response from the other side has been disappointing, underwhelming, or worse.

Within the world of "stuckness," though, there is a further analysis to help you decide how to navigate the complexities of a relationship where the differences might cut to the core of your values, self-worth, or sense of dignity.

At core, we acknowledge that in a world of diverse experience, viewpoint, and perspective, differences will abound, including irreconcilable ones. We also acknowledge and embrace that being conflict resilient means sitting *in relationship* with that deep discomfort.

Throughout this book, we've tried to emphasize that conflict resilience is an essential leadership and interpersonal skill—but not one that is deployed against one's safety, mental health, or security.

As you consider how to handle the "stuckness," we offer a key diagnostic question. Looking inward, ask yourself: *Have I truly tried to engage with the other person in a conflict-resilient way—with directness, compassion, deep listening, and effective assertion?*

If the answer is no, then ask yourself: *What is holding me back?*

If the answer is yes, consider the question: *What is keeping me stuck?*

In some cases, there might be an inertia based on tension between the "substance" and perhaps other more relational or emotional interests. In other words, your substantive BATNA is worse than staying or the status quo, even though from an emotional or relational consideration, you might prefer to exit. This leaves you stuck.

Take the example of an oil-and-gas executive—let's call him Xavi. He originally came to Bob for coaching on how to be more conflict resilient with his new boss, a young, ambitious executive with a background in renewable energy.

Over time, it became clear that Xavi's new boss was unlikely to be a collaborative colleague. And when we say "collaborative colleague" we don't mean someone who was prepared to agree with Xavi or share his vision—nice as that might have been. Instead, it became clear that the new exec had little interest in listening, engaging with Xavi, or having dialogue with him.

For months, Bob's coaching with Xavi felt a bit more like therapy. Xavi felt deeply unhappy professionally and yet trapped by a good pension plan and the final handful of years remaining before that pension plan kicked in after a twenty-five-plus-year run at an energy company he helped to start. Retirement was in sight, but still some years away. "Holding on" for a few more years seemed to be Xavi's goal. But for Bob, this sounded like *reservation value thinking*. In negotiation, this means focusing on the lowest potential benefit that is acceptable to you before deciding to walk away. Rather than focusing on his true interests and hopes, Xavi was focused on just silently gritting his teeth until retirement. Xavi couldn't see the possibility of reinventing himself at the age of sixty. Only over time did he see that the best way to get unstuck was to pursue opportunities outside his long-time employer, no matter how hard the attendant challenge and struggle. After a prolonged and earnest period of assessing his short- and long-term interests—substantive, relational, and emotional—Xavi realized that he had always deeply desired to be a pastry chef. He enrolled in a part-time pastry school. Soon he had an internship at a local bakery on weekends. Then, eighteen months into his part-time employment at the bakery, the longtime owners approached Xavi about the possibility of becoming a partial owner of the business as they transitioned to retirement. Imagine Xavi's surprise and delight at this! Today, Xavi's days in the oil-and-gas industry are history. He's now opening a second pastry shop in a nearby community. And he's never been happier.

There can be more complicated reasons for being "stuck." As complicated as it may be to improve your BATNA the way Xavi did, sometimes "improving your BATNA" isn't quite as straightforward or possible. If the other person involved in your "stuckness" is a family member, if there are circumstances that make complete exit nearly impossible or extremely costly, there are some additional questions to ask yourself as you decide how to move forward.

First, what keeps you in the relationship, even if you feel stuck? This can be a painful examination. But it's a worthwhile one. Perhaps it is economic dependence in some way. Maybe there is a sense of desperation, loneliness, and lack of agency. How many people do we all know who stay in unhappy relationships because of inertia or fear of loneliness? Maybe it is low self-confidence. On the flip side, maybe it is a sense of hope, whether appropriate or misplaced. Things can always get better, and there might be light just around the corner, right? Perhaps there is a fear of failure or disappointment. Identifying these very real challenges is the first step in assessing what to do next. There may be ambivalence that keeps you where you are. Good things that the relationship brings you. For all the pain and angst, there still may be moments of joy and connection. Or maybe it is your moral core and sense of ethics and family that compel you to stay. As you make these assessments in an honest and real way, you will need to engage the negotiation within.

Second, ask yourself, "What are the costs to me—emotional, relational, substantive—of staying in the relationship?"

Next, evaluate, "What would be the upsides of exit, if it were possible?" And then, "What are the costs and challenges of exit?"

Doing this in a structured way will provide more clarity on the wisdom of remaining in a relationship even if you've already decided not to engage certain topics with the other party.

Before making a final determination, though, there are some additional diagnostic questions to consider.

## ASSESS YOUR COUNTERPART

In evaluating whether to remain in a relationship or exit in the face of disagreement, it's important to consider the perspective and capacity of your counterpart. It's easy to chalk up the disappointing response of your counterpart to a myriad of nefarious intentions, bad faith, or just gross negligence and self-centered thinking.

It's also the case that a host of other reasons could explain why your best efforts are producing nothing but frustration, lack of comprehension, or, even worse, continued attacks and vitriol.

For example, one of the biggest challenges we have faced in our work involves bridging cultural and generational differences. In the 2017 romantic comedy *The Big Sick*, the protagonist, Kumail, an aspiring stand-up comedian, falls in love with an American woman. Raised in a Muslim family by Pakistani parents who immigrated to the United States, Kumail hides the fact of his White, American, non-Muslim girlfriend, Emily, until his mother tries to set him up with a Muslim woman whom he had already rebuffed.

His mother lets out a resigned sigh and says, "Kumi, if you don't want to be a lawyer, fine. If you want to do the stand-up comedy and embarrass us as a family, fine. There is only one thing that we have ever asked for you, Kumi. That you be a good Muslim and you marry a Pakistani girl. That is it. One thing." The room seems to contract around them as Kumi's shoulders straighten and his brow furrows. "Can I ask you something? Something that has never made sense to me? Why did you bring me here if you wanted me to not have an American life? We come here, but we pretend like we're still back there. That's so stupid."

His father cuts in. "Don't you talk to your mother like that."

Kumi goes on, confessing that he feels his parents don't care about what he thinks and just want him to follow their rules, which don't make sense to him. He doesn't even pray, and hasn't in years. His parents, in shock, question whether he believes in Allah. He responds honestly that he doesn't know what he believes and that he can't marry someone his parents find for him because he is in love with someone. "Her name is Emily and she's gonna be a therapist and right now she's very sick, but I couldn't tell you that. It makes me so sad that I couldn't tell you any of that. I really appreciate everything you've done for me.

I truly, truly, truly do. I really do. And I know Islam has been really good for you and it has made you good people, but I don't know what I believe. I just need to figure it out on my own."

His mother looks him in the eyes and says, "You're not my son."

No matter whom you find your heart sympathizing with here, it's hard not to feel tangibly the searing pain of both Kumi and his parents. While the above conversation could be played out with more skill, listening, and empathy on all sides, there is no denying that there exists here a deep gulf between first-generation parents and their bicultural son, one that is unlikely to be cleaned up simply with deploying some good conflict resilience skill. From Kumi's perspective, there is no way of making his hurt go away. Simply chalking up the misunderstanding to "generational" or "cultural" differences doesn't excuse his parents' unwillingness to see life from his perspective. At the same time, however, the generational and cultural difference must be part of Kumi's consideration of whether to stay or to go in his relationship with his parents. A failure to take that into account, in our view, is the opposite of what it means to be conflict resilient.

In assessing the intransigence or lack of reciprocity from a counterpart, there may be other mitigating factors to consider. We believe that everyone has a capacity—with skill, effort, and intention—to improve their skills of conflict resilience. At the same time, it's invariably the case that we are not all equally able to do so. Someone with a mental health condition or on the autism spectrum may be less capable of responding in the way that you might hope for or expect. The fact of the incapability does not wash away or obliterate the hurtful, confusing, and damaging impact on you. However, in our view, it's a factor that should be weighed in assessing whether to stay or go in a relationship.

Consider Lakeesha, whose mother suffered from a host of mental health conditions, including a tendency toward paranoia and extreme defensiveness. The situation was so severe that Lakeesha was often blamed for her mother spilling a glass of water.

"How is this my fault?" Lakeesha would ask.

"Oh, you are rushing me to drink the water. It's just stressful being around you."

Exchanges like this were frequent and incessant.

Repeated attempts by Lakeesha to engage her mother productively, to express concern about her mom's mental health, to show her support, and to offer to accompany her through the journey of treatment and care were universally rebuffed, often in the harshest and most emotionally abusive of ways.

Whether Lakeesha should stay in relationship with her mom was a genuinely painstaking deliberation. Outsiders could offer guidance, but only Lakeesha could evaluate her interests, values, and the terms on which she could stay or go. For our purposes, what does seem clear is that part of the analysis should be her mother's mental health condition and the mitigating impact that might have in the assessment.

In evaluating whether to remain in a relationship across painful lines of conflict or difference, it does matter whether extenuating cultural, situational, behavioral, generational, or health-related reasons may be contributing to the situation. They are categorically different from a simple lack of good faith, stubbornness, sloth, laziness, or knowing abuse of power.

Even as we write this, we acknowledge that assessing the intentions, capacity, and good faith of a counterpart is incredibly hard to do accurately. How do we *really* know what someone's capacity is to stretch themselves on conflict resilience? There is always a tension between the challenge to accept others as we find them and the desire and hope to see them at least trying to do the same hard work we are doing on conflict resilience, within the bounds of their capacity and limitation.

Making this assessment even more challenging is how we as human beings are prone to assume bad intentions, especially when we find ourselves in conflict with others and, particularly so, when that conflict centers on core values. Isn't it arrogant to even engage in this guessing game of understanding the mind and heart of the other?

For us, there is a danger of arrogance, but a necessity of at least trying to take the perspective of the other. Indeed, the entire act of listening and empathy is an act of trying to better understand and enter the mind, heart, perspective, and worldview of the other.

It is critically important that you bring a healthy dose of humility to the task of assessing the counterpart. It's also essential to push yourself to consider a full range of possible answers to questions of motivation, capacity, and context.

One of the lessons of Dolly Parton's story is that the decision to "stay" or "go" is not an "on/off" switch. There are ways we can calibrate our level of engagement or "staying" and our level of exit or "going." That careful calibration can lead to a deeper and more authentic connection in the domains where the relationship continues. And, at the very least, answering these questions with vulnerability and heart can help us get beyond the "unstuck" to something that better serves our short- and long-term interests.

As you stand at your own crossroads, unsure yet open to possibility, remember that your decision on whether to reach a deal, engage in conflict, or stay in the relationship is not just about the immediate situation. It's about the larger journey of growth, understanding, and the potential transformation that comes from facing these challenges head-on. Reflect on these insights and stories and let them guide you as you navigate the complex, yet potentially rewarding, terrain of conflict. Remember, whether you choose to courageously stay or courageously go, each choice in the face of conflict holds the potential for profound transformation and growth.

In our next and final chapter, we'll explore how—once we've undertaken our practice of strengthening our own conflict resilience—we can take the next step to embed conflict resilience into the fabric of our communities to transform disagreements into opportunities for collaboration and growth.

Chapter 9

# BUILDING CULTURE

Hardwire Conflict Resilience Everywhere

The dogmas of the quiet past are
inadequate to the stormy present.
The occasion is piled high with difficulty,
and we must rise with the occasion.
As our case is new, so we must think anew, and act anew.
We must disenthrall ourselves, and then
we shall save our country.

—Abraham Lincoln, Message to Congress, December 1, 1862

As you gradually level up your conflict resilience skills and become better equipped to manage conflict effectively, you may also start to feel a creeping, unsettling feeling that you stand alone in this capability, surrounded by friends, family, colleagues, bosses, organizations, and even (or especially) societal and organizational structures that fail to support—or even actively discourage—conflict resilience. Part of the motivation for this book is our own observation that we find ourselves in a societal ecosystem that actively encourages flight-or-fight, cocoons of comfort, cancellation, avoidance, and a quick escape from the discomfort of engagement and the difficult, but necessary, practice of conflict resilience.

Even worse, as you try to raise areas of disagreement with others in your organization or family, you may find yourself alienated and alone, viewed by others as a source of trouble and instigation.

Consider the plight of Joses. The owner of a downtown diner and a longtime dues-paying member of the local Chamber of Commerce, he finally decided it was time to give back and volunteer for service on the board of directors. Within six months of his election, Joses was surprised to notice the ways in which collective groupthink held the board back from long-range planning. There was a deep reluctance to question or rethink long-held assumptions. Attempts to do so were quickly dismissed as not part of the "culture" or "DNA" of the organization. A pattern emerged whereby new businesses in the community elected to not join the Chamber and fewer new business owners were willing to step forward to volunteer for leadership roles. Still, Joses wanted to make an impact. He started suggesting alternate ways forward, offering members data that showed the limitations of the association's patterns of groupthink. Instead of appreciating the extra time and energy he was investing in the new role—or even seriously considering his viewpoints—they started treating him as an annoying naysayer. Privately, a few board members pulled him aside to say that they largely agreed with his viewpoint. But when he brought up a new way of viewing an issue in a meeting, he was met with either silence or a one-line response along the lines of "That's not how we have typically done things here."

Despite the skill with which Joses raised different viewpoints, listened deeply, and sat with the discomfort, the organizational milieu penalized him for being willing to raise alternative viewpoints, ask questions, and propose new ways forward. He couldn't help feeling frustrated and exhausted, wondering whether his efforts were worth it.

Becoming conflict resilient is hard enough on its own. Doing it within an organization, workplace, or family ecosystem that lacks processes and structures to support your development is even tougher. Equally challenging can be the prospect of trying to engage differences constructively, especially when leadership is lacking or—even worse—works to actively undermine your efforts. Conflict resilience begins with individuals developing a new awareness and a new set of skills, but ideally and essentially, it depends on groups, organizations, and communities—whether a workplace, a local city council, a church, or your family—supporting and cultivating these skills too.

## A GREENHOUSE FOR CONFLICT RESILIENCE

Did you ever try growing tomatoes in a New England winter? How about sunflowers, petunias, or begonias? Corn, strawberries, watermelons, and grapes are all wonderful summer treats. But try growing them in February in Boston. Trust us! It doesn't work out too well. We all know that for many crops to thrive, the climate matters. That's why humans have created greenhouses—places where climate conditions can be controlled to allow crops to thrive and grow.

To create a culture of conflict resilience, you need to create greenhouse conditions that make the soil fertile for conflict resilience to take root.

## ASSESS THE SITUATION, TILL THE LAND, BUILD THE GREENHOUSE

To help build an organizational culture of conflict resilience, assessment is a critical initial step. In a large organization—a company, nonprofit, government agency—engaging a professional team to work through the questions above in a methodical way is the "gold standard" way forward.

Take, for example, Bob's experience working with Ross, the executive director of a legal and policy advocacy organization in Austin, Texas. Time and again, employees came to Ross with complaints of microaggressions and workplace bullying by various managers within the organization.

"Have you raised this directly with Florian?" Ross would ask the complaining employee.

"No, Ross, that's your job."

"OK. Well, may I share at least the broad contours of your concern with Florian?"

"No, I want this to remain completely anonymous and confidential."

"Hmm. OK. Help me understand how I can coach or talk with Florian about this without using any examples at all?"

"I have no idea. That's your job, not mine. I don't feel comfortable talking with Florian or even having you share that I came to you at all. I'm afraid of retaliation."

"Retaliation is a serious issue here. We have a strong policy against it. And if you were to become the target of retaliation, we will respond immediately."

"No, I still don't think it's my job to handle this kind of behavior. It's your job. I don't want to talk with Florian."

"Would you be open to mediation or something facilitated in some way?"

"Absolutely not. It's your job to solve. I'm exhausted."

Ross didn't know how to move forward. And, like Joses, he was exhausted. And at a loss.

In cases like Ross's (and so many others we've heard), this general pattern of avoidance, fear, and reluctance to engage in direct conversations signals that something is amiss within the culture of the organization quite apart from the details of even the specific problem that Ross was facing.

Rather than coach Ross to be more conflict resilient or suggest mediation, Bob suggested that the organization could benefit from a more comprehensive look at the systems, processes, and resources available to handle conflict productively.

As the executive director, Ross had the authority and the resources to make this happen. Bob and a team of conflict management professionals worked within the organization to set up an internal Conflict Management Team within the organization. Over a six-month period, they organized and ran focus groups, one-on-one interviews, and surveys for staff, management, and the board to learn the answers to the following questions:

- *When differences or conflicts come up within the organization, what formal and informal options are made available to employees?* This might include policies such as recourse to human resources, a Title IX office, an organizational ombuds, or face-to-face mediation, to name a few.

- *Apart from whatever formal processes are available, how do employees in a conflict situation typically handle conflicts within the organization?* For example, do they simply say nothing at all and avoid? Do they instead gossip within small groups or cliques on private Slack channels or around a proverbial (or real!) "water cooler"? Or instead, do they ask for a transfer to another department or manager? File a formal complaint? Leave the organization altogether? In answering these questions, it is important to observe the difference between the formal organizational processes that are available on paper and what people *actually* tend to do in practice.

- *Why might employees not be availing themselves of the formal processes and resources in place?* Perhaps the policies themselves are not well-known or advertised; alternately, perhaps the processes are well-known, but they are not seen as effective because of the specific personnel tasked with execution, or because of long delays, or administrative red tape; alternately, perhaps the processes are fine but there is a stigma or even an informal "penalty" imposed on anyone who avails themselves of a process.

Many years ago Bob worked with a local chapter of a university fraternity. On paper and in theory, the university and the fraternity had agreed upon a thoughtful and clear approach to handling allegations of bullying within the fraternity. In practice, no actual fraternity brother or pledge ever used any of the formal processes at all. Why? We wish it was because no such behavior ever occurred. Rather, we discovered that the culture of the fraternity was such that, if you chose to avail yourself of one of the processes laid out in the formal policy, you were immediately seen as a traitor and a loser. Culturally, there was a severe social penalty suffered by those who tried to buck the informal and traditionally accepted approaches to handling conflict. Despite efforts to create a system that would foster healthy conflict resilience, members of the fraternity resisted these efforts, and the culture of hazing and bullying persisted.

The assessment revealed that externally imposed processes were almost universally DOA—dead on arrival. Seen as part of decades-long efforts by the university to quash fraternity life, the on-paper dispute resolution and anti-hazing policy that looked so well designed was kryptonite for members internally. However, as part of the assessment, Bob and his team learned that tradition played an important role within the fraternity.

The key was to develop an approach to dispute-handling that deployed some of the language and framing that resonated within the history and culture of the fraternity—that called upon the noble ideals in its founding charter and governing documents. By creating an internal committee of members tasked with developing processes for handling conflict, and with coaching from Bob and his team, the committee was able to transform their culture by drawing on the best parts of the existing culture, history, and tradition of the fraternity. For example, the fraternity valued its alumni and, in particular, the role that they played in the organization. As part of initiation, the fraternity formalized a program that matched each new pledge with an alumnus between his fifth and his tenth reunion. The idea was that younger alums could still relate easily to undergraduates but also provide invaluable support and coaching through the undergraduate years. All mentors were required to participate in an online training on bullying, conflict, and harassment. Then, as part of the matchmaking process, pledges and recruits to the fraternity were told that their mentor alum could serve as a trusted resource to talk through issues related to bullying or interpersonal conflicts in the organization.

Framing the resource as part of the broader mentoring tradition within the fraternity reduced the social ostracization attendant to raising hard issues in the organization. Providing basic training to the mentors, especially training around conflict-handling, made them feel valued by their alma mater and the fraternity and helped them appreciate that mentoring was more than just helping their advisees land a job after graduation. Building on the tradition and values of the fraternity—that of mentoring and alumni engagement—proved a more effective way to provide support and resources around conflict resilience than having a top-down, university-imposed set of rules.

The upshot is that any good assessment of the climate for handling conflict has to look beyond what policies are currently in place. It also uncovers what real stakeholders are actually doing day-to-day when disagreements surface and why they may be engaging in non-productive and often dysfunctional methods to avoid conflict. Do they lack knowledge of anti-retaliation protections provided by their organization? Do they not trust them? Or are they simply using fear of retaliation as an excuse to avoid conflict?

Turning back to Bob's work with Ross, with the results of an assessment in hand, Ross was in a much stronger position to design a conflict-resilient system for managing differences within the organization. In addition to the information that the assessment provided, the process helped till the soil for the work ahead in the following ways:

- It offered *voice* to all staff, giving everyone an opportunity to be heard.
- It drew attention to the seriousness with which leadership was taking on hard issues related to conflict and differences within the organization.

- It helped identify what issues needed to be addressed the most—skills versus structures versus personnel versus education about processes and policies in place.

Following the assessment, the Conflict Management Committee at Ross's organization worked to design low-risk spaces and an integrated series of processes that would encourage and support conflict-resilient behaviors in the workplace. We could write an entire book about how to design and implement an organizational system of conflict-resilient processes within an organization (in fact, Bob and his colleagues already have in *Designing Systems and Processes for Managing Disputes*). For now, suffice to say that leadership from the top combined with inclusive, stakeholder-centered assessment work is an ideal first step in the effort to hardwire an organization for conflict resilience.

More practically, if you are volunteering with the local chapter of the ACLU or trying to determine if there's a way you can shift how your family handles where major holidays will be celebrated, you are clearly not going to be hiring "Conflict Consultants Inc." to help you out. But that doesn't mean you can't conduct an informal assessment on your own using the questions above, perhaps talking with some key stakeholders, or doing your own self-reflection to answer the questions. This kind of prep, whether on a grand organizational scale or in a more individualized approach, can make a real difference in the likelihood that you can build a new "greenhouse" that will allow conflict resilience to thrive.

## MAKE CONFLICT RESILIENCE A REQUIRED JOB COMPETENCY

Several decades ago, there was zero percent chance that "emotional intelligence" would be listed as a required professional competency in a job description. Now a surprisingly high percentage of middle and senior management positions expect candidates to have "emotional intelligence" as a prerequisite to serious consideration. When this competency is included in a leadership profile, an employer signals that they are looking for talent with more than just an ability to handle finances, enact strategy, raise money, direct a research agenda, manage a sales team, or be a substantive expert in artificial intelligence or the airline industry. They are also looking for someone who possesses a particular *management orientation* and a related *skill set* to make that happen.

As of the writing of this book, we are far away from seeing "conflict resilience" as a required professional competency for most leadership positions. But, if you are reading this in 2035 or 2050, we hope that has changed.

Behavioral interview questions are a tool to assess a candidate's suitability for a role, focusing on their past actions and performances as indicators of future behavior. This method delves into specific examples from the candidate's experience, aligning them with key competencies, such as leadership, maturity, accountability, and ownership. This is often followed with structured probing questions to gather additional detail. Unlike conversational interviews, which often lean on the interviewer's first impressions or instinctive judgments, behavioral interviews prioritize the applicant's responses, which increases the chances of a more objective and relevant evaluation of their skills and behaviors. This approach also minimizes the risk of drifting into irrelevant or even illegal questioning territories. The key to a successful behavioral interview lies in its structured nature, emphasizing job-relevant queries over casual conversation. This allows a fair and consistent assessment of all candidates.

Behavioral questions focusing on conflict resilience are particularly revealing; they allow the interviewer to rate responses along a spectrum of how well requirements are met.

Here are five sample behavioral interview questions and a straightforward rating system to evaluate responses consistently:

1.  Describe a time when you had to work through a stressful and uncomfortable conflict. How did you manage your emotions and reactions despite the discomfort?

    Specific Competency: Conflict tolerance

    Suggested Competency Ratings:

    1 The candidate showed difficulty in managing emotions, lacked self-awareness, or avoided the conflict.

    3 The candidate demonstrated basic emotional control and addressed the conflict but might have lacked depth in self-regulation.

    5 The candidate exhibited advanced emotional intelligence and self-regulation, using the conflict as a growth opportunity.

2.  Provide an example of a situation where you had to clarify and balance your short-term and long-term interests during a conflict. What was your approach?

    Specific Competency: Interest appraisal

    Suggested Competency Ratings:

    1 The candidate focused only on immediate gains or long-term goals without integrating both perspectives.

    3 The candidate showed an understanding of both short-term and long-term interests but might have struggled to integrate them effectively.

    5 The candidate skillfully balanced short-term and long-term interests, demonstrating strategic thinking in conflict resilience.

3.  Tell me about a time when you had to listen to someone with a completely opposite viewpoint. How did you handle it?

    Specific Competency: Deep listening

    Suggested Competency Ratings:

    1 The candidate exhibited close-mindedness or an inability to genuinely engage with opposing viewpoints.

3 The candidate listened and acknowledged the opposing viewpoint but might not have fully engaged or understood it.

5 The candidate demonstrated deep-listening skills, actively engaging, understanding, and reflecting the viewpoint to the counterpart to make them feel heard and seen.

4. Provide an example where you had to assert your point of view or your values in a conflict. How did you ensure you articulated your points with authenticity and in a way that maximized the chance that the other person could receive and appreciate the message?

Specific Competency: Effective assertion

Suggested Competency Ratings:

1 The candidate was either overly aggressive or too passive in asserting their viewpoint and interests, leading to misunderstandings.

3 The candidate asserted their viewpoint and interests adequately but might have lacked full effectiveness in communication.

5 The candidate effectively and empathetically asserted their perspective or viewpoint, exhibiting authenticity and sensitivity to how the counterpart could best receive it.

5. Describe a scenario where you designed a process or environment that created conditions that were conducive to open, respectful, and mutual dialogue. What approach did you take?

Specific Competency: Creative process design

Suggested Competency Ratings:

1 The candidate struggled to create a conducive environment for dialogue or lacked creativity in approach.

3 The candidate designed a functional process but might not have fully fostered conditions for deep listening and effective assertion.

5 The candidate excelled in creating an innovative and low-risk environment that promoted conflict resilience for all parties involved.

Organizations and other institutions that prioritize conflict re-silience in their selection processes not only equip themselves with individuals capable of navigating the complexities of modern-day chal-lenges, but they also foster environments in which innovation, per-sonal growth, and job satisfaction can flourish. Although starting at the stage of recruitment and building a team is ideal, we also believe that conflict resilience can be taught and developed—whether in your team or at home.

## BUT I'M NOT IN CHARGE: LEADING LATERALLY

We're guessing that reading the last few pages might leave some of you feeling frustrated and dejected. If you are not the executive director or CEO of your company, the head of school, the department chair, or the revered leader of your family or social clique, you might be feeling a bit low. Even worse, you may have little faith in your organization's for-mal leadership to make the kind of changes to the culture that would help cultivate organizational conflict resilience.

But don't lose hope. Here are three steps you can take wherever you sit within a family, company, department, or governing body to help cultivate organizational conflict resilience:

1. Capitalize on the power of one
2. Use guerrilla interventions
3. Create a market for change

### 1. Capitalize on the Power of One

The late Roger Fisher, one of the founders of the Harvard Negotia-tion Project and coauthor of *Getting to Yes,* understood the "power of one" to change an ecosystem. Though he was among the most influ-ential Harvard Law School professors of his day, Fisher was most effective in transforming culture when he eschewed formal authority and power and led by example. At the start of the semester, as students departed from Fisher's negotiation class, the desks in the large lecture room would often be littered with paper cups, plates, napkins. Without saying a word, at the end of each class as students filed out of the large lecture hall, Fisher would quietly start to walk up and down the rows, collecting left-behind garbage and recyclables. Even as students chatted with a classmate, packed their bags, or just filed out of the lecture hall, they nonetheless took notice of what their professor was doing. By the third week of the semester, Fisher could usually stop his garbage-collection duties. Because of his quiet example, in the course of a few weeks, students in the class were carrying their own garbage with them as they headed out the door to their next lecture. Without ever saying a word, making a rule, or chastising a soul, Fisher managed to shift a classroom culture for 144 Harvard Law students.

Setting a good example is one obvious way to reform organizational culture. When we navigate difference with poise, skill, and authenticity, people notice, and we start to transmit these vital skills and behaviors to those around us.

When Matteo, a third-year law student, visited Bob's office two months before graduation, he was physically shaking.

"Professor Bordone, I could use your help."

"OK. Um, are you all right?" Bob asked.

"Yes, but no. You see, I am from a very devout Catholic family. And my faith is really important to me and to my whole family. The thing is, my family is coming here to Cambridge for my graduation. And they don't know that I am dating a man. And I don't know how to talk to them about it all."

As you might imagine, Matteo's set of conflicts—both within himself and across the proverbial negotiation table with his family—was weighing on him. He was the middle child and the only boy in a very traditional Catholic family.

In the short term, Matteo needed a strategy for making it through graduation. It was clear to Bob that Matteo wasn't conflict resilient enough for a hard conversation before graduation. He was still grappling with his own negotiation within—the side of himself who knew that his sense of wholeness and integrity meant embracing his sexuality and his relationship with his boyfriend, and the other side of himself that desperately wanted to make his parents proud and live up to expectations. Not until Matteo could manage and integrate his internal conflict could he be ready for a genuine across-the-table conversation with his family. With Bob's help, Matteo took the brave step of engaging his "negotiation within" and developing a plan for managing the graduation events. This approach combined internal conflict resilience with a temporary but necessary use of "strategic avoidance."

Sometimes, short-term avoidance might be necessary as you do the hard work to make yourself ready for the discomfort of across-the-table disagreement and conflict. In Matteo's case, the short-term strategy meant saying nothing to his family at graduation. Instead, he coordinated with his boyfriend to host their families at the same restaurant for dinner on the evening of graduation. As excruciating as that felt in some ways, it helped Matteo avoid a hard conversation before he was ready and still at least be in the physical presence of his boyfriend for their graduation dinner.

Then, over a ten-month period, Matteo did the important mirror, chair, and table work to set up a series of conversations with family. The first of his difficult conversations was with his sister. A few months later, with his mom. And finally, the conversation that Matteo dreaded most—with his father. The last of the conversations didn't end how Matteo wished. His father expressed deep disappointment and even suggested conversion therapy. But that wasn't the end of the story.

Six years later, Bob beamed with pride witnessing Matteo marry the very same man he was dating at law school. Even more moving, the beautiful ceremony was punctuated by the deeply emotional and loving toast from Matteo's Catholic father, an active member of his own local parish.

But this story isn't just one of Matteo's conflict resilience journey. Like Roger Fisher picking up paper coffee cups after class, unbeknownst to himself, Matteo had become a role model to others too, creating a virtuous circle that extended well beyond Matteo's relationship with his father to the rest of his family. For example, since Matteo's coming out, one of his younger cousins found the courage to share with her family her story of dealing with a serious eating disorder on her own for many years; another family member had the courage to share their doubts about their faith and how they needed to take time away from the church. Even Matteo's mother found her voice as she shared for the first time the differences she had with Matteo's dad on key family decisions and preferences about national politics. In all these cases, though real differences persisted in the family, the ability to raise and discuss the hard issues drew the family closer, creating more authentic ties and making it easier to discuss them. Instead of secrets and gossip, the family had found a way to disagree without being disagreeable, to sit with the discomfort of disagreement, to become a conflict-resilient family. The power of one family member, Matteo himself—detached from formal authority—influenced the culture of his entire family. The shift was not toward greater unanimity or agreement with each other; it was toward more authenticity, more belonging, and more of a sense that different and uncomfortable views could find a home in the same tent.

## FROM MOMENTS TO MOVEMENTS

Roger Fisher and Matteo might not have known it, but their tactics are backed by science—social neuroscience, to be exact—and the idea that cultures evolve and adapt and have their own kind of resilience.

Imagine transporting a newborn from tens of thousands of years ago into the modern world. Surprisingly, this child would likely adapt with ease to contemporary skills, such as language, technology, and even complex tasks like algebra, internet use, and harnessing artificial intelligence. This reality illustrates a radical aspect of our evolution: while our biology has changed incrementally, our culture has undergone even more dramatic transformations.

At the heart of this cultural evolution is the concept of the *meme*, a term introduced by Richard Dawkins and expanded upon by Susan Blackmore. Memes are akin to biological genes, representing ideas or units of culture that pass socially from person to person. Their survival depends on their perceived utility or "fitness," which is akin to a cultural "survival of the fittest." Over time, certain valued skills or ideas within a community evolve into *traditions*, or distinctive patterns of behavior shared by a group. When these traditions accumulate, they form the foundation of a culture. This dynamic process is clearly demonstrated in experiments where groups improve upon tasks—like folding paper airplanes or building towers with raw spaghetti and marshmallows— through successive iterations, passing on enhanced techniques and knowledge. Over time, the paper airplanes fly longer and steadier, the towers grow taller and sturdier.

Unlike other species, humans possess the capability for more than just imitation—the mere copying of actions without knowledge of the goal of the action; humans can also understand the intentions and mental states behind the actions they copy. This deeper level of imitation, which sets us apart from other species, allows us to replicate both the actions and objectives of others.

Social neuroscience describes a phenomenon called "contagion," which is when innate repetitive behaviors, such as yawning or laughing, are replicated and spread across people (think of laugh tracks on TV shows). This adds an innate, almost instinctual layer to the dynamics of our social learning. Social learning could also be enhanced by a concept used often in marketing called "cognitive processing fluency," which basically means that the more you are exposed to something (like a behavior) the more readily available it is for your brain, and thus the more likely it is for you to select that behavior to achieve the outcome you want.

Understanding culture's evolutionary origins and the nuances of social learning versus imitation deepens our appreciation of the diversity of human behavior from cultural patterns in society. It also highlights the complexity and adaptability inherent in our nature. Our unique ability to imitate with an understanding of underlying intentions, combined with our capacity to enhance and transmit cultural memes, continues to evolve and adapt across generations. From these lessons in social neuroscience, we can harness some practical tips to help us be better role models in conflict resilience:

- *Use Effective Communication:* Leverage the power of language in transmitting cultural knowledge and traditions. Use clear, inclusive language to explain concepts and share knowledge, ensuring that your message is understood and can be effectively passed on. For example, instead of saying, "You need to listen even when people say stuff you can't stand," say, "As hard as it seems, when someone says things you can't stand, do your best to understand where they're coming from. You can do this without endorsing or supporting what they're saying. Sometimes, by making eye contact or asking an open-ended and genuinely curious question, or acknowledging the emotion behind what they're saying, you can show you've understood what they're trying to communicate and that may open space for them to listen to you better."
- *Attention with Intention:* Use stimulus enhancement strategies. That's a fancy way of saying that you need to draw attention to important aspects of a task or behavior you're modeling. This can involve physically pointing out or verbally emphasizing critical elements of an exchange or important step. These help observers focus on these key features and facilitate their own learning process. It also helps to highlight how the action relates to the goal.

So, when modeling a behavior or debriefing about what went well or what to do differently after a tense interaction, draw attention to the action, its context, and, especially, the end goal rather than just the process. This approach helps people's brains focus on the action you're modeling and understand the purpose behind these actions and generally when to apply the behaviors, which encourages them to adapt these goals into their context, rather than just copying your actions without understanding.

Consider Armando, who is a senior partner at a marketing agency. During a meeting reviewing progress on a campaign with one of their clients, another senior partner, Cynthia, makes a bold claim about what needs to be done to get the campaign back on track. Armando disagrees, but rather than just stating as such, he starts by paraphrasing what he heard Cynthia say and then asks an open question to better understand where Cynthia is coming from. After the meeting, his colleague Shonda thanks Armando for speaking up. Armando points out that he specifically was focused on practicing his deep-listening skills, approaching with genuine curiosity and working the Ladder of Inference by striving to understand the available data at the bottom of the ladder and the reasoning that led to Cynthia's conclusion. By explicitly highlighting for Shonda the specific aspects of his behavior that made that situation effective, he is making it much more likely that Shonda's brain will capture and integrate these skills, making her more able to apply those same techniques in future interactions with others.

- *Harness the Power of Social Contagion:* Be aware of the contagious nature of repeated behaviors, which can enhance your brain's ability to access and enact those past observed behaviors in the present. By consciously exhibiting these behaviors in repetitive ways, you can create a ripple effect, encouraging those around you to mirror the conflict resilience mindset and skills. Social network analysis conducted by Joel and other researchers has been uncovering how information—behaviors, physical and mental well-being—can flow through our social connections almost like a virus. Obesity, smoking habits, even happiness seems to spread this way.

Consider Emer's opportunities to disseminate conflict-resilient behaviors in her interactions with her family at reunions, dinners, and holiday get-togethers. When her teenage son became upset that he had to eat at a table with his younger cousins and not with the adults, Emer acknowledged her own frustration to his protest, paused and took a breath to manage the intensity of her physical reaction, and proceeded to more calmly acknowledge her son's feelings, sitting with him as he vented, offering an attentive ear without endorsing his position or immediately trying to fix the situation. At a family gathering at a restaurant, during a heated discussion incited by her vegan sister about the dinner menu options and the merits of forgoing meat, Emer (an avid carnivore) remained composed. She deeply listened to her sister's concerns about the lack of vegan options, reflecting her points back to ensure that she accurately understood what she was saying before asserting her own views on accommodating everyone's dietary needs. When her generally emotive father was reluctant to join a family photo on the day Emer introduced her newly adopted baby girl to the family, Emer wondered whether it had something to do with her new baby. She found a time to meet with her father a few days later, so she could sit beside him and engage in an open conversation about his feelings and what was behind his decision to refrain from being part of the family photo, without jumping to conclusions. Through her consistent demonstration of conflict resilience over time, Emer's behaviors gradually influenced some of her family members. Steadily, her son and her siblings began to mirror her approach and even some of her techniques, adopting more thoughtful and composed responses in their own interactions and a greater openness to be in the presence of conflict's discomfort.

## 2. Use Guerrilla Interventions

In addition to setting a personal example of conflict resilience, there are process-oriented moves you can make to help shift the way your company, organization, family, or group handles conflict. Because they occur with significant intention but little fanfare, these tactics have the quality of covert operations.

As part of a campaign in a city council election, you've been attending weekly team meetings for several months and observe the same stuck dynamic. A senior team member, Sareh, raises a troubling piece of polling data. Her boss Gary, the campaign manager, winces noticeably, downplays the importance of the issue, and refocuses the group on his preferred agenda. You notice through nonverbal body language and head nods that other colleagues seem supportive of Sareh's point. They too want to discuss Sareh's observation. But Gary's dismissive tone and pivot redirect the conversation and, after an awkward and tense moment, the team's attention returns to his agenda item.

It's easy to assume you are powerless in this moment. "Just get through the meeting and then debrief with others over lunch or through a private Slack channel," you say to yourself.

But exercising lateral leadership through a guerrilla intervention is another way forward, consistent with being conflict resilient.

For example, following the meeting you might reach out to Gary and ask for a chance to meet to ask a few questions to help you learn and to share a few observations from your vantage point.

In this meeting, you might follow an INQUIRE—SHARE—BRAINSTORM approach.

Now that you have observed a specific dynamic that seems to occur over time, the purpose of the meeting is to *inquire* about the purpose behind what you noticed and listen deeply. As you do this, it's important to be aware that your boss may not even have had much of a purpose. The dynamic you observed may be so "automatic" and ingrained that it's not showing up as something "strategic" or "intentional."

It might be more of "Well, this is what I always do, and it works just fine."

Whether or not your boss can articulate a purpose for what you observed, you would next *share* the impact, possible consequences (positive and negative), worries, advantages, disadvantages, risks, and opportunities of what you observed. It's important to do this in a neutral way—as if you are an analyst or "audience member" reviewing the situation from a balcony.

Then, if there is a positive or receptive reaction, you might suggest that you *brainstorm* together in a joint problem-solving mode, where you can identify different approaches to handling the situation. The brainstorming suggestion here can be critical. It helps reduce the social distance between the two of you, making it more likely that your counterpart will label you as part of the same group that naturally collaborates together—possibly by altering the activity of brain areas involved in how we form impressions of others and what we infer about their beliefs, goals, and intentions (dorsomedial prefrontal cortex and right temporoparietal junction). This makes it more likely that they will approach you as friend (and not foe) and any options you jointly create may also benefit from a positive halo effect, thus making it more likely that any proposed change in dynamic will be more likely to happen.

If you simply launch into your solutions, it may turn off your boss, the person who has the structural power to make decisions. At the same time, if you simply point out a problem or challenge, get the assent or agreement of the person in power, then walk away for them to solve it, the implicit message you are sending is "I have observed a deficiency and presented it to you to solve on your own."

Let's look at what the conversation between Gary and you might look like:

> **You:** Thanks so much for taking the time to meet with me, Gary. You know, I was hoping to share with you a dynamic that I've observed in some of our meetings. I hope that'd be OK?

**Gary:** Of course!

**You:** Great. I have two reasons for this. First, I'm genuinely curious to understand more about how you think about moments like this from a leadership perspective. And, secondly, I also want to share my own experience of this and how I think it might be impacting the team and get your reaction to it.

**Gary:** OK. Great. Go on, then.

**You:** Thanks. So, I've observed on occasion that when someone on the team raises an issue or decides to share some information that might be troubling or even negative, you often respond with a quick assent and an immediate pivot back to your agenda topic. Is this something you've noticed?

**Gary:** Hmm. Maybe. But go on, I want to hear more.

**You:** OK. Thanks. The thing is, at times, it seems to me that the person who has raised an issue can often feel discouraged and I get the sense that others may agree with them and may want a further conversation on the issue or new information their colleague has brought to light. I'm curious if you've observed this dynamic and, if so, how do you think about moments like this?

**Gary:** Hmm. I might have an idea of what you're talking about, but do you have any specific examples?

**You:** I do. Just to share one—last Wednesday at our weekly huddle, Sareh shared some of the polling data that indicated that some of the attack ads in our campaign are backfiring badly with the "under-25 demographic" that we need to support us in the election. You said something like "Well, the strategy needs more time, and we need to stay focused today. So let's just go back to the main goal—to ensure that our digital team stays on message."

**Gary:** Ah, yes. I remember that.

**You:** So, may I ask what makes you change the topic here in a situation that, at least for me, feels important?

**Gary:** Yeah—sure. So, here's the thing. Sareh is great. But she can't see the whole picture the way I do. If everyone shared all their micro concerns at these meetings, the meetings would last forever. And we'd never make any important decisions. So, my purpose in a moment like that is really to keep everyone focused and not get us distracted by something that should be handled in a small one-on-one conversation like this one.

**You:** Huh. It's helpful for me to get your perspective on this. From your vantage point, Sareh's observation can sometimes derail us from what we need to get done in the meeting. Plus, you're worried about everyone bringing forward all their concerns in an all-hands meeting in general. So, if I understand it right, for you, you'd rather see information like the polling data for young people brought up in a one-on-one just with you or the relevant players, not the whole team.

**Gary:** Yup. It's not like I don't appreciate her thoughts. It's just the wrong time and place. I mean, she can be overfocused on micro details at times. As we all can. It's just not the right time.

**You:** Right. Got it. And considering your purpose, what you're doing makes sense to me. One concern I have about this approach is that I think others on the team—like me, to be honest—sometimes take away a very different message. I know for me, I can sometimes see an intervention like this more as you not wanting to hear information you don't like. And that can feel demoralizing and, even worse, unproductive—unintentionally sending a signal that dissenting voices are disloyal and unwelcome, which, if I am hearing it right, you clearly don't want to do. What are your thoughts on this?

**Gary:** I never thought of that, but that's definitely not what I'm trying to convey.

**You:** Right. And that's great to hear. I wonder if we could come up with some ways to achieve your goal—which I hear as keeping us focused and efficient—in a way that doesn't leave people discouraged and feeling as if they shouldn't bring negative data or anything that is off your immediate game plan.

**Gary:** Yes. OK. You're right. We need to address this. What ideas do you have?

Note here the neutrality with which you, as senior manager, are speaking. You are describing your observation, inquiring about purpose, sharing the perceived meaning and potential impact of your observation, and then inviting a conversation about how to possibly address this. The role being offered to Gary here is inviting and positive. The dialogue is appropriately assertive: neither hesitant nor strident.

Admittedly, the example above is one with an extremely sympathetic, if somewhat unaware boss. We acknowledge that not every situation is as simple as this. But our broader point remains: even when you are lacking in formal power, you can exercise lateral leadership and influence dynamics to increase the likelihood that culture can change to better support conflict resilience. One thing that is for sure is that if you think the situation is hopeless, things are unlikely to change—at least on account of you. Assumptions you bring to a conflict situation or difficult conversation about having no agency or ability to make a difference have a curious way of being self-fulfilling.

Needless to say, not even the president of the United States can make every change they might prefer. And yet *even the most structurally disempowered person has some ability to influence other people around them*. And, if you made it this far in our book, we suspect and fervently hope that, deep down, you believe this too. No one reads a book about conflict and negotiation if they don't believe they have at least *some* ability to influence others and the environment in which they live and work.

The last thing we want to do is downplay the very real role that structural power and hierarchy have in creating a climate that is conflict-resilience-friendly—or the opposite. At the same time, individual agency gives everyone at least *some* capacity to influence an organizational or family dynamic. The key here is finding the right time and place to exercise your influence, to do so only after careful preparation, and to be brave enough to sit with your own discomfort around the possibility of disagreement and even failure.

### 3. Create a Market for Change

Stories of conflict resilience are not only touching, inspiring, and entertaining; they also serve a powerful purpose in shaping family, workplace, or other group dynamics. We share these stories frequently because they do more than just inspire feel-good emotions and a positive vibe.

When we narrate or listen to stories, our brains engage in a remarkable process. Not only are our brains programmed to vividly absorb and remember information when presented as a story, but storytelling also activates mirroring systems—these are neural mechanisms involved in empathy. This neural activity can lead to what's known as neural coupling and interbrain synchrony. In brief, during effective storytelling, the brain activities of the storyteller and listener can synchronize, leading to deeper empathetic connection and shared understanding.

As an added bonus, across 41 studies examining over 1,300 teams, it seems that greater interbrain synchrony is linked with better teamwork, presumably due to improved cooperation and understanding. So, stories that are well deployed and publicized can profoundly shape individual brains and, collectively, transform group culture for good—it's almost magical. By harnessing the power of sharing stories of conflict resilience we not only elevate the relevance of conflict resilient experiences, but also literally align our thinking, building a culture that upholds sitting and being with conflict as a positive social norm.

But let's face it: if you turn on local or national news, scroll the *New York Times*, or tune in to cable news, the lead story is frequently one of polarization, conflict, violence, or war. Stories of successful conflict resilience rarely make headline news. Even when agreement or consensus earns a bit of media coverage—"Congress Passes Infrastructure Bill" or "UPS Averts Major Strike" or "University and Campus Protesters Finally Reach a Détente!"—the story tends to get told as a drama with winners and losers, down-to-the-wire tactics, and back-against-the-wall compromises. In a media climate that is drawn to comic book narratives of good versus evil, where complexity and nuance are eschewed, it can be extremely hard to make the case for a more deliberative, thoughtful, and humanizing approach to handling conflict. And yet, if we want to hardwire conflict resilience into our community, politics, family, or workplace, this is exactly what we need to do. And it's the most purposeful and persuasive reason for telling stories of success.

Consider the work of the House Select Committee on the Modernization of Congress. Unlike most congressional committees, which have an uneven number of Republicans and Democrats (based on which party controls the chamber), this select committee was made up of an equal number (six) of Democrats and Republicans. In addition, unlike most House committees, which have separate Democratic and Republican staffs, this committee agreed to hire a single joint staff. In addition, the committee agreed to have a bipartisan planning retreat for its work. They also made intentional changes to the way they set up the physical space to encourage conversations across partisan divides. Instead of sitting on a dais with Republicans on one side and Democrats on another, they sat at a conference table together. They even scheduled to eat meals with each other.

These may sound like small, maybe even just ceremonial, moves. But they changed the nature and tenor of the conversations between Republicans and Democrats serving on the committee. By the time the committee ended its work four years after being formed, it had made 202 bipartisan recommendations—a stunning number given the gridlock in Congress that makes it hard to even pass a continuing resolution to fund basic functions, like paying salaries for air-traffic controllers. Even more notable, at the time of this writing more than one hundred of these recommendations had been either partially or fully implemented—a remarkable number in an age of gridlock and vitriol.

Consider another example: The World Trade Organization (WTO) operates on a unanimity-decision rule, meaning that any single country of the 166 member states can block an initiative with a single veto. In a global moment of increasing trade tensions—between China and the U.S., between Western countries and emerging global trade powers like India and Brazil, and due to greater collaboration and coordination among developing countries—a unanimity decision rule makes it virtually impossible to get anything done. A particularly challenging area of dysfunction is the way trade disputes get resolved within the WTO. For many years trade negotiators met bimonthly in Geneva to discuss ways to reform the complex dispute resolution system (called the Dispute Settlement Understanding, or DSU) that was rolled out when the WTO was created in 1995. In almost fifteen years of monthly meetings designed to reform the DSU, the only thing that the parties agreed upon was that *nothing got accomplished or agreed to*. Finally, a more conflict-resilient and interest-based approach was introduced to reform the negotiation process beginning in 2022. The result? In less than two years, diplomats were able to produce a fifty-plus-page report of agreed-upon reforms to the dispute resolution system. And, while final negotiations continue as of this writing, it's safe to say that, for the first time in many years, negotiators in Geneva felt a degree of optimism about the chances of reaching a result, reporting that, if nothing else, diplomats were actually talking to each other constructively and honestly for the first time in decades.

One way of reading these stories of conflict-resilient "greenhouses" being created in unexpected places is as a proverbial feel-good tag at the end of a newscast; it's there to leave the viewer feeling more hopeful in a darkening world. But the better reason, for us and you, to share stories of conflict resilience with other people is that doing so tends to build a virtuous cycle—a genuine market for success stories, not just epic dramas of good versus evil.

If we are to hardwire companies, institutions, and families for conflict resilience, we need to create a market for the change. That means telling the stories of transformation and success in ways that detail the hard work, all the challenges from the starting point to the victory, and the unlikelihood (as well as the possibility) of success at the start.

## TRANSFORMING VERSUS WORKING WITH CULTURE

In 2012, students at Harvard Law School had one of the rarest opportunities available for hardwiring conflict resilience into an organization—in this case, into a government agency. They were asked to design and propose a dispute resolution and appeals process for banks and other financial institutions that wanted to challenge findings of the Consumer Financial Protection Bureau (CFPB).

What made this opportunity so unique? It turns out that the CFPB was newly created in 2010, meaning that there was literally no "past system" or "current culture" for how disputes got resolved. The students had a fresh foundation on which to work. It's nearly impossible to imagine building a conflict-resilient culture from scratch in most of the contexts in which we find ourselves day-to-day. In virtually every real-life case—a company, a family, a political body, a synagogue, a bowling club—there is already some conflict-handling culture in place. Perhaps it's highly polarized. Or avoidant. Or vitriolic. Or passive-aggressive. Maybe resolution is very rules-oriented. Or top-down. Or Darwinian survival-of-the-fittest.

But in most cases, conflict resilience has to be injected into an existing organizational culture.

Where to begin? On one end of the spectrum would be an approach that says your goal must be to "Transform the old culture entirely!" On the other end your mantra might be "Respect and accept the culture as you find it."

Each of these one-liners may have some wisdom, depending on the context, timing, organization, and role in which you find yourself. At the time same, neither one-liner is particularly realistic or even preferable most of the time. Bob has worked to build conflict resilience capacity in various parts of the Catholic Church—from dioceses to parishes to religious orders' decision-making. Similarly, Joel has worked to build conflict resilience within various parts of the vast health care system in the U.S. Within the Catholic and health care universes— as in many hierarchical communities and contexts—conflict is coded negatively. In spaces where peace and harmony are seen as what it means to be "Christlike" or necessary to maintain order and efficiency, disagreeing with someone openly can be seen as disruptive and not being a team player. Even worse, if you disagree on key issues—in the religious context, think abortion, LGBTQ+ rights, the role of women, the justification of war, or the death penalty—your disagreement can be used as grounds to disqualify you from participation, promotion, or leadership. Indeed, encouraging dialogue on at least some issues in Catholic circles or in health care institutions might be the ultimate CLM—career-limiting move. This is compounded by a long tradition of hierarchical decision-making, where dissenters either leave (hello, Protestantism!), are silenced (sorry, Galileo!), or are booted out (doesn't take much open disagreement to get thrown out of an operating room at scalpel-point). You can appreciate why the aphorism "Transform the culture!" can feel a bit daunting.

The notion that it's possible to completely transform the culture of large institutions, especially at the global magnitude of the Roman Catholic Church or the behemoth that is American health care (17.3 percent of U.S. GDP in 2022), to create a greenhouse of "conflict-resilient" practice seems laughable. But process and structural reforms that support conflict-resilient disagreement and decision-making can happen.

In one case, Bob worked with a diocesan committee charged with identifying parishes for closure and merger. Mired in avoidance, the typical pattern of the committee was to delay decisions, forcing an otherwise collaborative bishop to issue last-minute edicts (against his will) that gave the impression that he was acting unilaterally. After undergoing training on the importance of discussing differences openly, along with effective process design and skilled facilitation, the advisory group's deliberations evolved from avoidance to competently and openly evaluating various parishes' strengths and weaknesses. This transformation led to greater transparency and enabled them to make well-reasoned, public recommendations to the bishop. While this instance doesn't represent a global or universal cultural transformation, it did open members' eyes to the value of conflict well handled instead of avoided. And it suggested other avenues where open dialogue and conflict could be used to drive a more direct, collaborative, and honest kind of decision-making instead of avoidance and then waiting for a hierarchical pronouncement from a bishop on high.

It's equally dangerous to say, "Take the culture as you find it." After all, in the case of the Catholic Church, it's exactly the culture of a historically male-dominated, top-down, hierarchical approach to governance, decision-making, and conflict-handling that has contributed to increasing toxic polarization both among American Catholics and among American Catholic bishops in recent years as well as to the colossal tragedy of the decades-long Catholic Church sexual abuse crisis in the United States.

Apart from whether you *could* transform a culture to make it more conducive to a conflict-resilient approach to handling differences, there are reasons to be cautious. Even a cursory history of European colonialism shows how efforts to force a Western law–based approach to conflict management on other cultures nearly squashed community-focused Indigenous approaches to conflict-handling that centered restorative practice, reconciliation, community involvement, and forgiveness.

## A CULTURE-SENSITIVE APPROACH

As you introduce some of the ideas and strategies we offer here to a workplace, a family, or a civic organization, we urge you to take a *culture-sensitive approach*. This requires two key dispositions: (1) genuine curiosity and openness and (2) humility.

### 1. Genuine Curiosity and Openness
Whether your intervention is in national politics, your immediate family, or the C-suite in your company, your effort to promote an organizational culture where differences are surfaced, discussed, and

held will land on more fertile soil if you take the time to learn more about the people, processes, traditions (formal and informal), and approaches to differences that are currently in place and valued.

In a highly pressured world of deadlines, it's tempting to skip or expedite the step of deep curiosity and learning. This would be a mistake, for a host of reasons. First, simply taking the time to learn about cultural norms is an act of respect that others will notice and appreciate. It increases your legitimacy when you do try to suggest changes. In addition, it helps you learn the "language" of influence within the ecosystem in which you are working.

Importantly, as you are open and curious about how a particular organizational ecosystem works, you will be able to identify what parts of the culture might already be the fertile soil in which you can plant the seeds of conflict resilience. You will learn what parts might be more amenable to change and modification and what parts might be resistant or hardened such that they must be managed rather than transformed.

Consider the dilemma faced by Dan, who was recruited from a large fast-food chain to head the HR function of a small but rapidly growing regional restaurant group. Upon his arrival, Dan discovered a dynamic that is not uncommon to start-ups growing from a small crew of entrepreneurial founders to a somewhat larger organization in need of more professionalized systems and processes for handling workplace differences. By spending time to learn the history of the company and get a handle on its culture and the preferred practices of the primary C-suite players, Dan was able to discover key elements that could help him nudge the company toward a culture that encouraged disagreement, that created low-risk space for divergent viewpoints, and that gave people the opportunity to build outstanding negotiation and conflict resilience skills.

Specifically, he learned that organizational leadership cared deeply about hiring outside, highly credentialed experts for professional development. The C-suite themselves were all graduates of elite universities and (whether deserved or not) they accorded great respect and deference to experts with similar credentials. Even though internally provided professional development might have been much cheaper for the organization, leadership neither valued nor respected it. Rather than make the economic case for a lower-cost model, Dan identified some of the world's leading and highly credentialed talent and brought them to the firm, which, despite being in the midst of raising funds for an IPO, found the means to retain this top talent. While the C-suite was willing to invest considerable resources to capacity-build senior managers right below them in how to handle conflicts, improve listening, and encourage productive disagreement, Dan observed what he coined "C-suite exceptionalism." Despite the sincere commitment to build their team's capabilities, the leadership actively resisted efforts to participate in the team's professional development activities or follow the protocols they themselves had said were important. This was an ongoing source of frustration, for sure.

If this dynamic sounds familiar, know you are not alone. One way of handling a dilemma like this would be to insist that the only way forward is to stop and get complete buy-in from the top. Any other approach would waste resources and time in a futile effort.

Another way forward would be to give up entirely. Without the C-suite modeling the conflict-resilient environment they said they wanted to create, efforts at culture-change and building organizational conflict resilience would only result in frustration.

But Dan saw it differently. He said yes to the "extended hand" of bringing in well-respected experts on conflict resilience for professional development and process design. He didn't stop there. Whenever he saw a breakthrough or innovative solution that could be tracked to the investment in conflict resilience, he made sure to use the example in C-suite meetings where he demonstrated the value of the approach in ways that were meaningful to the decision-makers. And when things failed or someone left because of conflict badly managed,

Dan artfully found a way to attribute the bad outcome to a breakdown in the ability of a team to handle differences. Did the culture wholly transform? Not exactly. But was there a meaningful and palpable shift? Without a doubt.

## 2. Humility

One of the toughest lessons that we have had to learn when working with individuals and organizations around conflict and differences is embracing genuine humility in our work. Almost all of us probably know of at least one couple who has gone through an awful divorce, marked by massive legal expenses, repeated attempts at retribution, and a seemingly unrelenting effort to impose pain on the other side. Typically, if you were not one of the members of the couple, you could probably offer each side a few very helpful pieces of advice on how to let go of the enmity long enough to get through the painful process, resolve the substantive issues in dispute, and move on. Indeed, part of the value each of us can bring as a trusted outsider to an organizational or family system in conflict is the equanimity of a third perspective.

This perspective is useful for sure, but it is also limited. When working within a family or organizational culture, it's critical to remember the limits of your role. Specifically, the wisdom of the solution is always found *within the community*, not outside it. In seeking to build a culture of conflict resilience within an organization or family or company, you likely have tools and skills for helping to create conditions that will help parties discover outcomes, solutions, and approaches that work within their cultural context. Where you are likely to get in trouble is when you think you have answers that are somehow better, wiser, or more enlightened than the wisdom found within the community itself. Cultivating a sense of humility in your work will guide you as you seek to understand an organizational culture and as you work within and through an existing culture to create conditions and processes and approaches to facilitate and support conflict resilience.

## WITH A LITTLE HELP FROM MY FRIENDS

Another aspect of evolving culture is the adoption of a trauma-informed approach. This framework involves understanding, recognizing, and responding to the effects of all types of trauma. It emphasizes physical, psychological, and emotional safety for everyone involved—both survivors and the people they interact with, such as health care providers, educators, or team members. The intent is to create opportunities for survivors to rebuild a sense of control and empowerment. This approach is grounded in an understanding of the vulnerabilities of trauma survivors that traditional approaches may exacerbate, so that services and programs can be more supportive and avoid retraumatization. This allows for an opportunity to foster a culture in which individuals are more likely to develop conflict resilience because they're in an environment where they can practice skills and be progressively challenged in a graduated manner without being overwhelmed. Below are a few key principles of a trauma-informed approach:

- **Safety:** Ensuring physical, psychological, and emotional safety for individuals.
- **Trustworthiness and Transparency:** Building trust with clear operations and expectations.
- **Peer Support and Mutual Self-Help:** Integrating the voices and experiences of trauma survivors.
- **Collaboration and Mutuality:** Recognizing that healing happens for survivors through relationships and in the meaningful sharing of power and decision-making.
- **Empowerment, Voice, and Choice:** Emphasizing individuals' strengths and experiences, ensuring their voices are heard and their choices respected.
- **Cultural, Historical, and Gender Issues:** Acknowledging the existence of cultural, historical, and gender issues and engaging

responsively. This includes taking into account the heterogeneity of cultural and gender-related experiences of individuals and creating environments that are mutually respectful, inclusive, and equitable and that foster a sense of belonging.

In essence, a trauma-informed culture recognizes the widespread impact of trauma and understands potential paths for recovery; recognizes the signs and symptoms of trauma in clients, families, staff, and others involved with the system; and fully integrates knowledge about trauma into policies, procedures, practices, and settings. To effectively create a trauma-informed culture, organizations and individuals can adopt a few best practices. These form the foundation of a supportive conflict-resilient environment:

1. **Educate and Train Everyone:** Provide comprehensive education and training on trauma's effects, signs, and appropriate responses to all members of the organization.

2. **Develop Supportive Policies:** Craft and implement organizational policies that reinforce a trauma-informed approach, maintaining transparency and collaboration consistently.

3. **Ensure Safety and Trust:** Establish and maintain an environment where both physical and psychological safety are prioritized, fostering trust at all levels.

4. **Involve Service Users in Decision-Making:** Actively include clients or service users in policy and practice development to ensure their needs and perspectives are addressed.

5. **Implement Peer Support Programs:** Establish peer support systems where individuals with lived-trauma experiences can offer empathy and understanding to others.

6. **Screen Regularly for Trauma:** Conduct routine trauma screenings in service settings to identify and address the needs of those affected. This can be done generally and anonymously, or as a part of more confidential one-on-one feedback sessions

to identify the presence and sources of trauma within your organization.

7. **Prevent Retraumatization:** Constantly review and modify practices and policies to avoid causing inadvertent retraumatization.

8. **Make Services Accessible:** Ensure that all services are accessible, regardless of cultural, economic, or social barriers.

9. **Evaluate and Seek Feedback Continuously:** Regularly assess the effectiveness of trauma-informed approaches and solicit feedback for ongoing improvement.

10. **Support Staff Self-Care:** Acknowledge the emotional impact on staff working with trauma survivors and provide adequate support and opportunities for self-care to safeguard against burnout.

Hardwiring conflict resilience into a culture is a multifaceted task. It requires awareness of existing cultural norms while actively working to transform them. By remaining curious and open, by cultivating our own humility, and by adopting a trauma-informed approach, we can create environments that are not only more productive but also more compassionate and apt to harness the value of the diverse experiences that shape our interactions.

## CONFLICT RESILIENCE: A SHARED CHALLENGE FOR POLARIZING TIMES

From COVID to George Floyd. From January 6 to October 7. From presidential candidates on opposing extremes, one election to the next. From congressional gridlock to raging wars around the world. From gender-affirming care to banning books and protecting parents' rights. From doxing to cancel culture. Everywhere we look on the domestic and international front, the forces of polarization and division are on the rise and are likely to continue to do so. Feeling threatened and under assault, we are prone to gather the brigades on our side and prepare for battle. A media environment obsessed with high drama, drawn to good-guy/bad-guy narratives, and dependent on drawing an audience that is more interested in having their assumptions and biases confirmed rather than challenged. These dynamics have created the most daunting crisis the United States has faced internally since the Civil War.

On the global front, the international order established at Dumbarton Oaks following World War II—the consensus that created the architecture for international institutions like the United Nations, NATO, and the WTO—has, despite manifold deficiencies, nonetheless succeeded in preventing the breakout of World War III or a full-blown superpower conflict. But that order is now under serious assault, viewed by many at times as woefully ineffective at promoting international peace, advancing healthy and fair global trade, or providing an adequate and coordinated response to existential threats like climate change or the proliferation of nuclear weapons into the hands of rogue states or terrorists.

Closer to home, families and friendships are torn apart over politics, or how to handle differences on issues related to gender, sexuality, immigration, free speech, education, gun rights, reproductive choices, climate, or even access to free and fair voting in a democracy.

As these conflicts intensify and as polarization increases, our brains react with anger and fear. Our most primal instincts drive us to those who are like-minded, to the clan who will protect us from the threat. But as we balkanize, defend, and prepare for battle, we lose the tools we need to ensure our long-term survival and our shared thriving in a world necessarily (blessedly!) full of difference, diversity, and conflict. The ease with which we can create our cocoons of comfort further makes the discomfort of sitting with conflict, difference, and disagreement less attractive or even plausible in some situations.

And yet, we *must reverse this trend*. We believe to our bones that failure to cultivate individual conflict resilience—both the capacity to sit with the discomfort of disagreement and the related skills to listen generously and assert authentically through conflict—will lead to the continued disintegration of our nation, workplaces, civic institutions, and families, and ultimately, perhaps, to our end as a society and as a species.

We are not arguing here that conflict resilience is all we need. It is necessary, but not sufficient. We opened this book with a story from Seeds of Peace, an organization that has brought young Israeli and Palestinian leaders together over many decades to engage in dialogue across conflict lines where deep and perhaps irreconcilable differences exist over even the basic factual narrative of the history and land of two peoples. It's easy to look at the current and gut-wrenching mess in the Middle East today and declare that conflict resilience—the efforts at dialogue and sitting with disagreement—have been a failure of epic proportions.

But that would be a mistake. Has the dialogue work of Seeds of Peace and other related organizations brought about peace between the Israeli and Palestinian people? Sadly, it has not. *But it has changed thousands of lives on both sides of the conflict*—spawning joint projects, creating relationships, inspiring new organizations and unexpected partnerships. And there is no doubt that the world—and the region itself—is profoundly better than it would otherwise be because of this organization's commitment to conflict resilience.

To become truly conflict resilient takes hard work. It's not something that can be done to you by reading this book, taking a workshop, or hiring a coach—though all these things may help. From both our experience and the science, we are persuaded that the return on investment of developing conflict resilience is worth the effort. It starts with you. But over time, as you commit to the internal and behavioral practice, as you find your voice, as you assess the places in your family and culture and workplace that you can influence by your example, we believe that a culture change is possible.

Polarization is not inevitable. Nor is balkanization, isolation, dehumanization, avoidance, violence, or war. All of these are choices—either of action or inaction. The only thing that is inevitable is that as long as human beings interact with each other, there will be conflict. How we embrace, use, mold, and grow with conflict are choices that will make the difference for the world in which we live and, truly, for the security, happiness, and fulfillment of our lives. This process often starts with a tiny first step: when you pause and appreciate, despite all hardship, how startlingly beautiful conflict can be.

We invite you to join us on this journey of building conflict resilience. And we leave you with the invocation of courage from one of our favorite poets:

**Blessing of Courage**
BY JAN RICHARDSON

*I cannot say*
*where it lives,*
*only that it comes*
*to the heart*
*that is open,*
*to the heart*
*that asks,*
*to the heart*
*that does not turn away.*

*It can take practice,*
*days of tugging at*
*what keeps us bound,*
*seasons of pushing against*
*what keeps our dreaming*
*small.*

*When it arrives,*
*it might surprise you*
*by how quiet it is,*
*how it moves*
*with such grace*
*for possessing*
*such power.*

*But you will know it*
*by the strength*
*that rises from within you*
*to meet it,*
*by the release*
*of the knot*
*in the center of*
*your chest*
*that suddenly lets go.*

*You will recognize it*
*by how still*
*your fear becomes*
*as it loosens its grip,*
*perhaps never quite*
*leaving you,*
*but calmly turning*
*into joy*
*as you enter the life*
*that is finally*
*your own.*

# ACKNOWLEDGMENTS

A book written by a committee hardly ever reads well. Nor does a book written without the wisdom and support of a community. We are blessed that the community that supported us in our writing journey is vast and wise. It extends across many years, draws from diverse academic, disciplinary, and applied backgrounds, and includes valued professional relationships as well as cherished personal friendships.

At heart, *Conflict Resilience* was born in and from the observations and experience we had in our own professional and personal communities. In the years preceding this amazing writing journey, we noticed increasing balkanization, polarization, and avoidance in the students, faculty, and patients with whom we worked as well as in our own circles of family and friends. The idea for the book was drawn from community as was our own collaboration: we met each other and became friends through our own membership in the LGBTQ+ and Harvard communities. There we nurtured the personal friendship that turned into a shared labor of love in this book.

*Conflict Resilience* itself draws from the lived experience of so many in our separate and our overlapping worlds. We are indebted to the many thousands of students, clients, and patients with whom we have collaborated and who shared their stories with us. And we stand in awe of the work from the interdisciplinary fields that inform prescriptions in this book: conflict resolution, negotiation, mediation, neuroscience, psychology, economics, business, public policy, and medicine (to name a few). And, of course, we appreciate deeply the richness and diversity of the family, friends, and colleagues who have helped us forge and shape our own conflict resilience day-to-day.

## FOR INSPIRATION AND IDEAS

Even before our collaboration was a subject of conversation between us, we each long aspired to author a book that might, if we were fortunate enough, make a real and positive difference in the lives of our readers. Hailing from academic worlds where groundbreaking scholarship and peer-reviewed articles matter more than general readability, we also occupied unique niches as scholar-clinicians in that ecosystem. We each worked with and learned from mentors and colleagues who broke new ground by translating theory and research to action in their work.

Bob feels fortunate for his many years of association with the Harvard Program on Negotiation and the lineage of groundbreaking and impactful books that emerged from the program since its founding in 1983 and that continue to transform the way leaders negotiate, advance peace and diplomacy, resolve conflicts, and forge deals. He spent more than twenty years on the full-time faculty of Harvard Law School, learning from not only colleagues but also from legions of talented and generous students too numerous to name.

The late Roger Fisher, a founder of Harvard's Program on Negotiation and co-author of *Getting to Yes*, would often ask Bob as he considered writing an article, paper, or op-ed: "Would anyone in the world do anything different because of what you are planning to write?" Ensuring that the answer to that question is a "yes" for this book has been a personal North Star for Bob in the writing process.

Apart from the inspiration, we are grateful to a pantheon of leaders and mentors in the negotiation and dispute resolution academic world with whom we've had the honor of working with and learning from through the years. They include the late Roger Fisher and the late Frank E.A. Sander, as well as Sheila Heen, Craig McEwen, Carrie Menkel-Meadow, Bob Mnookin, Michael Moffitt, Bruce Patton, Nancy Rogers, Dan Shapiro, Ron Shapiro, Doug Stone, Larry Susskind, Bill Ury, and Mike Wheeler.

We are also grateful for mentors and leaders in the field of neuroscience and the immense contributions they continue to make, especially Michael Banissy, Lisa Feldman Barrett, Lisa F. Berkman, Jud Brewer, David Caplan, Tracey Cho, Merit Cudkowicz, Nancy Donovan, Guy Itzchakov, Tracey Milligan, V.S. Ramachandran, Dorene Rentz, Allan Roper, Jonathan Rosand, Natalia Rost, Lee Schwamm, Sudha Seshadri, Reisa Sperling, Jamie Ward, Jamil Zaki, and the late Martin Samuels.

Standing on the shoulders of such giants in our respective fields, we've sought to contribute to the ongoing conversations, with the hope of building something that resonates.

In a special way, we thank our colleagues at the Cambridge Negotiation Institute for their ideas and support as they accompanied us in the writing of this book: Toby Berkman, Amy Cohen, Florrie Darwin, Krista deBoer, Dan Del Gobbo, Daniel Doktori, Sarah Doktori, Charles Ferrara, Kyle Glover, Lauren Gore, Tristan Jones, Leah Kang, Kevin Keystone, Esther Lin, and Zoe Segal-Reichlin. This collection of professionals are the best-of-the-best, drawn in large part from a pool of amazingly accomplished Harvard Law School negotiation students over two decades of Bob's teaching and running the Harvard Negotiation & Mediation Clinical Program. We appreciate their ideas for the book and their ongoing collaboration in our work together.

In a world more-and-more torn asunder by the kind of conflict that keeps us apart, polarizes, and incites violence and division, the transformative work of Seeds of Peace, a leadership program founded in 1993 that brings young leaders together for dialogue across lines of difference, gives us enduring hope and schools us in how to sit with the discomfort of disagreement. If you want to know what it means to be conflict resilient, you need look no further than the young people who have been part of this extraordinary leadership program over the past thirty-plus years.

Our book is filled with vignettes about imaginary characters from Carrie and Miranda to Katie to Trevor and Kendra and Danilo.

While no story (besides the ones about ourselves and public personalities like Pete Buttigieg, Anthony Fauci, and Dolly Parton) represents an actual "real-life" person, the situations and dilemmas are amalgams of real life situations, drawn from the thousands of students, patients, clients, and friends whom we have been blessed to teach, coach, serve, support, befriend, and learn from. We are ever grateful for the people and relationships behind the stories and for the insights, patterns, and strategies that emerged from the courage and conflict resilience they showed.

## FOR FEEDBACK

Though we don't often think of it this way, soliciting feedback in a genuine way—where you really want to hear "what works" and "what stinks"—is an invitation to conflict! Despite the societal trends toward avoidance, we are grateful for a team that didn't hold back in offering their best advice on everything from word choice (i.e., "Stop saying 'by dint of' so much. No one speaks that way!") to cover design (i.e., "I don't mean to offend you, but I think that cover design looks AI-generated. You can't use it!"). Long before we wrote the first word of the book, we solicited feedback using an extensive list of questions—from "Is there a book here? We don't want to do a rewrite of the literature already out there!" to "How do we evaluate publisher offers?" to "What do you think of the flow of the chapters and framework?"

Our efforts to land on a title were at once deeply frustrating and oh-so-helpful. In our first round of soliciting feedback on the title, not a single person we reached out to liked *any* of our top five titles. In these dispiriting moments, we always knew that if we leaned in with deep listening, we'd be the beneficiaries of insight that would give us and you a better book, a more attractive cover, and a title that spoke to the urgency and relevance of the content.

We can't thank you enough, dear community, for the coaching to make this book what it is.

The great Bob Barnett of Williams & Connolly helped us navigate the tricky auction process, as did Harvard Business School Professor Emeritus Michael Wheeler. Karen Dillon was indispensable at every step of this process, from the auction right through to publication. More than that, she has been a cheerleader of our ideas and of the possibility that the book could make a difference in the world.

In addition to the Cambridge Negotiation Institute colleagues above, we also thank, Eva Armour, Cynthia Drescher, Ashley Fougner, Antoine Issaly, Laura Erickson-Schroth, Dan Garodnick, Alex Grodd, Elaine Lin Hering, Chris Lawton, CSP, Ricky Manalo, CSP, Kevin Michael Murphy, Annie Olinick, Mark Stoltenberg, MD, Amy Uelman, PhD, Jeff Wetzler, and Sandra Wijnberg. Through challenging questions, candid critiques, or heartfelt encouragement, you played a key role in refining our ideas and helping us stretch our thinking.

In addition to the community of colleagues and friends cheering us on and critiquing us along the way, we are grateful that we had the best in the business at our side.

To our agent, Roger Freet at Folio: thanks for believing in us and in this project from our very first conversation. Your wise counsel every step of the way helped us navigate the bewildering world of book publishing with confidence and aplomb!

Miles Doyle spent countless hours helping us shape our key ideas and stopping us from oversharing pointless details in our stories, whether they be about a personal story of conflict or a fine point of cutting-edge neuroscience. Your patience with us and your discerning eye made this book so much better.

To our publisher and editor, Hollis Heimbouch: When we were deciding with whom to work, everyone we spoke with told us, "Hollis is the best in the business." You were not undersold. You somehow found a way to keep us moving even when we stagnated and to do so in a way that reminded us that we could pull this book off. We're especially grateful to you for the workshop session that helped us build out the framework for the book that would, as you rightly said, "then write itself." Thank you for believing in us and in this project. We hope that this book will make the impact that you and we both believe it can.

We extend additional thanks to Heather Drucker, Jessica Gilo, Rachel Kambury, and the entire team at HarperCollins.

It matters little if you write a great book that no one picks up, reads, or listens to. We are ever grateful to Mark Fortier, Norbert Beatty, and the team at Fortier Public Relations for providing the strategy that helped us introduce our ideas to the world. Heidi Gross also provided invaluable support and counsel as we built our Book Launch Village. Your passion for our topic and the steadfast persistence in helping us bring this to the world means so much to us! Thank you for partnering with us.

## FOR SUPPORT

Feelings are a big part of conflict and a big part of writing a book. As most authors can attest, most of what gets written remains unseen. And we had many writing days of nothing—or almost nothing—to show for it. Through the ups-and-downs of the process, we are grateful for friends and family who have and who continue to support us. Many of them are already mentioned above. But there are some special others who have been closer to the process.

Though Bob's partner, Robert MacArthur, arrived on the scene in the latter months of completing this manuscript, he patiently endured countless hours of agonized writing and rewriting and multiple pronouncements that, "The book is finally done!" only to have to sit through a new round of work, edits, or assignments a few weeks later. Your patience, calm, and support through the anxiety and hand wringing—as well as your constant affirmation for this work and the belief that it matters in the world—calms Bob's soul and grounds him. Thank you for being the Chasten to Bob's Pete in all the ways that it matters most.

In addition, Bob's parents, Robert M. and Mary Bordone, have believed in him and his capacity to write a book that could make a difference long before Bob himself thought it to be possible. For a lifetime of love, encouragement, and unconditional support, a million thanks could not be enough.

Jared Hatch, Joel's partner, deserves more gratitude than he could ever express here. Throughout the many long days and nights spent writing, editing, and revising, you offered Joel not only your unwavering support but also the gift of patience. Whether it was enduring stretches where we missed quality time together, allowing Joel to work through weekends or during trips, or simply being a steadfast source of calm during the inevitable ups and downs of this journey, you made sure that this book could make its way to the public. Your understanding allowed Joel the time and mental space he needed to dive deeply into this work, and for that, Joel is endlessly grateful.

Also, to Joel's family—Armando, Norma, Rainier, Scarlett, and Jay— your love and encouragement mean more than words can express. Thanks also to Kaitlyn Hova and Laura Erickson-Schroth for your friendship and your honest perspectives and support.

Though they can't read these words, we are both blessed by loyal four-legged companions who forewent hours of attention and stayed by our side as we wrote and edited. To Bob's golden retriever Rosie— you are God's direct emissary to me, reminding me of unconditional love and support. Joel is equally thankful to his long-haired Chihuahua, Waffle. A factory full of Greenies could never repay the debt we owe you!

## FOR THE PAST, PRESENT, AND FUTURE

Finally, to everyone who has touched us or been touched by us, anyone who is part of this journey of sitting in the discomfort of conflict to build a more vibrant and dynamic world—thank you for being part of our community of curiosity and learning.

We imagine that not everyone who reads our book will agree or like all or even much of it. But we want your feedback, suggestions, and yes, your disagreement. We promise to listen deeply and to learn from the experience of those who take on the challenge of becoming conflict resilient. The errors and missteps in this book are ours; the victories, improved relationships, and ongoing growth in the journey are yours—and we celebrate and offer thanks for them all!

# NOTES

## Introduction

4   *termed* conflict resilience: R. C. Bordone, "Building Conflict Resilience: It's Not Just About Problem-Solving," *Journal of Dispute Resolution* (2018): 65.

7   *quadrupled from 3.9 percent to 15 percent:* E. E. McGinty, R. Presskreischer, H. Han, and C. L. Barry, "Trends in Psychological Distress Among US Adults During Different Phases of the COVID-19 Pandemic," *JAMA Network Open* 5, no. 1 (2022): e2144776.

7   *closer to 1 in 5:* E. E. McGinty, R. Presskreischer, H. Han, and C. L. Barry, "Psychological Distress and Loneliness Reported by US Adults in 2018 and April 2020," *JAMA* 324, no. 1 (2020): 93–94.

7   *a recent Gallup poll:* "Satisfaction with the United States," Gallup, 2024, https://news.gallup.com/poll/1669/general-mood-country.aspx.

8   *perceive physical injuries and attacks:* G. Tabibnia and M. D. Lieberman, "Fairness and Cooperation Are Rewarding: Evidence from Social Cognitive Neuroscience," *Annals of the New York Academy of Science* 1118 (2007): 90–101; A. W. Cappelen, T. Eichele, K. Hugdahl, K. Specht, E. O. Sorensen, and B. Tungodden, "Equity Theory and Fair Inequality: A Neuroeconomic Study," *PNAS* 111, no. 43 (2014): 15368–72.

8   *neuroplasticity and synaptogenesis:* S. Schmidt, S. Gull, H. Herrmann et al., "Experience-Dependent Structural Plasticity in the Adult Brain: How the Learning Brain Grows," *Neuroimage* 225 (2021): 117502; R. G. O'Connell and I. H. Robertson, "Plasticity of High-Order Cognition: A Review of Experience-Induced Remediation Studies for Executive Deficits," 2011.

8   *fire together, wire together:* S. Lim, "Hebbian Learning Revisited and Its Inference Underlying Cognitive Function," *Current Opinion in Behavioral Sciences* 38 (2021): 96–102.

14   *enhances an organization:* D. Chrobot-Mason and N. P. Aramovich, "The Psychological Benefits of Creating an Affirming Climate for Workplace Diversity," *Group & Organization Management* 38, no. 6 (2013): 659–89.

14   *across every metric:* Q. M. Roberson, "Diversity in the Workplace: A Review, Synthesis, and Future Research Agenda," *Annual Review of Organizational Psychology and Organizational Behavior* 6 (2019): 69–88.

14   *advantageous conflict:* J. Armache, "Diversity in the Workplace: Benefits and Challenges," *Conflict Resolution & Negotiation Journal* 1 (2012).

## Chapter 1: Getting Past Excuses to Diagnoses

31   *predictions of the future:* K. M. Lee, F. Ferreira-Santos, and A. B. Satpute,

"Predictive Processing Models and Affective Neuroscience," *Neuroscience & Biobehavioral Reviews* 131 (2021): 211–28.

32 *perceiving-predicting system:* M. J. Kim, P. Mende-Siedlecki, S. Anzellotti, and L. Young, "Theory of Mind Following the Violation of Strong and Weak Prior Beliefs," *Cerebral Cortex* 31, no. 2 (2021): 884–98.

35 *less distressing for her:* A. Rawat, N. Sangroula, A. Khan et al., "Comparison of Metacognitive Therapy Versus Cognitive Behavioral Therapy for Generalized Anxiety Disorder: A Meta-Analysis of Randomized Control Trials," *Cureus* 15, no. 5 (2023): e39252.

35 *almost a decade:* S. Solem, A. Wells, L. E. O. Kennair, R. Hagen, H. Nordahl, and O. Hjemdal, "Metacognitive Therapy Versus Cognitive-Behavioral Therapy in Adults with Generalized Anxiety Disorder: A 9-Year Follow-up Study," *Brain and Behavior* 11, no. 10 (2021): e2358.

## Chapter 2: Rethinking Your Relationship with Conflict

40 *award-winning documentary* Seeds: *Seeds,* directed by Owen Long, released 2019, available at www.seedsthemovie.com.

45 *listen to what they're saying:* L. Miller, *The Ashes on the Lawn,* podcast, WNYC Studios, December 18, 2020, https://radiolab.org/podcast/ashes-lawn/.

## Chapter 3: Understanding Your Conflict Tolerance

54 *in recent years:* M. T. Hawes, A. K. Szenczy, D. N. Klein, G. Hajcak, and B. D. Nelson, "Increases in Depression and Anxiety Symptoms in Adolescents and Young Adults During the COVID-19 Pandemic," *Psychological Medicine* 52, no. 14 (2022): 3222–30.

54 *remain unclear:* E. Hoge, D. Bickham, and J. Cantor, "Digital Media, Anxiety, and Depression in Children," *Pediatrics* 140 (Suppl 2) (2017): S76–S80; T. Alvi, D. Kumar, and B. A. Tabak, "Social Anxiety and Behavioral Assessments of Social Cognition: A Systematic Review," *Journal of Affective Disorders* 311 (2022): 17–30.

54 *interpersonal dilemmas:* J. Davila and J. G. Beck, "Is Social Anxiety Associated with Impairment in Close Relationships? A Preliminary Investigation," *Behavior Therapy* 33, no. 3 (2002): 427–46.

54 *keeping relationships:* N. A. Tonge, M. H. Lim, M. L. Piccirillo, K. C. Fernandez, J. K. Langer, and T. L. Rodebaugh, "Interpersonal Problems in Social Anxiety Disorder Across Different Relational Contexts," *Journal of Anxiety Disorders* 75 (2020): 102275.

54 *school and work:* I. M. Aderka, S. G. Hofmann, A. Nickerson, H. Hermesh, E. Gilboa-Schechtman, and S. Marom, "Functional Impairment in Social Anxiety Disorder," *Journal of Anxiety Disorders* 26, no. 3 (2012): 393–400.

62 *our own devices:* I. Carlsson, P. E. Wendt, and J. Risberg, "On the Neurobiology of Creativity: Differences in Frontal Activity Between High and Low Creative Subjects," *Neuropsychologia* 38, no. 6 (2000): 873–85; K. M.

Heilman, "Possible Brain Mechanisms of Creativity," *Archives of Clinical Neuropsychology* 31, no. 4 (2016): 285–296; A. U. Patil, S. Ghate, D. Madathil, O. J. L. Tzeng, H. W. Huang, and C. M. Huang, "Static and Dynamic Functional Connectivity Supports the Configuration of Brain Networks Associated with Creative Cognition," *Scientific Reports* 11, no. 1 (2021): 165.

62 *your experience:* C. J. Price and H. Y. Weng, "Facilitating Adaptive Emotion Processing and Somatic Reappraisal via Sustained Mindful Interoceptive Attention," *Frontiers in Psychology* 12 (2021): 578827.

62 *positive or negative emotions:* E. Constantinou, M. Van Den Houte, K. Bogaerts, I. Van Diest, and O. Van den Bergh, "Can Words Heal? Using Affect Labeling to Reduce the Effects of Unpleasant Cues on Symptom Reporting," *Frontiers in Psychology* 5 (2014): 807; E. Levy-Gigi and S. Shamay-Tsoory, "Affect Labeling: The Role of Timing and Intensity," *PLoS One* 17, no. 12 (2022): e0279303; J. Liang and H. Lin, "Current and Lasting Effects of Affect Labeling on Late Positive Potential (LPP) Amplitudes Elicited by Negative Events," *Brain and Behavior* 13, no. 7 (2023): e3065; S. G. Shamay-Tsoory and E. Levy-Gigi, "You Name It: Interpersonal Affect Labeling Diminishes Distress in Romantic Couples," *Behavior Therapy* 52, no. 2 (2021): 455–64.

63 *sleep-deprived:* P. Cernadas Curotto, V. Sterpenich, D. Sander, N. Favez, U. Rimmele, and O. Klimecki, "Quarreling After a Sleepless Night: Preliminary Evidence of the Impact of Sleep Deprivation on Interpersonal Conflict," *Affective Science* 3, no. 2 (2022): 341–52; L. F. Barrett and W. K. Simmons, "Interoceptive Predictions in the Brain," *Nature Reviews Neuroscience* 16, no. 7 (2015): 419–429.

63 *bodily sensations:* C. D. Wilson-Mendenhall, A. Henriques, L. W. Barsalou, and L. F. Barrett, "Primary Interoceptive Cortex Activity during Simulated Experiences of the Body," *Journal of Cognitive Neuroscience* 31, no. 2 (2019): 221–35.

64 *research:* R. Waite and N. S. McKinney, "Enhancing Conflict Competency," *ABNF Journal* 25, no. 4 (2014): 123–28; S. Mustafa, J. K. Stoller, S. B. Bierer, and C. F. Farver, "Effectiveness of a Leadership Development Course for Chief Residents: A Longitudinal Evaluation," *Journal of Graduate Medical Education* 12, no. 2 (2020): 193–202.

72 *selective attention biases:* G. Prat-Ortega and J. Rocha, "Selective Attention: A Plausible Mechanism Underlying Confirmation Bias," *Current Biology* 28, no. 19 (2018): R1151–R1154.

73 *their behaviors:* S. Kelly, S. Martin, I. Kuhn, A. Cowan, C. Brayne, and L. Lafortune, "Barriers and Facilitators to the Uptake and Maintenance of Healthy Behaviours by People at Mid-Life: A Rapid Systematic Review," *PLoS One* 11, no. 1 (2016): e0145074.

75 *process physical pain:* M. Richter, J. Eck, T. Straube, W. H. R. Miltner, and T. Weiss, "Do Words Hurt? Brain Activation During the Processing of Pain-Related words," *Pain* 148, no. 2 (2010): 198–205; P. A. Kragel, L. Koban, L. F. Barrett, and T. D. Wager, "Representation, Pattern Information, and Brain Signatures: From

Neurons to Neuroimaging," *Neuron* 99, no. 2 (2018): 257–73; N. I. Eisenberger, M. D. Lieberman, and K. D. Williams, "Does Rejection Hurt? An fMRI Study of Social Exclusion," *Science* 302, no. 5643 (2003): 290–92.

75   *breathwork is crucial:* G. W. Fincham, C. Strauss, J. Montero-Marin, and K. Cavanagh, "Effect of Breathwork on Stress and Mental Health: A Meta-Analysis of Randomised-Controlled Trials," *Scientific Reports* 13, no. 1 (2023): 432.

75   *feel more calm:* D. C. Mathersul, K. Dixit, R. J. Schulz-Heik, T. J. Avery, J. M. Zeitzer, and P. J. Bayley, "Emotion Dysregulation and Heart Rate Variability Improve in US Veterans Undergoing Treatment for Posttraumatic Stress Disorder: Secondary Exploratory Analyses from a Randomised Controlled Trial," *BMC Psychiatry* 22, no. 1 (2022): 268.

76   *neurotransmitter called GABA:* A. C. Bonham, "Neurotransmitters in the CNS Control of Breathing," *Respiratory Physiology* 101, no. 3 (1995): 219–30.

76   *One study:* M. Y. Balban, E. Neri, M. M. Kogon et al., "Brief Structured Respiration Practices Enhance Mood and Reduce Physiological Arousal," *Cell Reports Medicine* 4, no. 1 (2023): 100895.

76   *mindful meditation alone:* Balban, Neri, and Kogon.

76   *restore calm:* C. F. Chick, A. Singh, L. A. Anker et al., "A School-Based Health and Mindfulness Curriculum Improves Children's Objectively Measured Sleep: A Prospective Observational Cohort Study," *Journal of Clinical Sleep Medicine* 18, no. 9 (2022): 2261–71.

76   *holding capability:* Balban, Neri, and Kogon, "Brief Structured Respiration Practices."

84   *reactive parts of our brains:* Y. Y. Tang, B. K. Holzel, and M. I. Posner, "The Neuroscience of Mindfulness Meditation," *Nature Reviews Neuroscience* 16, no. 4 (2015): 213–25; B. Bremer, Q. Wu, M. G. Mora Alvarez et al., "Mindfulness Meditation Increases Default Mode, Salience, and Central Executive Network Connectivity," *Science Reports* 12, no. 1 (2022): 13219.

84   *you might be experiencing:* P. M. McEvoy, "Metacognitive Therapy for Anxiety Disorders: A Review of Recent Advances and Future Research Directions," *Current Psychiatry Reports* 21, no. 5 (2019): 29; R. L. Brown, A. Wood, J. D. Carter, and L. Kannis-Dymand, "The Metacognitive Model of Post-Traumatic Stress Disorder and Metacognitive Therapy for Post-Traumatic Stress Disorder: A Systematic Review," *Clinical Psychology & Psychotherapy* 29, no. 1 (2022): 131–46.

85   *kind behaviors:* H. Y. Weng, A. S. Fox, A. J. Shackman et al., "Compassion Training Alters Altruism and Neural Responses to Suffering," *Psychological Science* 24, no. 7 (2013): 1171–80.

87   *bigger, better offer:* J. Brewer, "How to Break Up with Your Bad Habits," *Harvard Business Review*, December 5, 2019, https://hbr.org/2019/12/how-to-break-up-with-your-bad-habits.

88   *experiences and predictions:* Weng, Fox, and Shackman, "Compassion Training."

89   *prefrontal cortex:* Tang, Holzel, and Posner, "The Neuroscience of Mindfulness Meditation"; Bremer, Wu, and Mora Alvarez, "Mindfulness Meditation."

## Chapter 4: Embracing Your Negotiation Within

97   *In his memoir:* The Shortest Way Home: Pete Buttigieg, *The Shortest Way Home: One Mayor's Challenge and a Model for America's Future* (New York: Liveright Publishing, 2019).

99   *In their 2009 book,* Immunity to Change: Robert Kegan and Lisa Laskow Lahey, *Immunity to Change: How to Overcome It and Unlock the Potential in Yourself and Your Organization* (Boston: Harvard Business Press, 2009).

102  *physical pain:* A. Stegemann, S. Liu, O. A. Retana Romero et al., "Prefrontal Engrams of Long-Term Fear Memory Perpetuate Pain Perception," *Nature Neuroscience* 26, no. 5 (2023): 820–29; M. Noel, T. M. Palermo, C. T. Chambers, A. Taddio, and C. Hermann, "Remembering the Pain of Childhood: Applying a Developmental Perspective to the Study of Pain Memories," *Pain* 156, no. 1 (2015): 31–34; B. McCarberg and J. Peppin, "Pain Pathways and Nervous System Plasticity: Learning and Memory in Pain," *Pain Medicine* 20, no. 12 (2019): 2421–37; Tang, Holzel, and Posner, "The Neuroscience of Mindfulness Meditation."

102  *form lasting memories:* J. M. Fitzgerald, J. A. DiGangi, and K. L. Phan, "Functional Neuroanatomy of Emotion and Its Regulation in PTSD," *Harvard Review of Psychiatry* 26, no. 3 (2018): 116–28.

103  *Harvard Negotiation and Mediation Clinical Program:* R. C. Bordone, T. C. Berkman, and S. E. del Nido, "The Negotiation Within: The Impact of Internal Conflict Over Identity and Role on Across-the-Table Negotiations," *Journal of Dispute Resolution* (2014): 175.

109  *first introduced by Bob and his coauthors:* Bordone, Berkman, and del Nido.

110  *called "loss aversion":* C. K. De Dreu, P. J. Carnevale, B. J. Emans, and E. Van De Vliert, "Effects of Gain-Loss Frames in Negotiation: Loss Aversion, Mismatching, and Frame Adoption," *Organizational Behavior and Human Decision Processes* 60, no. 1 (1994): 90–107.

113  *bodily self:* B. M. Herbert and O. Pollatos, "The Body in the Mind: On the Relationship Between Interoception and Embodiment," *Topics in Cognitive Science* 4, no. 4 (2012): 692–704.

113  *body identity integrity disorder:* H. Gillmeister, N. Bowling, S. Rigato, and M. J. Banissy, "Inter-Individual Differences in Vicarious Tactile Perception: A View Across the Lifespan in Typical and Atypical Populations," *Multisensory Research* 30, no. 6 (2017): 485–508.

114  *when not handled well within:* C. Shi, Z. Ren, C. Zhao, T. Zhang, and S. H. Chan, "Shame, Guilt, and Posttraumatic Stress Symptoms: A Three-Level Meta-Analysis," *Journal of Anxiety Disorders* 82 (2021): 102443; L. Shen, "The Evolution of Shame and Guilt," *PLoS One* 13, no. 7 (2018): e0199448; J. A. Rudy, S. McKernan, N. Kouri, and W. D'Andrea, "A Meta-Analysis of the Association

Between Shame and Dissociation," *Journal of Trauma Stress* 35, no. 5 (2022): 1318–33; L. Muller-Pinzler, S. Krach, U. M. Kramer, and F. M. Paulus, "The Social Neuroscience of Interpersonal Emotions," *Current Topics in Behavioral Neuroscience* 30 (2017): 241–56; S. Mantzoukas, S. Kotrotsiou, M. Mentis et al., "Exploring the Impact of Shame on Health-Related Quality of Life in Older Individuals," *Journal of Nursing Scholarship* 53, no. 4 (2021): 439–48; D. M. Candea and A. Szentagotai-Tatar, "Shame-Proneness, Guilt-Proneness, and Anxiety Symptoms: A Meta-Analysis," *Journal of Anxiety Disorders* 58 (2018): 78–106.

120  *purpose and meaning:* C. Rousseau, M.-F. Gauthier, L. Lacroix et al., "Playing with Identities and Transforming Shared Realities: Drama Therapy Workshops for Adolescent Immigrants and Refugees," *Arts in Psychotherapy* 32, no. 1 (2005): 13–27; B. H. Hough and S. Hough, "The Play Was Always the Thing: Drama's Effect on Brain Function," *Psychology* 3, no. 6 (2012): 454–56; C. Hertzog, A. F. Kramer, R. S. Wilson, and U. Lindenberger, "Enrichment Effects on Adult Cognitive Development: Can the Functional Capacity of Older Adults Be Preserved and Enhanced?" *Psychological Science and the Public Interest* 9, no. 1 (2008): 1–65; S. Rabe, T. Zoellner, A. Beauducel, A. Maercker, and A. Karl, "Changes in Brain Electrical Activity After Cognitive Behavioral Therapy for Posttraumatic Stress Disorder in Patients Injured in Motor Vehicle Accidents," *Psychosomatic Medicine* 70, no. 1 (2008): 13–19.

120  *different pathways:* W. A. J. Vints, O. Levin, H. Fujiyama, J. Verbunt, and N. Masiulis, "Exerkines and Long-Term Synaptic Potentiation: Mechanisms of Exercise-Induced Neuroplasticity," *Frontiers in Neuroendocrinology* 66 (2022): 100993; G. Neves, S. F. Cooke, and T. V. Bliss, "Synaptic Plasticity, Memory and the Hippocampus: A Neural Network Approach to Causality," *Nature Reviews Neuroscience* 9, no. 1 (2008): 65–75; G. H. Diering and R. L. Huganir, "The AMPA Receptor Code of Synaptic Plasticity," *Neuron* 100, no. 2 (2018): 314–29.

120  *navigate our lives:* Z. Yang, D. J. Oathes, K. A. Linn et al., "Cognitive Behavioral Therapy Is Associated with Enhanced Cognitive Control Network Activity in Major Depression and Posttraumatic Stress Disorder," *Biological Psychiatry: Cognitive Neuroscience and Neuroimaging* 3, no. 4 (2018): 311–19; H. Shou, Z. Yang, T. D. Satterthwaite et al., "Cognitive Behavioral Therapy Increases Amygdala Connectivity with the Cognitive Control Network in Both MDD and PTSD," *NeuroImage: Clinical* 14 (2017): 464–70; S. Scaini, R. Belotti, A. Ogliari, and M. Battaglia, "A Comprehensive Meta-Analysis of Cognitive-Behavioral Interventions for Social Anxiety Disorder in Children and Adolescents," *Journal of Anxiety Disorders* 42 (2016): 105–12; Z. M. Manjaly and S. Iglesias, "A Computational Theory of Mindfulness-Based Cognitive Therapy from the 'Bayesian Brain' Perspective," *Frontiers in Psychiatry* 11 (2020): 404; M. A. Chalah and S. S. Ayache, "Disentangling the Neural Basis of Cognitive Behavioral Therapy in Psychiatric Disorders: A Focus on Depression," *Brain Science* 8, no. 8 (2018).

## Chapter 5: Cultivating Genuine Curiosity

137 *listen well:* M. Zeljko, P. M. Grove, and A. Kritikos, "Implicit Expectation Modulates Multisensory Perception," *Attention, Perception, & Psychophysics* 84, no. 3 (2022): 915–25; W. J. Hall, M. V. Chapman, K. M. Lee et al., "Implicit Racial/Ethnic Bias Among Health Care Professionals and Its Influence on Health Care Outcomes: A Systematic Review," *American Journal of Public Health* 105, no. 1 (2015): e60–76.

137 *common ground:* I. W. Maina, T. D. Belton, S. Ginzberg, A. Singh, and T. J. Johnson, "A Decade of Studying Implicit Racial/Ethnic Bias in Healthcare Providers Using the Implicit Association Test," *Social Science & Medicine* 199 (2018): 219–29.

140 *medical malpractice context:* G. W. Lester and S. G. Smith, "Listening and Talking to Patients: A Remedy for Malpractice Suits?" *Western Journal of Medicine* 158, no. 3 (1993): 268–72.

141 *urge to litigate:* Lester and Smith.

141 *extreme of their attitude:* G. Itzchakov, N. Weinstein, M. Leary, D. Saluk, and M. Amar, "Listening to Understand: The Role of High-Quality Listening on Speakers' Attitude Depolarization During Disagreements," *Journal of Personality and Social Psychology* 126, no. 2 (2024): 213–39.

141 *Joel has conducted a study:* J. Salinas, A. O'Donnell, D. J. Kojis et al., "Association of Social Support with Brain Volume and Cognition," *JAMA Network Open* 4, no. 8 (2021): e2121122.

142 *thousands of individuals:* Salinas, O'Donnell, and Kojis.

142 *feelings of isolation:* G. Itzchakov, A. N. Kluger, and D. R. Castro, "I Am Aware of My Inconsistencies but Can Tolerate Them: The Effect of High-Quality Listening on Speakers' Attitude Ambivalence," *Personal and Social Psychology Bulletin* 43, no. 1 (2017): 105–20; G. Itzchakov, K. G. DeMarree, A. N. Kluger, and Y. Turjeman-Levi, "The Listener Sets the Tone: High-Quality Listening Increases Attitude Clarity and Behavior-Intention Consequences," *Personal and Social Psychology Bulletin* 44, no. 5 (2018): 762–78.

142 *overall physical health:* F. R. Lin, J. R. Pike, M. S. Albert et al., "Hearing Intervention Versus Health Education Control to Reduce Cognitive Decline in Older Adults with Hearing Loss in the USA (ACHIEVE): A Multicentre, Randomised Controlled Trial," *Lancet* 402, no. 10404 (2023): 786–97.

144 *including your brain:* R. Zefferino, S. Di Gioia, and M. Conese, "Molecular Links Between Endocrine, Nervous and Immune System During Chronic Stress," *Brain and Behavior* 11, no. 2 (2021): e01960; L. D. Sher, H. Geddie, L. Olivier et al., "Chronic Stress and Endothelial Dysfunction: Mechanisms, Experimental Challenges, and the Way Ahead," *American Journal of Physiology–Heart and Circulatory Physiology* 319, no. 2 (2020): H488–H506; R. Schulz and S. R. Beach, "Caregiving as a Risk Factor for Mortality: The Caregiver Health Effects Study," *JAMA* 282, no. 23 (1999): 2215–19; J. K. Kiecolt-Glaser and R. Glaser, "Chronic Stress and Mortality Among Older Adults," *JAMA* 282, no. 23 (1999): 2259–60; R. P. Juster, B. S. McEwen, and S. J. Lupien, "Allostatic Load Biomarkers

of Chronic Stress and Impact on Health and Cognition," *Neuroscience and Biobehavioral Review* 35, no. 1 (2010): 2–16; S. Hassamal, "Chronic Stress, Neuroinflammation, and Depression: An Overview of Pathophysiological Mechanisms and Emerging Anti-Inflammatories," *Frontiers in Psychiatry* 14 (2023): 1130989; N. E. Adler and K. Newman, "Socioeconomic Disparities in Health: Pathways and Policies," *Health Affairs (Millwood)* 21, no. 2 (2002): 60–76.

144 *you can grow:* A. O. Malik, P. Peri-Okonny, K. Gosch et al., "Association of Perceived Stress Levels with Long-term Mortality in Patients with Peripheral Artery Disease," *JAMA Network Open* 3, no. 6 (2020): e208741.

145 *2020 study:* G. Itzchakov, N. Weinstein, N. Legate, and M. Amar, "Can High Quality Listening Predict Lower Speakers' Prejudiced Attitudes?" *Journal of Experimental Social Psychology* 91 (2020): 104022.

146 *self-esteem:* G. Itzchakov and N. Weinstein, "High-Quality Listening Supports Speakers' Autonomy and Self-Esteem When Discussing Prejudice," *Human Communication Research* 47, no. 3 (2021): 248–83.

146 *Prior studies:* Itzchakov, Kluger, and Castro, "I Am Aware of My Inconsistencies"; J. F. Dovidio, S. L. Gaertner, and K. Kawakami, "Intergroup Contact: The Past, Present, and the Future," *Group Processes & Intergroup Relations* 6, no. 1 (2003): 5–21.

146 *backlash effect:* J. F. Heller, M. S. Palla, and J. M. Picek, "The Interactive Effects of Intent and Threat on Boomerang Attitude Change," *Journal of Personality and Social Psychology* 26, no. 2 (1973): 273.

146 *personal growth:* Itzchakov, Kluger, and Castro, "I Am Aware of My Inconsistencies."

146 *in the study:* Itzchakov et al., "Can High-Quality Listening Predict Lower Speakers' Prejudiced Attitudes?"

148 *Dr. Helen Weng and others:* Weng et al., "Compassion Training."

153 *frontal lobe:* S. Channon, A. Rule, D. Maudgil et al., "Interpretation of Mentalistic Actions and Sarcastic Remarks: Effects of Frontal and Posterior Lesions on Mentalising," *Neuropsychologia* 45, no. 8 (2007): 1725–34.

153 *limbic system:* H. T. Uchiyama, D. N. Saito, H. C. Tanabe et al., "Distinction Between the Literal and Intended Meanings of Sentences: A Functional Magnetic Resonance Imaging Study of Metaphor and Sarcasm," *Cortex* 48, no. 5 (2012): 563–83.

153 *your left ear:* T. Harada, S. Itakura, F. Xu et al., "Neural Correlates of the Judgment of Lying: A Functional Magnetic Resonance Imaging Study," *Neuroscience Research* 63, no. 1 (2009): 24–34.

153 *truthfulness:* Harada et al.

153 *ourselves and others:* E. Winner, H. Brownell, F. Happe, A. Blum, and D. Pincus, "Distinguishing Lies from Jokes: Theory of Mind Deficits and Discourse Interpretation in Right Hemisphere Brain-Damaged Patients," *Brain and Language* 62, no. 1 (1998): 89–106.

153 *ability to dampen:* T. Shany-Ur, P. Poorzand, S. N. Grossman et al., "Comprehension of Insincere Communication in Neurodegenerative Disease: Lies, Sarcasm, and Theory of Mind," *Cortex* 48, no. 10 (2012): 1329–41.

155 *effective listening behaviors:* Itzchakov et al., " The Listener Sets the Tone"; G. Itzchakov, "Can Listening Training Empower Service Employees? The Mediating Roles of Anxiety and Perspective-Taking," *European Journal of Work and Organizational Psychology* 29, no. 6 (2020): 938–52; R. Bordone, "Listen Up! Your Talks May Depend on It," *Negotiation: The Newsletter of the Harvard Program on Negotiation* 10, no. 5 (2007): 9–11.

163 *Walensky said:* "Meet the New CDC Director with Rochelle Walensky." *In the Bubble with Andy Slavitt*, podcast, Lemonada Media, October 5, 2020, https://lemonadamedia.com/podcast/meet-the-new-cdc-director-with-rochelle-walensky.

163 *2019 study:* N. Singh Ospina, K. A. Phillips, R. Rodriguez-Gutierrez et al., "Eliciting the Patient's Agenda—Secondary Analysis of Recorded Clinical Encounters," *Journal of General Internal Medicine* 34 (2019): 36–40.

164 *published a study:* J. R. Curhan, J. R. Overbeck, Y. Cho, T. Zhang, and Y. Yang, "Silence Is Golden: Extended Silence, Deliberative Mindset, and Value Creation in Negotiation," *Journal of Applied Psychology* 107, no. 1 (2022): 78.

165 *communicate care and concern:* S. M. Jones and B. R. Burleson, "The Impact of Situational Variables on Helpers' Perceptions of Comforting Messages: An Attributional Analysis," *Communication Research* 24, no. 5 (1997): 530–55.

165 *mutual vulnerability:* S. M. Jones and K. Guerrero, "The Effects of Nonverbal Immediacy and Verbal Person Centeredness in the Emotional Support Process," *Human Communication Research* 27, no. 4 (2001): 567–96.

165 *person-centeredness:* S. Jones, "Putting the Person into Person-Centered and Immediate Emotional Support: Emotional Change and Perceived Helper Competence as Outcomes of Comforting in Helping Situations," *Communication Research* 31, no. 3 (2004): 338–60.

165 *experience of the speaker:* Jones and Burleson, "The Impact of Situational Variables."

**Chapter 6: Giving Voice**

176 Without Giving In: R. Fisher, W. L. Ury, and B. Patton, *Getting to Yes: Negotiating Agreement Without Giving In* (New York: Penguin, 2011).

184 *Master and her team:* S. L. Master, D. M. Amodio, A. L. Stanton, C. M. Yee, C. J. Hilmert, and S. E. Taylor, "Neurobiological Correlates of Coping Through Emotional Approach," *Brain, Behavior, and Immunity* 23, no. 1 (2009): 27–35.

185 *physical and mental health:* Master et al.

186 *results of the study:* Master et al.

187 *Heidi Kane:* H. S. Kane, J. F. Wiley, C. Dunkel Schetter, and T. F. Robles, "The Effects of Interpersonal Emotional Expression, Partner Responsiveness, and Emotional Approach Coping on Stress Responses," *Emotion* 19, no. 8 (2019): 1315–28.

187 *fewer negative emotions:* Kane et al.

194 *interpersonal trust among colleagues:* A. Yu, J. M. Berg, and J. J. Zlatev, "Emotional Acknowledgment: How Verbalizing Others' Emotions Fosters Interpersonal Trust," *Organizational Behavior and Human Decision Processes* 164 (2021): 116–35.

194 *"costly signal":* Yu, Berg, and Zlatev.

195 *positive ones:* Yu, Berg, and Zlatev.

195 *strengthen bonds and build trust:* Yu, Berg, and Zlatev.

197 *Ladder of Inference:* C. Argyris, *Overcoming Organizational Defenses: Facilitating Organizational Learning* (Boston: Allyn & Bacon, 1990).

197 *top of the ladder:* A. Fiester, "The 'Ladder of Inference' as a Conflict Management Tool: Working with the 'Difficult' Patient or Family in Healthcare Ethics Consultations," paper presented at HEC Forum 2024.

## Chapter 7: Setting the Table

213 *dispute resolution processes and systems:* N. H. Rogers, R. C. Bordone, F. E. Sander, and C. A. McEwen, *Designing Systems and Processes for Managing Disputes* (Aspen Publishing, 2018).

218 *use of time:* R. D. Van Hoek, M. DeWitt, M. Lacity, and T. Johnson, "How Walmart Automated Supplier Negotiations," *Harvard Business Review*, November 8, 2022, https://hbr.org/2022/11/how-walmart-automated-supplier-negotiations; H. A. Schroth, "Hey ChatGPT, Can You Help Me Negotiate My Salary?" *California Management Review,* 2023.

221 *"Fitting the Forum to the Fuss":* S. Goldberg and F. Sander, "Fitting the Forum to the Fuss," *Negotiation Journal* 10, no. 1 (1994).

233 *evaluating every idea:* B. Obama, *A Promised Land* (New York: Crown, 2020).

243 *negotiator's dilemma:* D. Lax and J. Sebenius, "The Manager as Negotiator: The Negotiator's Dilemma: Creating and Claiming Value," *Dispute Resolution* 2 (1992): 49–62.

246 *reactive devaluation:* L. Ross, *Reactive Devaluation in Negotiation and Conflict Resolution,* Stanford Center on Conflict and Negotiation, Stanford University, 1993.

247 Getting to Yes: Fisher, Ury, and Patton, *Getting to Yes.*

## Chapter 8: Deciding the Future—Together or Apart

268 *rapport with colleagues:* R. E. Nisbett and L. Ros, "Human Inference: Strategies and Shortcomings of Social Judgment," 1980.

269 *the "sunk costs" or "escalation of commitment" problem:* K. A. Diekmann, A. E. Tenbrunsel, P. P. Shah, H. A. Schroth, and M. H. Bazerman, "The Descriptive and Prescriptive Use of Previous Purchase Price in Negotiations," *Organizational Behavior and Human Decision Processes* 66, no. 2 (1996): 179–91; M. H. Bazerman and M. A. Neale, "Heuristics in Negotiation: Limitations to Effective Dispute Resolution," 1986.

285 *past decades:* "Understanding the Difference Between a Difficult Moment and a Trauma," NYU Langone Health, 2020, https://nyulangone.org/news /understanding-difference-between-difficult-moment-trauma.

285 *fear or helplessness:* A. Pai, A. M. Suris, C. S. North, "Posttraumatic Stress Disorder in the DSM-5: Controversy, Change, and Conceptual Considerations," *Behavioral Science (Basel)* 7, no. 1 (2017); American Psychiatric Association, *Diagnostic and Statistical Manual of Mental Disorders*, 5th ed. (Washingon, DC: American Psychiatric Association, 2013) (DSM-5).

285 *fade away:* "Understanding the Difference."

287 *PTSD:* DSM-5.

287 *significant symptoms:* "Understanding the Difference."

287 *daily life:* DSM-5.

288 *post-traumatic growth:* R. G. Tedeschi and L. G. Calhoun, "The Posttraumatic Growth Inventory: Measuring the Positive Legacy of Trauma," *Journal of Trauma and Stress* 9, no. 3 (1996): 455–71.

288 *around them:* R. G. Tedeschi, "The Post-Traumatic Growth Approach to Psychological Trauma," *World Psychiatry* 22, no. 2 (2023): 328–29.

288 *catalysts for growth:* "Understanding the Difference."

288 *PCL-5:* C. A. Blevins, F. W. Weathers, M. T. Davis, T. K. Witte, and J. L. Domino, "The Posttraumatic Stress Disorder Checklist for DSM-5 (PCL-5): Development and Initial Psychometric Evaluation," *Journal of Trauma and Stress* 28, no. 6 (2015): 489–98.

290 *having PTSD:* Blevins et al., "The Posttraumatic Stress Disorder Checklist for DSM-5."

291 *conducted a study:* P. J. Jones, B. W. Bellet, and R. J. McNally, "Helping or Harming? The Effect of Trigger Warnings on Individuals with Trauma Histories," *Clinical Psychological Science* 8, no. 5 (2020): 905–17.

291 *the study:* P. J. Jones, B. W. Bellet, and R. J. McNally, "Helping or Harming? The Effect of Trigger Warnings on Individuals with Trauma Histories," *Clinical Psychological Science* 8, no. 5 (2020): 905–17.

292 *reevaluated:* B. W. Bellet, P. J. Jones, C. A. Meyersburg, M. M. Brenneman, K. E. Morehead, and R. J. McNally, "Trigger Warnings and Resilience in College Students: A Preregistered Replication and Extension," *Journal of Experimental Psychology: Applied* 26, no. 4 (2020): 717–23.

293 *Dolly Parton:* J. Abumrad, *Dolly Parton's America*, podcast, WNYC Studios, October 22, 2019, https://www.wnycstudios.org/podcasts/dolly-partons-america /episodes/i-will-always-leave-you.

## Chapter 9: Building Culture

310 *already have:* Rogers, Bordone, Sander, and McEwen, *Designing Systems and Processes for Managing Disputes.*

311 *indicators of future behavior:* S. J. Motowidlo, G. W. Carter, M. D. Dunnette et al., "Studies of the Structured Behavioral Interview," *Journal of Applied Psychology* 77, no. 5 (1992): 571.

318 *Richard Dawkins:* R. Dawkins, *The Selfish Gene* (Oxford: Oxford University Press, 2016).

318 *Susan Blackmore:* S. Blackmore, "Evolution and Memes: The Human Brain as a Selective Imitation Device," *Cybernetics & Systems* 32, nos. 1–2 (2001): 225–55; S. Blackmore, *The Meme Machine* (Oxford: Oxford University Press, 1999).

318 *techniques and knowledge:* J. Ward, *The Student's Guide to Social Neuroscience* (London: Psychology Press, 2022).

318 *actions they copy:* D. C. Penn and D. J. Povinelli, "On the Lack of Evidence That Non-human Animals Possess Anything Remotely Resembling a 'Theory of Mind,'" *Philosophical Transactions of the Royal Society of London B: Biological Sciences* 362, no. 1480 (2007): 731–44.

318 *yawning or laughing:* R. R. Provine, "Contagious Yawning and Laughter: Significance for Sensory Feature Detection," *Social Learning in Animals* 179 (1996).

319 *outcome you want:* N. Schwarz, "Metacognitive Experiences in Consumer Judgment and Decision Making," *Journal of Consumer Psychology* 14, no. 4 (2004): 332–48; A. J. Flanagin and Z. Lew, "Individual Inferences in Web-Based Information Environments: How Cognitive Processing Fluency, Information Access, Active Search Behaviors, and Task Competency Affect Metacognitive and Task Judgments," *Media Psychology* 26, no. 1 (2023): 17–35.

321 *like a virus:* K. P. Smith and N. A. Christakis, "Social Networks and Health," *Annual Review of Sociology* 34 (2008): 405–29.

321 *Obesity:* N. A. Christakis and J. H. Fowler, "The Spread of Obesity in a Large Social Network over 32 Years," *New England Journal of Medicine* 357, no. 4 (2007): 370–79.

321 *smoking habits:* N. A. Christakis and J. H. Fowler, "The Collective Dynamics of Smoking in a Large Social Network," *New England Journal of Medicine* 358, no. 21 (2008): 2249–58.

321 *happiness:* J. H. Fowler and N. A. Christakis, "Dynamic Spread of Happiness in a Large Social Network: Longitudinal Analysis over 20 Years in the Framingham Heart Study," *BMJ* 337 (2008): a2338.

323 *collaborates together:* M. Sherif, "Superordinate Goals in the Reduction of Intergroup Conflict," *American Journal of Sociology* 63, no. 4 (1958): 349–56; M. Sherif, O. Harvey, B. White, W. Hood, and C. Sherif, *Intergroup Conflict and Cooperation: The Robbers Cave Experiment,* vol. 10 (Norman, OK: University Book Exchange, 1961).

323 *right temporoparietal junction:* M. J. Kim, P. Mende-Siedlecki, S. Anzellotti, and L. Young, "Theory of Mind Following the Violation of Strong and Weak Prior Beliefs," *Cerebral Cortex* 31, no. 2 (2021): 884–98.

323  *not foe:* M. J. Kim, P. Mende-Siedlecki, S. Anzellotti, and L. Young, "Theory of Mind Following the Violation of Strong and Weak Prior Beliefs," *Cerebral Cortex* 31, no. 2 (2021): 884–98.

323  *positive halo effect:* B. Park and L. Young, "An Association Between Biased Impression Updating and Relationship Facilitation: A Behavioral and fMRI Investigation," *Journal of Experimental and Social Psychology* 87 (2020); B. L. Hughes, J. Zaki, and N. Ambady, "Motivation Alters Impression Formation and Related Neural Systems," *Social Cognitive and Affective Neuroscience* 12, no. 1 (2017): 49–60.

328  *presented as a story:* R. Scheurich, C. Palmer, B. Kaya, C. Agostino, and S. Sheldon, "Evidence for a Visual Bias When Recalling Complex Narratives," *PLoS One* 16, no. 4 (2021): e0249950; I. Davidesco, E. Laurent, H. Valk et al., "The Temporal Dynamics of Brain-to-Brain Synchrony Between Students and Teachers Predict Learning Outcomes," *Psychological Science* 34, no. 5 (2023): 633–43.

328  *empathy:* L. Peled-Avron, E. Levy-Gigi, G. Richter-Levin, N. Korem, and S. G. Shamay-Tsoory, "The Role of Empathy in the Neural Responses to Observed Human Social Touch," *Cognitive, Affective, & Behavioral Neuroscience* 16, no. 5 (2016): 802–13; H. Gillmeister, N. Bowling, S. Rigato, and M. J. Banissy, "Inter-Individual Differences in Vicarious Tactile Perception: A View Across the Lifespan in Typical and Atypical Populations," *Multisensory Research* 30, no. 6 (2017): 485–508.

328  *neural coupling:* G. J. Stephens, L. J. Silbert, and U. Hasson, "Speaker-Listener Neural Coupling Underlies Successful Communication," *PNAS* 107, no. 32 (2010): 14425–30.

328  *interbrain synchrony:* M. Zhang, H. Jia, and G. Wang, "Interbrain Synchrony of Team Collaborative Decision-Making: An fNIRS Hyperscanning Study," *Frontiers in Human Neuroscience* 15 (2021): 702959.

328  *cooperation and understanding:* C. Reveille, G. Vergotte, S. Perrey, and G. Bosselut, "Using Interbrain Synchrony to Study Teamwork: A Systematic Review and Meta-Analysis," *Neuroscience & Biobehavioral Reviews* 159 (2024): 105593.

332  *17.3 percent of U.S. GDP in 2022:* National Health Expenditure Data: Historical, Centers for Medicare & Medicaid Services, 2024, https://www.cms .gov/data-research/statistics-trends-and-reports/national-health-expenditure -data/historical#:~:text=The%20data%20are%20presented%20by,For%20 additional%20information%2C%20see%20below.

# INDEX

# ABOUT THE AUTHORS

ROBERT C. BORDONE (Bob) is an internationally recognized expert, author, speaker, and teacher in negotiation, conflict resolution, mediation, facilitation, and conflict resilience. As the founder and principal of The Cambridge Negotiation Institute, Bob consults with C-suite executives, government officials, and leaders at universities and across a wide range of industries to help them navigate their toughest conflicts and negotiations.

Currently a senior fellow at Harvard Law School, Bob served on the full-time faculty at Harvard Law for more than twenty years as the Thaddeus R. Beal Clinical Professor of Law and as the director and founder of the Harvard Negotiation and Mediation Clinical Program. He continues to teach as an adjunct professor of law at Georgetown University Law Center and as faculty for the Division of Continuing Education at Harvard University.

Bob is the coauthor of two previous books: *Designing Systems and Processes for Managing Disputes* and *The Handbook of Dispute Resolution*. He has published in leading business and law journals, including the *Harvard Business Review* and the *Harvard Law Review*. Bob's writing and commentary have appeared in print and broadcast media outlets, including NBC News, the *Washington Post*, the *Wall Street Journal*, and CNN's Situation Room.

Bob earned his J.D., cum laude, from Harvard Law School, and his A.B., summa cum laude, from Dartmouth College. He currently resides in Cambridge, Massachusetts, with his golden retriever, Rosie. You can follow him on X @bobbordone, on his YouTube channel at http://bit.ly/YouTubeBob, and through bobbordone.com or cambridgenegotiationinstitute.com.

\*\*\*

JOEL (pronounced 'joh-EHL') SALINAS, M.D., MBA, MSc, FAAN, is a Harvard-trained behavioral neurologist, speaker, author, and researcher with expertise in how brain science can inform human connection and conflict resilience. As founder and chief medical officer of Isaac Health, Joel has pioneered innovative approaches in brain health care. His research, funded by the NIH, explores the role of social relationships in brain health and how understanding these dynamics can help us live happier, healthier, and more fulfilling lives.

Joel has authored over forty peer-reviewed academic papers and contributed to eight books on evidence-based practice of neurology. He is the author of the bestselling memoir *Mirror Touch*, in which he examines the brain's potential for empathy and how it shapes the way we navigate complex human interactions. His work has been featured in the *New York Times*, *Forbes*, and national broadcast outlets.

Joel is also clinical assistant professor of neurology and the former Lulu P. and David J. Levidow Assistant Professor of Neurology at the NYU Grossman School of Medicine. Prior to being at NYU, he was assistant professor in neurology at Harvard Medical School and Mass General and was clinical director of the McCance Center for Brain Health.

Joel lives in New York City, where he can be found wandering around Central Park walking his long-haired chihuahua, Waffle. You can follow him on X @joelsalinasmd or through joelsalinasmd.com and isaac.health.

***

**Interested in learning more?** Bob and Joel offer compelling keynotes, conflict resilience trainings, and personalized coaching and consulting in negotiation and conflict resilience. To learn more, check out our website for resources and how to contact us: **conflictresiliencebook.com**.